Heal Yourself with Emotional Freedom Technique

John Freedom

D1023680

John Freedom, CEHP, is an educator and EFT practitioner and trainer. He serves as research coordinator for the Association for Comprehensive Energy Psychology. He holds a Master's Level Certification in Neuro-Linguistic Programming, with additional certifications in Emotional Freedom Technique, Thought Field Therapy, Eye Movement Desensitization and Reprocessing and Acupuncture Detox (auricular acupuncture). A former radio talk-show host and magazine editor, he teaches seminars in EFT, Energy Psychology and related topics throughout the US and in Europe. He makes his home in Tucson, Arizona, where he devotes his time to teaching, writing, hiking, piano and raising chickens. His website is www.JohnFreedom.com.

'This is a wonderful book – as joyously and generously facilitating as EFT itself. Freedom writes as a seasoned veteran of the field of "energy psychology", a participant in this new paradigm of healing from its beginnings. He knows EFT thoroughly, and his guidance can be trusted. EFT is the most simple and user friendly of the energy psychology methods, with wide applications to both emotional and physical distress. I recommend this book both to those seeking effective self-help and to professional practitioners who are learning EFT.'

Phil Mollon, PhD, psychoanalyst, psychotherapist and Clinical Psychologist; consultant practitioner in the British National Health Service

'This book will be of interest to anyone who wants to heal body, mind or spirit, which is pretty much all of us. Whether you are well versed in Emotional Freedom Techniques or just want to learn the basics, this book will give you the information you need to put these powerful practices into effect in your life. This is absolutely the best book I've read on the subject. It's easy to read, yet comprehensive in scope.'

Jed Diamond, PhD, LCSW, author of *Source Power: Unleash Your Inner Vitality Through the Secrets of Energy Medicine*

'As someone who uses EFT in the world of elite sport performance, I can certainly lay claim to the positive changes that occur in the athletes I work with. This book provides lots of case studies, practical exercises and descriptions of how and why EFT works. As someone who likes easy books to read, this book is right up my street and will hopefully help you to overcome your inner challenges.'

Dr Mike Rotheram, performance psychologist with the British short-track speed skating team and England Netball

'John Freedom shares his knowledge of EFT in an easily readable and understandable voice that will inform and inspire both EFT newcomers and experienced tappers. This book is good to dip in and out of, as I have done, and will reward thorough study and complement other sources.'

Gwyneth Moss, EFT Master

'A great book. Easily accessible, it's filled with information, tips and case studies, so you can see how EFT works in the real world with real people. If you want to know about EFT and how to use it, this book is ideal.'

Jaqui Crooks, EFT Master

'The fields of "energy medicine" and "energy psychology" evoke both praise and scorn. For curious people who simply want to learn about these fields, there is no more articulate book than this. The book is reader-friendly and provides readers with an opportunity to "tap" their own acupuncture points in an attempt to unblock energy and allow it to "flow" more easily. The author contends that stress is a key factor in human distress and that "tapping" can help to "unwind" stress-related conditions.... Many people will begin this book with skepticism; they might be guided by the old adage, "Try it. You may like it."'

Stanley Krippner, PhD, co-author of *Personal Mythology*

Heal Yourself with Emotional Freedom Technique

John Freedom

e Also available in ebook

This book is dedicated to you:
the reader, the explorer, the healer.
Remember to share the gift.

Acknowledgements

Every book is the work of many hands and minds. This book would not exist but for the creative genius and efforts of hundreds of people, of whom I can name but a few.

I wish to acknowledge the pioneers of Energy Psychology, including Roger Callahan, Gary Craig, John Diamond and George Goodheart.

Stanley Krippner, my first mentor, for introducing me to the scientific study of subtle energies; David Feinstein, for his invaluable assistance compiling and interpreting research in Energy Psychology and Energy Medicine; Phil Friedman, for assistance with research on optimism and positive psychology; Michael Galvin for coaching me on time management skills; Jerry Isaacs for schooling me in NLP; Lorna Minewiser for acting as such a sensitive sounding board; and Greg Nicosia, for his inspiration and mentoring me in this field.

Several pioneers in the field of understanding and treating trauma, including Bruce Ecker, Peter Levine, Ron Ruden, Robert Scaer, Francine Shapiro and Bessel van der Kolk.

My friends and family, who love, support and encourage me, despite my faults: Janetta Bensing, Nancy Cohen, John Dommisse, Franny and Bob Gryl, Noel Hargreaves, Marie Kearney, Marina Koshelev, Kewaunee Lapseritis, Ingrid Lephardt, Jeannie and Tom Maldonado, Rebecca Rizzo-Freedom, Bruce Silvey, Jim and Cherie Sohnen-Moe, Marie Ueda, Marty Woerner and Jay Yasgur.

The practitioners who generously contributed cases and stories, including Martina Becher, Meryl Beck, Judy Byrne, Jaqui Crooks, Alina Frank, Mary Hammond, Susan Hannibal, Crystal Hawk, Rhonda Heyns, Lindsay Kenny, David Lake, Karen Ledger, Ashley Mann, Steve Manire, Lorna Minewiser, Gwyneth Moss, Betsy Muller, Cassandra Noel, Jeraldine Peterson-Mark, Barbara Rattenborg, Caroline Sakai, Mary Stafford, Holly Timberlake, Stacey Vornbrock, Greg Warburton, Yves Wauthier-Freymann, Steve Wells, Phyllis Winslow and Susi Wolf.

My colleagues in the fields of Energy Psychology and Energy Medicine: Dan Benor, Liz Boath, Dawson Church, Melinda Connor, Tina Craig, Jed Diamond, Jenny Edwards, Helena Fone, Jacqui Footman, Fred Gallo, Sandra Hillawi, Kristin Holthuis, Norman Katz, Willem Lammers, Rollin McCraty, David MacKay, Phil Mollon, Mike Rotheram, Jack Rowe, Ron Ruden, Thornton Streeter and Helen Walker.

My friends and colleagues in the Association for Comprehensive Energy Psychology: Ann Adams, Tiffany Barsotti, Suzanne Connolly, Cheryl Cross, John Diepold, Shirley Eckes, Marty Frantz, Michael Galvin, Patricia Hodge, Kristin Holthuis, Bob and Lynne Hoss, Philippe Isler, Jim Lane, Karen Ledger, Lorna Minewiser, Betsy Muller, Lynne Namka, Greg Nicosia, Bob Pasahow, Gary Peterson, George Pratt, Jack Rowe, April Rubino, Bob Schwarz, Robin Smith, Carole Stern, Judith Swack, Sharon Toole, Robin Trainor, Debby Vajda, Greg Warburton, Julie Weiner and Andrew Winkler.

My 'team' in New Mexico: Susan Barrera, Tammy Bredy, James and Joan Burnett, Mary Carafelli, Halima Christy, Patricia Flasch, Chery Klairwator, Sylvia Machado, Eugenia Manrique, Anne McGoey, Jean Meltesen and Shirley Schaan.

And finally, my clients and students, whom I am acknowledging anonymously; I feel grateful for all you have shared with me.

The author and publisher would like to thank the following for their permission to reproduce material in this book:

Figures 1–6 used with permission © Energy Psychology Press; Figure 7 © Abramova Kseniya – Shutterstock.

Graphs in Chapter 2 and Figures 12 and 16 © Cenveo® Publisher Services.

Figures 8–11 and 13–15 © Barking Dog Art.

Quoted passage in Chapter 11 © Steve Wells; quoted passage in Chapter 13 © Gary Craig.

Disclaimer

The information contained in this book, including ideas, suggestions, exercises and other materials, is provided only as general information and is solely intended for your own self-improvement and personal growth. It is not meant to be a substitute for medical or psychological treatment and does not replace the services of healthcare professionals. If you experience emotional distress or physical discomfort using any of the ideas, suggestions or exercises contained in this book, you are advised to stop and to seek professional care, if appropriate.

While Emotional Freedom Technique and meridian tapping have been found to be effective for many people with common forms of emotional distress, it is not intended to be a self-treatment for severe mental illness. If you are experiencing severe anxiety, depression, multiple personalities, hearing 'voices' or having suicidal thoughts, please consult a mental health professional.

Publishing of the information contained in this book is not intended to create a client–therapist or any other type of professional relationship between the reader and the author. The author does not make any warranty, guarantee or prediction regarding the outcome for any individual using this book for any particular purpose or issue.

You agree to assume and accept full responsibility for any and all risks associated with using any of the ideas, suggestions, exercises or meditations described in this book and agree to accept full and complete responsibility for applying what you may learn from reading this book.

Contents

Introduction: The promise of Emotional Freedom Technique

> There is a giant asleep within every man. When that giant awakens, miracles happen.
>
> Frederick Faust

This book, like all books, is a story. It is the story of one of the most exciting breakthroughs in the history of psychotherapy and personal growth. Chances are you've heard about Emotional Freedom Technique (EFT) already. You may have heard of 'tapping', seen it on the internet or YouTube and/ or heard some of the astonishing successes people are having with it. This book is my personal story; a story about the pioneers who discovered meridian tapping; and the stories of many people who are discovering the power of EFT and Energy Healing for themselves and changing their lives for the better. Perhaps it will become your story as well.

This is also a book about healing. While its primary focus is emotional healing, when we shift and heal emotionally, there are often dramatic shifts and changes in our bodies as well. When we think of healing, we may be reminded of Jesus and stories in the Bible of wondrous and miraculous healings. Some people think of healing as being some kind of special and magical power that only doctors and healers and special people have. And still others dismiss this as being superstition, old wives' tales or New Age woo.

What these people are ignoring is the fact that we *all* have tremendous healing powers available to us, right at the tips of our fingers. And you do not need to gifted, special or a 'healer' in order to do this. EFT is a self-help, self-healing technique that everyone can do. These techniques are very easy to learn and apply and available to all of us.

EFT is a form of meridian therapy, a novel method for rapidly releasing and resolving emotional distress, simply by tapping on acupoints. These techniques address the fundamental causes of emotional distress by releasing blockages in the body's energy system. Thousands of people around the world are using these techniques to release fears and phobias, overcome anxiety and depression, improve academic and athletic performance and live happier and healthier lives.

EFT and Energy Healing are Gifts for all Mankind. It is my privilege to share their story with you.

Releasing the djinns

In the East there are many stories of djinns, or genies, powerful spirits trapped in bottles or caves. In these stories an explorer unwittingly opens the cave or breaks the bottle, thus releasing the genie, who, in his tremendous gratitude, grants the explorer a magical Wish (or sometimes even three Wishes). The explorer wishes for great wealth, great power or a harem of beautiful women, gets all his Wishes fulfilled and lives happily ever after.

While we can smile at the naivety of stories like this and dismiss them as childish fantasies and wish-fulfilment, they are metaphors, symbolizing inner truths; and like all stories and metaphors, they reveal powerful truths about ourselves.

Deep within each of us lies incredible, unlimited promise and potential. Yet, just like the genies in the myth, our almost-infinite potential has been 'locked in a bottle', denied and repressed and disowned, in the process of 'growing up', 'getting real' and becoming 'good boys and nice girls'. Through years of education we are conditioned and brainwashed into becoming good servants of the system, and in so doing we often lose and forget our Selves. Later in life we encounter walls, limits and 'glass ceilings', which appear to be 'out there'. Yet the limitations we find ourselves in, whether physical, emotional or financial, are but reflections of our inner bottles.

There are many books on self-help and inner healing on the market today. Many of them urge us to meditate or visualize, breathe deeply or practise yoga, eat healthily, think positively, practise the 'Law of Attraction' etc. But very few address this fundamental issue.

This book is about a new field called Energy Psychology. It will introduce you to your inner Genie, reveal the nature of the 'bottles' that have kept you locked up and how to break through the locks and blocks that have kept you smaller and less powerful than you know you truly are. It is about breaking the bottles and releasing the power and potential you know you have within you. It is about setting yourself free.

How to use this book

This book is designed and formatted as a teaching tool. Experience is the best teacher and so it is set up as a series of exercises that build upon each other. An experience is worth a thousand words; and you will learn and gain much more by going through the exercises and experiences than by skipping and skimming.

However, having been a rebel myself, I am well aware that many people do not follow instructions and instead feel more comfortable skipping ahead, and picking and choosing as they feel moved. If you're feeling rebellious (or adventurous!), feel free to skip ahead to Chapter 5 and begin tapping right away. After experiencing the power of EFT, you may want to go back and review the earlier material and exercises in Chapters 1–4.

EFT and the different forms of meridian tapping are very robust techniques and work on many issues for many people. This book presents many ideas and powerful techniques you can use to heal yourself, your friends and your family. It is up to you to experiment with these tools and see which ones work best for you.

Sprinkled throughout this book are personal stories and case studies. I have included these to show the many different kinds of issues that meridian tapping may be applied to, as well as to pique your interest and motivation to tap tap tap! for yourself. If other people have successfully applied EFT to difficult and seemingly impossible issues, perhaps you can too. For those interested in scientific research in this area, you will find a brief discussion with references in Appendices 1 and 2.

In any event, adapt this book to yourself and your own needs. Each of us is conditioned and programmed a little differently and we all see the world through different lenses. *This is your book! Adapt it to yourself and make it your own.*

A few words about words

I attempt to speak and write as accurately as I can. While I love words and enjoy painting pictures with colourful phrases, I'm also acutely aware of their shortcomings. Words are concept-symbols representing ideas, which themselves are concepts attempting to represent 'real' phenomena. Thus words are two orders of reality removed from the phenomena they attempt to describe. As the Polish-American semanticist Alfred Korzybski noted, 'The map is not the territory', or as someone else once said, 'The menu is not the meal'. Please be aware that my attempts to represent and symbolize these very subtle phenomena are simply that. It will be helpful, if you find yourself grappling or struggling (or arguing!) with these ideas, to rephrase what I've written as 'or perhaps something like this…'

While the ideas and techniques I describe in these pages are very powerful and work for many people much of the time, they are still poorly understood. Language, for all its beauty and richness, is inherently metaphoric; modern physics and neuroscience have yet to fully and accurately describe and elucidate the mechanisms underlying these techniques. Also, I have simplified some concepts to avoid pedantic discussions and to fit this subject within the covers of a popular book. This book is what mathematicians call a 'first approximation'; there will be many upgrades and revisions, in both theory and practice, in the years to come. The astute reader will be aware that the delicate, multi-dimensional realities I am attempting to map are much more subtle and sophisticated than my feeble attempts to describe them succinctly.

Throughout this book I will be using the terms 'EFT', 'tapping' and 'meridian tapping' somewhat interchangeably. This is not strictly accurate; there are differences between them and each technique's devotees (and founders!) will protest that their method is the most effective. Strictly speaking, EFT refers to the original Emotional Freedom Technique developed by Gary Craig; for information and its most recent revisions, go to www.emofree.com. I use these three terms partly to avoid using the term 'EFT' repetitiously, but also to make the point that all the different varieties of tapping, such as EFT, Thought Field Therapy (TFT), Touch and Breathe (TAB), and other meridian tapping therapies (MTTs), can be effective. For more information about the many flavours of tapping, see Chapter 14.

Becoming all we are meant to be

We all have incredible, almost unlimited potential. We can sense this incredible potential in infants; their little minds and bodies are not yet fully formed and so they are open to being and becoming almost anything. We have approximately 100 trillion (100,000,000,000,000) neurons in our brains. Although that is a very large number, it is still finite and limited. One measure of creativity is the ability to conceive of things in different ways. The number of possible ways we can think about anything, the number of possible combinations of neuro-circuits in our brains, is virtually infinite. This implies that our creativity is virtually unlimited as well.

The seeds of Greatness lie within each of us.

Walking out in the countryside, I always enjoy exploring and simply observing the trees, plants and living things all around us. Observe anything – a flower, a bush or a mighty oak or elm – given sufficient soil, water and sunlight, it grows by itself in accordance with its innate design. Within all living things lies an inner blueprint, an inner Wisdom, a field of innate Intelligence, which guides and directs that plant to grow and fulfil its destiny.

As the therapist and author David Richo writes:

> There is a natural and inviolable tendency in things to bloom into whatever they truly are in the core of their being. All we have to do is align ourselves with what wants to happen naturally and put in the effort that is our part in helping it happen.

The same is no less true of our selves. We, too, have an inner blueprint, an inner Wisdom and Intelligence that guides and shapes us. We are hard-wired to learn arithmetic and languages, to develop skills and talents, to succeed in careers and professions. We have within us what Carl Jung called the process of *individuation* and what Abraham Maslow termed the drive towards *self-actualization*. We are meant to grow and blossom and flourish, to become all we are meant to be. *We are here to be happy.*

But sometimes, something happens. Just as trees can have their growth stunted and distorted, sometimes circumstances stunt our growth and distort our potential. Many of us have thought of our selves as 'damaged goods', and feared that the damage was permanent. For many years, scientists and psychologists agreed with them.

You may be familiar with the work of Konrad Lorenz. Lorenz was a Swiss biologist, who won a Nobel prize for his study of imprinting in birds. Species of birds like geese 'imprint' onto the first thing they encounter, whether alive or inanimate, and thereafter will try to bond and mate with it. We human beings are also imprinted by the events of our lives. But while birds and geese are imprinted forever, we can overcome the effects of trauma and negative imprinting.

Just as the energies released from nuclear fusion are far more powerful than dynamite, so the inner energies released with EFT and energy healing are far more powerful than those used in ordinary methods. This book will give you the tools to touch and release your own inner energies and to liberate your own inner Genie/Genius.

To begin this journey, turn to Chapter 1…

John Freedom

May 2013

1

Why Emotional Freedom Technique?

Your emotional health, your success in the world and your level of joy can all be dramatically enhanced by shifting the energies that regulate them. This is the promise of the fascinating new field of energy psychology.

David Feinstein, *The Promise of Energy Psychology*

In this chapter you will learn:

▶ *what Emotional Freedom Technique (EFT) is*

▶ *what EFT can be used for*

▶ *the history of EFT and Thought Field Therapy*

▶ *why stress can be harmful*

▶ *why we have emotions*

▶ *the power of intention.*

I'm teaching an EFT Level 1 training seminar in Columbus, Ohio.

> Unbeknown to me, one of this group of 25 people has a severe phobia of heights, to the extent that she will not get on an airplane. I tell the trainees to focus on a 'recent, upsetting experience, *not* your worst trauma'. 'Leslie' ignores my instructions and focuses on her fear of heights while I guide the group through the tapping sequence. After repeating an affirmation of self-acceptance and tapping on several acupoints, I 'check in' with the group, to see how they're doing.

> 'I gotta see if this really works!' Leslie walks outside the meeting room, which is on the second floor of the hotel, and leans over the balcony, looking down. 'I still have some fear, but it's better,' she tells me. I stand next to her and we do three more rounds of tapping. After each round she leans over the balcony and 'checks in' with me. After the last round, she leans over the balcony for a long time, takes a deep breath and takes in the huge lobby below her. 'This is amazing,' she says. 'I'm totally OK now, there's no fear at all.'

EFT Master Gwyneth Moss from Yorkshire shares this story:

> 'In my trainings we spend the first day learning how to use the tool of EFT and by the end of the afternoon the trainees tap with each other for a current situation in which they feel nervous or annoyed. "June" partnered with another newcomer to EFT and told him that she became very nervous on the slip road to a motorway and would stop and get stuck; as a consequence she never drove on motorways. Working together the two uncovered several aspects and cleared them using EFT. Two weeks after the training June called to say that she had driven from Yorkshire to Plymouth and back on the motorways with complete confidence. When on the return journey she had to face her biggest fear, driving in a thunderstorm, she pulled over and got the whole family tapping with her and then drove on despite the lightning and thunder.'

I'm leading an EFT Level 2 training seminar in Santa Fe, New Mexico.

'Jocelyn' suffered a stroke 11 years previously. Since her stroke, in addition to the left side of her body being disabled (she walks with a shuffle), she often stammered and experienced what she called 'a delay' in her speech. She described it as 'knowing what I want to say, but not being able to express it in words.' This issue was disconcerting for her, because she had been a public speaker prior to the stroke.

Over the weekend, I tap with her a couple of times, for 15–20 minutes each time, on emotional issues: her fear and guilt about her disability, her self-consciousness about her speech, her disappointment in herself, comparing herself to her husband and two adult sons etc. By the time we finish the weekend, she's speaking as freely and easily as you and I.

Albuquerque life coach and EFT practitioner Susi Wolf shares this story about a woman with a sugar addiction:

'I was teaching EFT to 26 teachers in Roswell, New Mexico. After teaching them the Basic Recipe, I brought out some chocolate and asked for a volunteer who had a sugar addiction. One of the group volunteered and we tapped on her cravings for chocolate and sugar. That night she went home to a surprise; her husband had bought her favourite goodies for her and there on the table were chocolate chip cookies, chocolate cake and chocolate ice cream. She looked at all the chocolate, took a bite out of a cookie, realized that she didn't want it and just stood there, amazed at her reaction, as well as at her new-found freedom.'

I'm teaching another training seminar in Seattle.

'Harry' is a successful, apparently confident executive at an aerospace company. But underlying his confident persona is a dogged perfectionism, fuelled by a terror of making mistakes. This fear has motivated him to compensate by striving for excellence in all areas of his life. He has been very successful, but at tremendous cost in terms of stress and anxiety, affecting his health and family.

I taught the class how to tap and Harry applied this to his perfectionism issues, stemming from his mother.

'Even though my mother tried to control every aspect of my life and even though now I'm doing the same thing, I deeply and completely accept myself.' With the same dogged persistence, he practised his tapping routine every morning.

A couple of months later he called me. 'John,' he said, 'You won't believe what I just did. For years I've never been able to throw any contracts or documents away, for fear that I might need them. This morning I spent a couple of hours going through my files, tossing any documents more than five years old.' 'That's wonderful,' I replied. 'Yes, it is. But the most wonderful part of this is that I feel so much younger. I can do things now that I simply could not do before.'

This is something I hear from my students, clients and colleagues repeatedly: *I can do things now that I simply could not do before.*

Results like these are not unusual. In every training seminar, people 'pop' like popcorn, with shifts and Aha's, with sighs and giggles of release and laughter. Any EFT trainer can share many stories like these. I must emphasize that they do not happen for every person, every time. But they happen often enough that we have two names for them in the tapping world: 'one-minute wonders' and 'one-minute miracles'.

What is EFT?

EFT, also called 'tapping', is a novel method for rapidly releasing and resolving emotional distress, simply by tapping on acupoints. Thousands of people around the world are tapping to release fears, phobias, blocks, anger, guilt, cravings, stress, self-sabotage etc. EFT can also be used to enhance and improve academic and athletic performance, self-confidence and self-esteem, health and wellness, psychic and intuitive abilities, sex and relationships etc. EFT can be applied to improve virtually every aspect of human behaviour.

▶ EFT is a revolutionary new method for rapidly resolving emotional distress.

▶ EFT is a tapping technique (not a talking technique).

▶ EFT is a self-help and self-empowerment tool that people can use for themselves, their friends and their families.

EFT and meridian tapping:

- are highly effective
- work rapidly
- work on a wide variety of issues
- are painless with no side effects.

When people tap on specific points on the body while focusing on an upsetting memory or issue, several things often happen.

- The emotional distress lightens or releases entirely.
- They become more present in their bodies.
- Other symptoms sometimes release as well.
- They spontaneously experience a new perception, a fresh point of view.
- They feel lighter, clearer and freer.

The shifts and changes that people experience are palpable and often permanent.

What can EFT be used for?

- phobias
- traumas
- stress
- insomnia
- grief
- guilt
- self-sabotage
- shame
- anger
- upsets
- resentment
- asthma
- anxiety
- allergies
- depression
- cravings
- addictions
- rashes
- bee stings
- some health conditions
- attention deficit disorder (ADD)
- learning issues
- pre-menstrual syndrome (PMS)
- post-traumatic stress disorder (PTSD).

EFT can also improve and enhance:

- grades
- test scores
- academic performance
- focus
- concentration
- sports performance
- intuition
- psychic abilities

- musical performance
- health
- well-being
- relationships
- self-esteem
- communication
- self-improvement
- spiritual growth.

Gary Craig, the founder of EFT, enthusiastically urges us to 'try it on everything!'

Key point

Virtually all aspects of human behaviour can be improved with EFT and meridian tapping.

Where did EFT come from?

EFT was developed by Gary Craig, an American engineer and businessman. In the early 1990s Craig heard reports of something that sounded unbelievable; people were relieving long-standing mental and emotional problems just by tapping on acupressure points. He called Dr Roger Callahan, the developer of what is now called Thought Field Therapy (TFT), and questioned him about his methods. Although it seemed too good to be true, Craig decided to attend one of Callahan's training seminars. He had one reservation; he was not a doctor or licensed therapist. Callahan's response was, 'That's not a problem at all. You'll have that much less to unlearn.'

Craig attended Callahan's basic and advanced training and realized that here was the key to one of mankind's oldest and most vexing problems: how to rapidly and effectively relieve emotional pain.

EFT is a simplified, more user-friendly version of TFT. Where did TFT come from? Ah, that's a story...

A SERENDIPITOUS DISCOVERY

In the early 1980s Roger Callahan was practising psychology in Palm Springs, California. Like the psychologist-turned-author Wayne Dyer, Callahan had grown up in foster homes, which fuelled a life-long desire to help people relieve their emotional pain. One of his patients, 'Mary', had a fear of water even while bathing and refused to go out of the house when it was raining. He had been treating her for over a year, with very little progress.

Mary often experienced nausea just thinking about water. At this time Callahan was studying applied kinesiology, a healing system which involves testing the strength of different muscle groups, also called 'muscle testing'. Applied kinesiology was developed by an American chiropractor, Dr George Goodheart. One of his discoveries was that certain muscles were associated with specific acupuncture meridians. When the meridian was 'out of balance', the corresponding muscle would test 'weak'; when he corrected the meridian imbalance, the corresponding muscle would then test 'strong'. Goodheart developed detailed charts and protocols for correcting these meridian imbalances.

Callahan knew from his study of kinesiology that nausea, which is in the stomach, was associated with the stomach energy meridian. He asked Mary to think about water while he gently tapped on Stomach 1, two meridian points on the bony orbits under her eyes. Within a minute or so Mary reported that 'the sick feeling in her stomach' was gone, as he expected; but so also was her long-standing phobia, which he did not expect. Callahan decided to test the results by asking Mary to go outside to the swimming pool. He reported what happened next as follows:

'I fully expected her to resist as usual, but to my surprise, I had to hurry to keep up with her on the way to the pool. For the first time, she looked at the water, put her head near it and splashed water in her face... I watched in amazement as she joyfully shouted, "It's gone, it's gone!"'

Like many other discoveries in science, his finding was both fortunate and serendipitous. Callahan then began doing extensive muscle testing with every one of his patients. Over time he noticed certain patterns, and developed treatment protocols of tapping on meridian points in sequences, which he codified into what is now Thought Field Therapy (TFT).

ANOTHER DISCOVERY

As Callahan developed his new system, he found that it worked about 65–70 percent of the time. Why didn't it work 100 percent of the time? As all human beings are hard-wired the same way, if a principle or procedure works some of the time, in theory at least it should potentially work all the time. In muscle testing some people, he found that they would muscle test 'weak' when he would ask them say 'I wish to be healthy,' and muscle test strong when asked to say 'I wish to be sick' (the reverse of the way they should test). He realized that there was a blockage to getting better at work, which he called a 'psychological reversal'. Using physical procedures to address and correct these 'reversals', his reported success rate in treating emotional disorders increased to over 90 percent.

These results are astounding, to say the least and incurred a lot of scepticism. Callahan sought to gain attention for his methods through the media. He appeared on a series of call-in radio shows, offering to treat phobias. His success rate in treating people with phobias on the radio (people who were not even in his physical presence!) was 97 percent (66 successes out of a total 68 callers). This demonstration was repeated on call-in radio shows nine years later by a colleague, Dr Glenn Leonoff, whose success rate was also 97 percent (66 successes out of 68 callers). One difference was the amount of average time spent with each caller. Dr Leonoff's average time was just over six minutes, while Dr Callahan's average time was only four minutes and 34 seconds.

TFT is a very powerful system, but its popularity has remained limited. One possible reason for this is that it is designed primarily for mental health professions; TFT contains numerous 'algorithms', different sequences of meridian points to be tapped for different issues. Like the standard medical model, it is a robust but complex system, consisting of different treatments for different conditions.

One of Callahan's many students was Gary Craig. Interestingly, Craig was not a psychologist or doctor or therapist; he was an engineer-turned-businessman who had a passion for helping people achieve their peak performance. He studied with Callahan for a couple of years and realized that the way Callahan was marketing his techniques was limiting its spread and acceptance. Asking himself how he could make the tapping system simpler and more user-friendly, Craig came upon the idea of having people tap on one sequence of points rather than many. After experimenting with this 'one size fits all' model, he came out with EFT in the early 1990s. EFT grew rapidly through Craig's seminars, presentations and website and meridian tapping continues to grow rapidly to this day.

EFT and the other forms of meridian tapping are part of a new movement in psychology, called Energy Psychology. Energy Psychology is a field of innovative interventions that balance, restore and improve human functioning by stimulating the human 'subtle energy system'. These techniques are spreading rapidly around the world (largely via the internet) and have been known to catalyse rapid, dramatic and lasting changes in feelings, beliefs, mental states and behaviours.

The invisible epidemic

Our understanding of stress, also called *the general adaptation response*, is based on the work of the Canadian physician Hans Selye. He conducted a series of studies in which he exposed rats to stressors such as extreme heat or cold, electric shocks and pulling their tails. He discovered that even with different stressors the rats exhibited the same basic physiological response: weight loss, stomach ulcers, weakening of their immune systems and enlargement of their adrenal glands. After numerous studies he came to realize that all these changes were the result of an innate, adaptive mechanism that had been overactivated.

Stress is a condition in which environmental demands exceed the natural regulatory capacity of an organism. Our bodies have an inner wisdom and are continually moving towards and maintaining *homeostasis*, a condition of physiological equilibrium, a state of good health. It is estimated that upwards of 80–90 percent of all illnesses are stress-related.

It is important to recognize that stress is not 'out there', nor is it 'all in your mind'. The stress response, also called 'fight or flight', is an innate physiological response designed to help us survive. However, stress is extremely stressful on our bodies! Adrenaline and cortisol levels rise, the heart races, blood pressure increases, blood flow is diverted from our internal organs to our limbs and we either fight or flee. For those rare emergencies when our lives are threatened by lions, tigers or bears, it works superbly well.

Key point

The stress response, also called 'fight or flight', is extremely stressful on our bodies. For rare emergencies, it works superbly well. But when triggered every day, it becomes maladaptive and destructive.

However, when our stress response is triggered repeatedly – by deadlines, ringing phones, demanding customers – we do not have time to readapt and the stress response becomes maladaptive. Over time, the body's capacity to adapt is depleted, leading to adrenal fatigue and exhaustion. When blood is diverted to the limbs for fight or flight, our digestive, immune and reproductive systems shut down to conserve energy for survival. When we are repeatedly stressed without time to recover, these systems become chronically impaired. One result of this is the rise of the gastrointestinal, autoimmune, menstrual and chronic fatigue problems that many people are experiencing today.

The 'fight or flight' response also shunts blood flow away from the prefrontal cortex (seat of rational thinking) to our limbic system (emotional brain). When people say things like 'I couldn't think straight' or 'I wasn't in my right mind', this is literally true. When in fight or flight modes, all our resources are focused on surviving and we are not thinking or behaving rationally or normally.

To call stress an epidemic is an understatement. Millions experience symptoms of stress every day, from headaches and heartburn to heart disease and high blood pressure. Stress also contributes to other health problems, including insomnia and irritable bowel syndrome. Emotional symptoms include anxiety, nervousness, panic attacks, lack of appetite or overeating, loss of energy or enthusiasm, irritability and depression.

To combat these symptoms, doctors wage war with their arsenal of anti-medicines: anti-biotics, anti-inflammatories, anti-depressants and anti-anxiety meds. These medicines can be lifesaving when used in the short term but become problematic when used for extended periods. While doctors are busy writing prescriptions, many healthcare practitioners are recommending practices like yoga, meditation, t'ai chi and deep breathing. Meanwhile, many seek to manage their stress with alcohol, tobacco and drugs, whether prescribed or recreational.

Activity: Unwinding stress

This activity may be done holding your own head or with a partner.

1 Sit comfortably in a chair with your ankles crossed and eyes closed.
2 Cover your forehead with one hand, while cradling the back of your head, right at the top of the neck, with the other.
3 While breathing deeply and gently, notice any stress or tension in your body.
4 Give the stress a name (3–5 words) and rate its intensity from 0–10 (0 = no stress and 10 = overwhelming).
5 Pay attention to the subtle sensations and feelings, noticing where they are and their feeling quality.
6 Follow the sensations with your attention, as they move, shift or change.
7 Continue holding, attending and breathing until the stress has shifted and dissipated.

As you gently cradle your head in your hands (no pressure is necessary), you may feel your hands growing warmer as the energy moves and circulates. As you progress, the felt experience may get stronger or weaker, or it may shift from one emotion to another, as you process layers of experience. Or it may move from the chest to another part of the body etc. Any change is positive and is a sign that the stress is releasing and unwinding.

This technique is called *Frontal/Occipital Holding* and is a gentle yet effective method for defusing stress. Note that this practice is meditative; EFT tends to work much faster.

Yoga, meditation, t'ai chi and breathing exercises are powerful practices and I myself meditate and do yoga stretches every day. But they are *practices* and to be effective need to be practised for at least 30–90 minutes every day. This is their downside; in our hyperactive, multitasking society, many people believe they 'don't have the time'. The single biggest reason people give for not exercising, eating well or generally taking care of themselves is lack of time.

EFT is a one-minute practice. You can do one full round of the Basic Recipe in less than one minute. Stress can often be defused in 1–3 rounds and you can sometimes clear entire issues within a few minutes. Another advantage is that while yoga, meditation and deep breathing are global practices, meridian tapping is very specific – it targets the specific stress that's at a high level for you in each moment.

Key point

EFT is a one-minute practice. You can do the EFT Basic Recipe in one minute, and you can sometimes clear issues within a few minutes.

The emotion–immune connection

Your emotions affect every cell in your body. Mind and body, mental and physical, are intertwined.

Dr Thomas Tutko, the 'father of sports psychology'

For many years it was believed that our immune systems were purely physiological and were essentially 'immune' to the ups and downs of our emotional states. It is now documented that our thoughts and emotions affect our brains and immune systems directly and immediately. It is fascinating, for example, that neurotransmitters such as serotonin, epinephrine and dopamine, also bind to receptors in our immune systems. Conversely, there are receptor sites in the brain for the major immunotransmitters. This suggests that there are direct, two-way connections between our emotions and our immune system. This is why we are most likely to catch a cold when we're stressed. Chronic stress, sadness and worry suppress the immune system, while love, laughter and social connections strengthen it. In short, happiness affects our health, and our health affects our happiness.

Key point

What we think and feel impacts our immune system directly and immediately. Happiness affects our health, and our health affects our state of mind.

Activity: The mind–body connection

Get a pen and piece of paper and jot down five things you feel angry or upset about. Read your list aloud several times. What emotions and sensations do you notice and feel in your body?

Then take another piece of paper and jot down five to ten things you feel grateful for. Read your list aloud several times. What emotions and sensations do you notice and feel in your body now?

Why do we have emotions?

Emotions can seem like unwelcome intruders which get in the way of trying to live our lives peacefully. Sometimes they are like little pests that bug and bite and annoy us; sometimes like our parents (and partners!), who frustrate the heck out of us; and sometimes like unexpected outbursts that shock and surprise others (or even ourselves). Moods can be like storms that appear out of nowhere, or like grey clouds of depression that block our enthusiasm and seem to last forever. Even when we try to be positive, 'keep a stiff upper lip' and maintain control, we can feel them stirring and stewing. We have our 'outer' persona, the professional appearance we present to the world, but beneath the surface lie these subterranean currents, just waiting to erupt or explode, to betray or bewilder.

Feelings are feedback. They are very primal, non-verbal, almost instantaneous communications which help us thrive and survive. They are emotional thermostats, continually monitoring our well-being, motivating us to meet our needs. When we need food or water, we feel hungry or thirsty. When we're threatened, fear motivates us to flee or seek safety. When we lose someone we love, we grieve as a way of calling for love and reassurance and reconnection. When we're treated unjustly, anger motivates us to correct the injustice and 'set things straight'.

Key point

Feelings are feedback. They are primal, non-verbal, almost instantaneous communications which help us thrive and survive.

We have two aspects to our brains, one that thinks and one that feels. Rational thought and decision making take place primarily in the prefrontal cortex, while our feelings are processed by the limbic system, the seat of our emotional brain. Our emotional processing system works much faster than our cognitive processing system. If we had to wait while we ponder and figure out the best strategy for dealing with a tiger, we'd be lunch. Our feelings motivate us to fight or flee, to meet our survival needs, much faster than thoughts trickling down from our rational brain.

People sometimes complain about all the 'negativity' in the tabloids and news media. This is largely a function of biology; we are hard-wired to react to threats, violence and danger. Sensationalism sells; news that presses our fear, anger or betrayal buttons has much more emotional impact than dry statistics or a thousand random acts of kindness.

Under normal circumstances, our emotions can be overridden by our cognitive brains – we've all learned how to 'suck it up' and 'keep a stiff upper lip'. But the converse is also true; when we feel threatened, the limbic system is activated, stress hormones flood the body, and blood flow to the prefrontal cortex is reduced, with the result that rational thinking and decision making are temporarily impaired. To use Daniel Goleman's colourful phrase in *Emotional Intelligence* (1995), our brain is 'hijacked' by the limbic system. Emotions temporarily trump reason; this is why we can't 'think straight' when we're stressed or upset.

Key point

When we're feeling stressed, blood flow to the prefrontal cortex is reduced and our capacities for rational thinking and decision making are temporarily impaired.

Case study: James's story

'James' had a lot going for him. A young executive at an internet technology firm, he had a promising career ahead of him. He was also a talented musician and had posted a rap video on YouTube that had gotten 50,000 hits. He was very fit and well-built as a result of regular workouts at the gym for years. Yet despite his abilities and accomplishments, he had chronic social anxiety.

In my office he told me that he avoided looking people in the eyes. He believed that people didn't like him and that they were 'always' talking about him. Despite the fact that he was respected at work and had recently gotten a raise, he believed that people saw him negatively. His chronic social anxiety was a symptom of this.

'I HATE anxiety,' he told me. 'It's interfering with my life. I just want it to go away.'

Stuck alarms

While our emotions are an amazingly sensitive biofeedback system, like any form of electronic signalling mechanism, they can get 'stuck'. We've all had the experience of hearing someone's car or house alarm go off accidentally. The siren blares on and on annoyingly, sometimes for hours, until the owner comes and turns it off. The sound of an insistent siren is so loud and invasive that it's not possible to think or feel anything else while it's blaring. Similarly many of us experience stuck emotions, chronic anxiety, inconsolable grief or seething resentment that continue blaring and sounding long after the original emergency has passed. Like Sleeping Beauty waiting for her Prince to awaken her, stuck emotions are waiting for someone with the key to come and turn them off.

Stuck emotions can also be like 'stuck pedals', constantly revving our engines at high speed, wearing us out in the process. Stuck emotions can cause chronic stress, wear and tear on our 'engines' and relationships, fatigue and exhaustion, and illness and 'dis-ease'.

Rather than dealing with the emotion directly, many of us are taught from an early age that emotions are not acceptable. We learn that 'children should be seen but not heard', and that 'little girls don't get angry' and 'big boys don't cry'. As we get older we 'get with the program', and learn to 'tough it out', 'keep a stiff upper lip', and 'not be wimps or sissies'. Thus we are systematically taught to ignore and tune our emotions out, with the result that we are no longer sensitive to our bodies, our feelings or our needs. As we get older we get better and better at tuning our 'negative' feelings out by drinking, drug-taking or distracting, or by overeating and attempting to feed vague hungers we've lost touch with.

How do you know when an emotion is 'stuck'?

When we observe children, we see how fluid their emotions are. A child will fall, feel hurt and scared and start crying. She'll run to her mum for comfort and reassurance; and after being reassured that she's OK, stop crying and return to her play, all within a few minutes. There are occasions, such as the death of a loved one or anger at an ongoing injustice, where the emotion will last longer. But in general, if the emotion lasts longer than a few hours, you know that it's 'stuck'.

If you can relate to any of this, this book is for you. It will reveal the cause of blocks and stuck emotions, and how to turn stuck alarms off. You will learn powerful tools for overcoming blocks and walls, freeing yourself from emotional bottles and bondage. More than that, you may even find yourself feeling happier, healthier and able to live and love more fully than you had thought possible. This is the promise of energy healing with EFT.

Who can do EFT?

YOU! If you can follow directions, feel your feelings, use your fingers and desire to live a healthier, happier life, you can and will do EFT successfully.

Key point

This book is based on a simple premise: Feeling is healing. What you feel, you can heal.

EFT and the other forms of meridian therapy have been controversial in academic and professional circles, in part because of early enthusiastic claims that had not (at that time) been validated by research. Even now (2013), research is only just beginning to demonstrate efficacy for the different forms of meridian tapping. While thousands of people have used EFT successfully for many kinds of issues, please note that EFT is not a panacea. As with any other self-help technique, EFT and meridian tapping work for many people, for many issues, much of the time. EFT can be applied to a wide range of issues and concerns. With intention, practice and persistence, your success will increase. You will learn how to improve your success rate with the hints in Chapter 7.

Key point

EFT is not a panacea. Meridian tapping works for many people, for many issues, much of the time. However, you can improve your success rate with intention, practice and persistence in using the methods described in this book.

Intentions

Everything we do, we do to satisfy an Intention: something we intend to do for some purpose. Meridian tapping is an investment of your valuable time and energy. You will get more out of EFT and meridian tapping, or any other self-help technique, if you get clear about your intentions, i.e. what you are doing this for.

For many people, their initial intention may be to free themselves from emotional or physical pain. For others it may be to change an unhealthy or destructive habit. For some it may be to improve their relationships or to become 'better' people. And for some it will be to flourish: to 'be all they can be', to actualize their almost-infinite human potential.

Getting clear about and writing down your intentions will increase your motivation to practise and aim you in the direction toward achieving your goals.

Activity

Write down 3–5 responses to complete this phrase: 'My intentions in learning and practising EFT are...'

Things to remember

The main points to remember from this chapter are:

* the Emotional Freedom Technique is a novel method for rapidly releasing and resolving emotional distress, simply by tapping on acupoints
* EFT and meridian tapping are highly effective, work rapidly, work on a wide variety of issues and are painless with no side effects
* what we think and feel impacts our immune system directly and immediately. Mental states impact our health and our health affects our state of mind.
* feelings are feedback. They are primal, non-verbal communications which help us thrive and survive. They are emotional thermostats, continually monitoring our well-being, motivating us to meet our needs.
* feeling is healing: what you feel, you can heal
* EFT is not a panacea. EFT works for many people, for many issues, much of the time.
* if you can follow directions, feel your feelings and use your fingers, you can and will do EFT successfully.

The healing power of touch

> We cannot touch something without being touched by it in the very same instant. We cannot be touched without touching. Walking barefoot, our feet kiss the earth with every step and the earth kisses right back and we feel it.
>
> Jon Kabat-Zinn, *Coming to Our Senses*

In this chapter you will learn:

- ► *why touch was our first medicine*
- ► *why touch is a fundamental biological need*
- ► *how to listen to your body*
- ► *how we can change even 'involuntary' behaviours*
- ► *how to engage the relaxation response.*

Touching was our first medicine. Long before we had aspirin and antibiotics, we had our hands and each other. When babies cry, their mothers walk over, pick them up and embrace them. Some of our earliest, fondest memories are of being held and rocked in the warmth of our mother's arms. Hugging, snuggling, kissing, rocking and other forms of touching are the most primal ways we share and express love for each other. We all need several doses of 'Vitamin T' every day. Touching is both nurturing and healing.

Touching is the most primal way we have of healing and soothing ourselves. When someone hurts or is in pain, it's instinctive to touch and hold them. How do you know when you love someone, when you feel close to them? We get physically close, we hug and touch and hold them. Touching is loving.

The skin is our largest organ, containing millions of nerve receptors. Our hands are particularly rich in nerve receptors, which is why they are exquisitely sensitive to touching and being touched. The word 'touch' has one of the longest entries in the Oxford English Dictionary, even longer than the entry for 'love'. Touch involves both physical sensations in our bodies and emotional feeling. Our experience of feeling is rooted in the sense of touch. When we speak of 'being touched', especially by an act of beauty or sympathy, we are describing the state of being emotionally moved.

'Touch is the primary language of compassion, love and gratitude – emotions at the heart of trust and cooperation – even more than facial expressions and voice. Touch is the central medium in which the goodness of one individual is shared with another. Touch is the original contact high,' writes the social psychologist Dacher Keltner. We are hard-wired to touch and be touched.

Touch is not a luxury, reserved for those who can afford a weekly massage. Tactile stimulation is necessary for our growth and development. Baby mice and rats that are not licked by their mothers often fail to thrive and die. During the 19th and early 20th century, most infants in institutions died in their first year of life from what was called 'infantile atrophy'. After hospitals instituted rules that babies should be picked up and rocked and 'mothered' several times a day, mortality rates dropped dramatically. 'The manner in which the young of all mammals snuggle and cuddle against the body of the mother and against the bodies of their siblings strongly suggests that cutaneous stimulation is an important biological need,' notes Ashley Montagu, in his seminal book *Touching*.

Touch is a fundamental biological need, along with food, clothing and shelter. Many of us grew up in emotionally 'cold' families, where touching was discouraged. Some parents did not want to give in to or spoil their children, so they left them in cribs or with nannies. As a result many people feel touch-deprived and experience what has been called 'skin hunger'. This is one reason why many men and women become promiscuous or have affairs; they will do anything just to be held and touched.

Key point

Touch is a fundamental biological need. Babies who were not touched or rocked in infancy have died in infancy.

Regular touching:

► decreases anxiety

► lowers blood pressure

► increases endorphins (our feel-good chemicals)

► helps us rest and sleep better

► helps us bond and connect with others.

The importance of touch was vividly demonstrated by a research study conducted by Harry Harlow and associates. In this experiment he presented infant rhesus monkeys with surrogate 'mothers', one made from soft cloth and the other made from wire. In the first group, the wire mother held a bottle with food while the cloth mother held no food; in the other, the cloth mother held the bottle while the wire mother held nothing. Overwhelmingly, the baby monkeys preferred spending their time clinging to the cloth mothers. Even when the wire mothers provided food, the infants visited her only to feed. Harlow concluded that this 'contact comfort' was essential to the healthy development of both monkeys and children.

Touching is also profoundly healing. We are living in a 'golden age' of healing, where many forms of body work and somatic healing are being revived and new ones are being discovered. Besides well-known modalities like massage, chiropractic and physical therapy, there are Oriental therapies such as shiatsu, acupressure and acupuncture, as well as Rolfing, the Alexander technique, trager work, Touch for Health etc. There are also many energy-based techniques such as reiki, healing touch, laying on of hands, therapeutic touch, pranic healing etc. New healing modalities are being discovered and developed every day.

EFT and meridian tapping are forms of natural bio-destressing. They are methods for triggering the relaxation response and self-soothing (rather than self-medicating!) ourselves when upset. They work by tapping acupoints on our bodies, activating receptors in our skin that soothe and calm us down. They are powerful methods for tapping into our own natural, innate mechanisms for healing.

The language of the body

It has been estimated that our senses receive 11 million bits of information every second (Tor Nørretranders, 1998), of which our conscious mind is aware of approximately 40. That's a tiny percentage! We cannot attend to all the stimuli flooding our senses 24/7 and so we 'tune in' and 'tune out'. We are continually making choices about what we're 'tuning in' to, whether that's our friends, music, Facebook or politics. But while we're busy 'tuning in', we're also 'tuning out'. With years of practice many of us have mastered the fine art of tuning out: our parents, our partners, the opposition party – and our own bodies. We then wander around less than fully awake and aware, ignoring cues from without and within.

Our bodies are continually talking to us. Our bodies speak to us in dreams, images, feelings, sensations and symptoms. Our touch is more eloquent than our words. Many of us are fluent in two or three languages or adept at navigating our iPads, iPods and iPhones. Yet trying to understand our bodies' communications can seem like trying to read Chinese.

Key point

Images, feelings, somatic sensations and symptoms are the language of the body. If we want to 'hear' and communicate with our bodies, we need to attend to and listen to their sensations and symptoms.

You are likely familiar with biofeedback. This technology provides immediate, real-time information about our physiology that enables us to regulate autonomic functions such as muscle tension, heart rate or brainwaves. An amazing aspect of biofeedback is that even involuntary, 'unconscious' behaviour can be changed; it simply needs to be amplified and associated with a sensory signal such as a musical tone. We can learn to change even seemingly involuntary and 'unconscious' behaviours by attuning to subtle signals in our bodies and bringing them back into balance.

Biofeedback is based on a very powerful principle: that whatever we are aware of, we can change.

Key point

We cannot change what we are unaware of. But whatever we become aware of, we can change.

EFT is a body-mind, psychosensory technique. We can enhance success with EFT by attuning to subtle somatic sensations – the 'wisdom of the body' underlying the chatter of our minds. One reason why many of us experience anxiety is because we ignore our bodies' messages. Then, like little children, our bodies clamour ever more loudly, trying to get our attention. When we listen to our bodies and start to get their messages, they calm down and we feel more connected – because we are.

Activity: Listening to the body

Close your eyes, breathe several deep breaths and attune to your body. Now think of an emotion you experience often and rate its intensity from 0–10, as you experience it now.

Then ask yourself each of the following questions slowly and wait for a response to arise; where in your body do you feel it? What are its

Every person is unique and every person's experience will be
different. Take and accept what your body gives you; whatever
you experience is right for you.

The relaxation response

Herbert Benson, Professor of Medicine at Harvard Medical School,
began investigating the effects of Transcendental Meditation (TM)
in the 1960s. He found that during TM meditators experienced
lower heart and breathing rates, lower blood pressure and muscle
relaxation. Their EEG brainwave patterns resembled those of
someone asleep even though they were wide awake. He eventually
realized that this response was not unique to TM; that modalities
such as hypnosis, autogenic training and other forms of meditation
could elicit this state as well. These different methods were
triggering an innate, self-healing mechanism, parallel to the fight/
flight stress response. He named this the 'relaxation response'.

The relaxation response is a natural, innate antidote to the fight/
flight response. It helps people counteract the toxic effects of
chronic stress by slowing their breathing rate, relaxing muscles
and normalizing autonomic functioning. Consciously engaging
the relaxation response is an effective way to give our body-minds
needed rest and relaxation and to balance our sympathetic (active
arousal) and parasympathetic (rest and rejuvenate) nervous systems.

Fight/flight response	Organ	Relaxation response
Rate increased	Heart	Rate decreased
Blood pressure increased	Heart	Blood pressure decreased
Bronchial muscle relaxed	Lungs	Bronchial muscle contracted
Breathing rate increased	Lungs	Breathing rate slower
Pupil dilation	Eye	Pupil constriction
Motility reduced	Intestine	Motility increased
Sphincter closed	Bladder	Sphincter relaxed
Decreased urine secretion	Kidneys	Increased urine secretion

There are a number of different ways to elicit the relaxation response. Besides meditation, other practices include yoga, deep breathing, reiki, acupuncture, massage and the different touch therapies – including tapping.

Key point

The relaxation response is a natural, innate antidote to the fight/flight response. It counteracts the toxic effects of chronic stress by slowing the breathing rate, relaxing muscles and normalizing autonomic functioning.

Activity: Engaging the relaxation response

Either lie on your back on a bed or couch or sit back in an easy chair. Cross your ankles over each other, put your right hand with the palm turned up under your tailbone (coccyx) and your left hand cradling the base of the skull (occiput) at the top of the back of your neck. Close your eyes and breathe slowly and deeply for 3–10 minutes, paying attention to your internal body sensations.

What did you notice?

This is a simple yet effective method, called the Eeman Relaxation Circuit, for turning on the relaxation response and balancing our nervous systems. It can be used in the middle of the day in place of a power nap (or to start a nap), or any time you feel the need to unwind mentally and reconnect with yourself.

Touching ourselves

It is instinctual to touch and hold ourselves (and our loved ones) when we're hurting physically or emotionally. Touching is a self-soothing behaviour that activates nerve receptors in our skin and calms us down. When feeling upset, some people drum their fingers on their desks, some hold their chin in their hands, some stroke their face or hair, some rub their temples, and some cross their arms and hold themselves.

Where do you touch yourself when you're feeling upset?

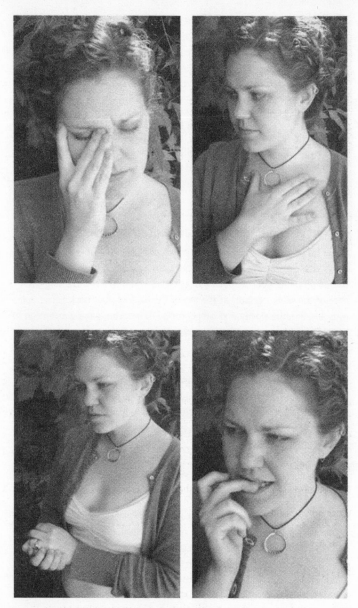

Figures 1–6: Unconscious self-soothing behaviours

Activity: How do you soothe yourself?

Think of how you touch yourself to calm down when feeling upset. Then think of a recent upsetting experience, notice where you feel it in your body and rate its intensity from 0–10. Recall the memory in your mind and feel it in your body while breathing and touching yourself as you normally do, for about a minute or so, until you feel a shift. (If you don't touch or hold yourself when upset, try gently rubbing your temples, holding your head in your hands or crossing your arms and hugging yourself while breathing, feeling and recalling the experience.)

Then sit up straight, shake out your hands and look around.

What do you notice now?

Rockin' and rollin'

A particularly soothing way to touch is rocking. When we were scared or crying as small children, our mothers soothed our fears away by picking us up and gently rocking us. We recognize repeated rhythmic motion as healing. Even though much of modern music can be very loud, dissonant and seemingly chaotic, it is experienced (by some!) as soothing and reassuring. Whether in the forms of rocking, drumming or dancing, repeated rhythms create resonances in mind and body that we find soothing and healing.

We intuitively understand the language of rhythm. Both children and adults will often rock themselves when distressed, as there is a deep comfort and security in rhythmic movement. Gentle rocking evokes body-memories of being in the womb, where we were subjected to gentle rhythmic pulsation, and of being cradled and rocked during infancy. Rhythmic movement is hypnotic and we experience rocking, drumming and dancing as both nurturing and healing. When we rhythmically tap on ourselves, we're giving ourselves a non-verbal message that everything is OK, that we're safe and that we're loved.

Repeated rhythmic movement is very powerful, especially when done in a group or community. You can literally feel the energy when people come together to dance or drum. At the right rhythm, repeated movement creates resonance, where the wave motions that are repeatedly reinforced get stronger and stronger. Just like the story of the bridge that began swaying and collapsed in resonance with the marching soldiers and like the Italian tenor Enrico Caruso shattering wine glasses with his voice, so also rhythmic movements like drumming, toning (chanting and making healing sounds) and tapping can break through and release blockages in our bodies and minds.

Key point

Rhythmic movements like drumming, toning and tapping can 'break through' and release blockages in our bodies and minds.

The Institute of HeartMath has done some fascinating research showing that positive emotions have immediate effects on both our heart and brain rhythms. The wave patterns of 'positive' emotions like joy, love and gratitude are more coherent than those of 'negative' emotions. Dr Rollin McCraty, Director of Research for HeartMath, describes the state of coherence as 'the ordered or constructive distribution of power within a waveform. The more stable the frequency and shape of the waveform, the higher the coherence… coherence describes the degree of order and stability in the rhythmic activity generated by a single oscillatory system.'

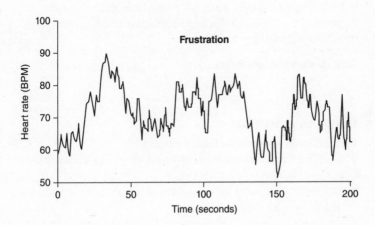

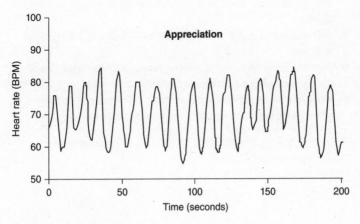

Source: Institute of HeartMath

Activity: Rocking and tapping through feelings

Think of a recent, mildly upsetting memory or situation, attune to its sensations in your body and rate it from 0–10 (0 = not upsetting at all, 10 = overwhelming).

Sit on a chair with your feet flat on the floor and your arms crossed, with the right hand on the left upper arm and the left hand on the right upper arm. While still feeling the sensations and emotions in your body, begin rocking left and right, slowly and gently, while alternately and rhythmically tapping your hands on your arms and breathing comfortably, for at least 1–2 minutes.

What do you notice now?

Things to remember

The main points to remember from this chapter are:

* touch is a fundamental biological need. Babies who were not touched or rocked in infancy have died in infancy.
* we cannot change what we are unaware of. But whatever we become aware of, we can change.
* we can learn to change even seemingly involuntary behaviours by attuning to subtle signals in our bodies and bringing them back into balance
* the relaxation response is a natural, innate antidote to the fight/flight response
* rhythmic movements like drumming, toning and tapping can break through and release blockages in our bodies and minds
* resonance between heart and brain can create a state of coherence, where heart, brain and emotions are working together.

It's all energy

Do you remember how electrical currents and 'unseen waves' were laughed at? Knowledge about man is still in its infancy.

Albert Einstein

Something unknown is doing we don't know what.
    Sir Arthur Eddington, commenting on quantum physics

In this chapter you will learn:

▶ *how we are bathed in an ocean of energy*
▶ *the structure of the human energetic anatomy*
▶ *principles of energy healing*
▶ *exercises for sensing energy in our bodies*
▶ *ways to enhance energy healing.*

Some days we feel GREAT, like we're 'on top of the world', and everything is flowing our way. Other days we feel 'blah', we're 'out of synch', we're just 'not connecting', and we 'don't know what's wrong'. Have you ever wondered why that is?

It's all energy. When we're tuned in, turned on and connected, then not only are our inner energies connected, but we're in synch: with ourselves, with others and with the Universe around us. When we're tuned out, turned off and dis-connected, we're out of synch: with ourselves, with others and with the Universe.

This chapter explores this fascinating topic and will show you simple ways to tune in, turn on and connect with the energy all around you.

Bathing in the ocean of energy

We are bathed in fields of energy, in the forms of gravity, light, heat and cosmic radiation from the sun and the earth's electromagnetic field. We are also bathed in man-made fields of energy, from radio and television, AM and FM waves, and the electromagnetic fields of all our appliances, computers, microwaves and cell phones. We absorb energy from the living Universe all around us: from the sun, the air, the food we eat and the water we drink. We also receive and exchange energy with everyone around us, whether 'good vibes' or 'bad'. We are surrounded by an invisible, energetic universe, nourished and supported by fields of energy within us and all around us.

We have been taught and conditioned to see everything as 'things', i.e. as individual objects separate from each other and from the greater universe. But all 'things' exist only in relationship to each other. Just as male cannot exist without female and up cannot exist without down, so matter and energy, waves and particles are two sides of the same quantum coin.

The biologist Bruce Lipton writes:

> Quantum physicists discovered that physical atoms are made up of vortices of energy that are constantly spinning and vibrating... . The fact that energy and matter are one and the same is precisely what Einstein recognized when

he concluded: $E = mc^2$... . The Universe is *one indivisible, dynamic whole* in which energy and matter are so deeply entangled it is impossible to consider them as independent elements. (2005; my italic)

Key point

The Universe is one indivisible, dynamic whole in which energy and matter are so deeply entangled that it is impossible to consider them as independent elements.

Underlying all physical phenomena is a field pregnant with potential energy. Although the definition of a vacuum is 'a space from which all matter has been removed', vacuums are not really empty. Even when all the matter has been removed, there remains a zero point field, full of potential energy. It is estimated that every cubic metre of 'empty' space contains 10^{113} Joules per cubic metre (Milloni, 1994). This is roughly equivalent to the amount of energy expended by 100 billion stars shining for one million years! This zero point field undergirds what we think of as our solid, physical bodies as well.

The prevailing scientific paradigm holds that we human beings are our bodies, that our bodies are composed of cells made of proteins, which are large chains of molecules grouped together. These molecules are made of atoms, composed of protons, neutrons and electrons, themselves made up of infinitesimally smaller subatomic particles, some of which are bleeping in and out of existence in a few millionths of a second. This paradigm holds that all our metabolic and behavioural functions, including consciousness itself, are a result of biochemical interactions.

But even though we have bodies, we are not our bodies. We have personalities, but we are not our personalities. Who we are most essentially is something insubstantial and non-material, that has been called 'soul', 'spirit' or 'consciousness'. We are energetic beings in an energetic universe, individualized fields of awareness in inter-penetrating fields of energy.

Key point

Who we are, most essentially, is something called 'soul' or 'spirit'. We are energetic beings bathed in fields of energy.

Just as magnets, motors and electric circuits have electromagnetic fields around them, so also all living things have a biofield around them. First called L-fields (or Life-fields) by the scientist and Yale professor H. S. Burr, these fields are believed to organize and coordinate the functioning of all living processes simultaneously. In addition to the fields around our bodies, every organ and every cell has its own field as well. These cells are themselves composed of atoms and electrons, surrounded by their own infinitesimally subtle fields. We are surrounded and supported by an interactive, interpenetrating hierarchy of fields within fields within fields. Some people who are sensitive can see or feel these fields, as halos and auras. We are only in the beginning phases of being able to map, measure and understand these subtle fields of energy, both all around as well as inside ourselves.

Figure 7

Our energetic anatomy

Just as our physical bodies have an anatomy, consisting of the skeleton, muscles and fascia, internal glands and organs, so also our 'energetic body' has an anatomy. This energetic body consists of:

▶ circuits or pathways called meridians

▶ the seven major energy centres

▶ the human aura, also called the biofield or human energy field.

Just as the circulation of blood and neural impulses is vital for good health and optimal functioning, so also the circulation of subtle energies through our 'energy circulatory system' is vital for physical, emotional and spiritual health. 'Meridians carry energy the way arteries carry blood,' says Donna Eden, the author of *Energy Medicine* (1998).

The human biofield, or aura, has been known for thousands of years. If you look at the sacred art and iconography of different religious traditions, including Christian, Hindu and Buddhist, there are numerous depictions of halos around Jesus, Mary, Buddha and the saints and spiritual masters. The fact that these depictions are seen in different religious traditions worldwide points to a common, cross-cultural reality.

Another aspect of our subtle energy system are the various energy centres. These centres, called *chakras* by the Hindus, have also been described in several religious traditions, including the Ayurvedic, Chinese and Sufi traditions. While not as widely recognized as the biofield, they have been depicted in the artwork of both religious and traditional healing systems.

The origins of acupuncture and traditional Chinese medicine are lost in prehistory, but are thought to be around 5,000 years old. The Chinese discovered a complex system of internal energy circuits we now call *meridians*. Knowledge of the meridian pathways was not exclusive to China, but it was here that it reached its highest development. The first written mention of it is found in the *Huang Ti Nei Ching Su Wen* (The Yellow Emperor's Classic of Internal Medicine), which dates back to the second century BCE.

There is a long tradition of understanding subtle energy in the East. Called *chi* or *qi*, internal energy is literally at the heart of all things. Each of us is given a certain amount of energy as part of our constitution. This inner energy can be conserved and cultivated using ancient practices such as the martial arts *t'ai chi* and *pa kua*, as well as in the healing arts of *qi gong*.

When we talk about 'energy' or a 'subtle energy system', some people roll their eyes and think that this is superstition. But consider how many phenomena there are which we know exist but cannot see, such as X-rays, radio and television frequencies, microwaves, heat waves, subatomic particles etc. In fact, virtually all forms of energy are invisible. All the forms of energy we are familiar with and take for granted today – electric, magnetic, nuclear – were at one time unknown. Should we be so arrogant as to think that everything that exists has already been discovered? Less than 150 years ago X-rays and microwaves were unknown and unsuspected, so there are many forms of subtle energy that we are only now beginning to research and understand.

Key point

Virtually all forms of energy are invisible.

We cannot see energy directly, but we can measure it with voltmeters, ammeters, photo-voltaic meters and oscilloscopes. Doctors measure electrical activity in the heart and brain with ECG and EEG devices. Similarly, we can now measure the energy of the human biofield using sophisticated instrumentation such as the Biofield Viewer, Electro Photonic Imaging, Tri-axial meter and and other systems. Dr Thornton Streeter and his colleagues at the Centre for Biofield Sciences are at the forefront of exploring these new technologies (see www. biofieldsciences.com). But even though we cannot see energy, we know it from its effects. The same is true for the subtle energies in our bodies.

There are many names for subtle energy in different traditions. It has been called *chi*, *qi*, *mana*, *prana*, *mojo orgone*, vital force, vital energy, biofield etc. A survey in 1977 found that

97 cultures have names for the human energy field (White & Krippner, 1977). All these different names and concepts point to a shared human experience.

Figure 8: Feeling the field

Activity: Feeling the field

Sit comfortably with your back straight and legs uncrossed. Hold your hands about shoulder-width apart with the palms facing. Breathe slowly and deeply. Now slowly bring your hands towards each other, with the palms facing but not touching, until you sense the energy field between them. Then slowly pull them apart several inches, and then bring them back together (but not touching) again. Repeat several times.

After feeling the field between your hands, hold your hands around your head, chest and shoulders and 'explore' feeling the field around your body. This exercise is also fun to do with another person.

What did you sense and notice?

People experience the field in different ways. Some experience it as warmth, some as 'resistance', and others as being like the sensation of stretching a rubber band. Whatever you experience is right for you.

Principles of energy healing

The principles of energy healing are as follows.

1 Energy follows intention.

2 Health is our natural state. It is natural and normal to feel alive, happy and healthy. When we feel unhappy or unhealthy, something is blocked or out of balance.

3 Health, Energy and Aliveness are synonymous. When our inner energies flow freely, we experience joy, aliveness, health and well-being. When the flow of our inner energies is blocked or disrupted, we experience anxiety, fatigue, frustration and 'dis-ease'.

4 Energy fields carry information. Just as radio waves carry signals that our radios, televisions and cell phones receive, so also the energy flows in our meridians carry information about our state of well-being.

5 The cause of negative emotions is a disruption in the human subtle energy system.

6 Healing is connecting. Dis-ease is a symptom of disturbance, disruption or imbalance.

7 The body heals itself. When we remove the blockages and disruptions, our vital energies flow freely and our bodies heal themselves spontaneously.

Key point

Health is our natural state. It is normal and natural to feel alive, happy and healthy. When we feel unhappy or unhealthy, something is out of balance.

These principles were summarized by the qi gong master Hong Liu (Perry, 1997) in this way:

> Qi is the fundamental life force that permeates all things. Qi connects and animates everything in the universe. When the flow of qi is impaired, there is low energy, fatigue and dis-ease. When the flow of qi is free and unimpaired, there is abundant energy and radiant health.

Key point

Energy Flow is Aliveness.

When our inner energies flow freely, we experience joy, aliveness and well-being. When the flow of our inner energies is blocked or disrupted, we experience anxiety, fatigue, frustration and dis-ease.

Activity: Feeling the flow

Lie in bed, place one hand under the back of your head and the other hand on your heart, and breathe gently and deeply. Listen for your heartbeat (you may or not be able to feel it; either way is OK). Gently hold your hands in place for 2–5 minutes, until you can feel a sense of warmth, an energy pulse or flow or tingling between your hands.

What did you sense and notice?

This exercise will balance the energy between your head and heart and is especially delicious to do lying in bed on a Sunday morning! You can also do it with a partner. Hold your hands on their heart and under their head while breathing deeply, until you feel the flow. Then switch roles with your partner and receive.

Figure 9: Feeling the flow

Imagine a mountain stream flowing through a green valley. It flows and meanders easily and smoothly, as its nature is to flow and follow gravity on its journey back to the sea. Now suppose that there's an avalanche and several boulders come crashing down and fall into the middle of the stream. They don't block the stream entirely, but now the water ripples as it rushes past the boulders. They are causing an interference pattern, which is seen as ripples in the wave-patterns. Similarly, traumas act as boulders in our inner energy flows, disturbing and distorting the normally smooth waves of energy and emotion in our meridians. These disturbances cause ripples of emotional interference until the boulders/traumas are removed. When we remove the blockages and disruptions, our vital energies flow freely and our bodies heal themselves spontaneously.

Key point

The body heals itself. When we remove the blockages, our vital energies flow freely, and our bodies heal themselves spontaneously.

Moving the energy

Healers talk about 'moving the energy' and there are many ways to do this, including physical movement, dancing, drumming, deep breathing, acupuncture needles, qi gong, massaging, chanting, toning, touching and tapping. Common to all these methods is an intuitive understanding of energy and how it works.

The simplest way to channel and move energy is to touch. Our arms and hands are jump leads; by placing a hand on one part of the body and the other hand on another part, within a few moments energy will flow from one hand to the other. When doing energy healing with another person, you can place one hand on their abdomen and the other hand over their heart. You can also 'make a hand sandwich' and place one hand on their abdomen and the other directly opposite, under their back. Then breathe deeply, think healing thoughts and allow the energy to flow by itself.

Different people experience this in different ways: as heat, as a moving current or as tingling or pulsing sensations. Whatever you experience is right for you.

Key point

Our arms and hands are jump leads; by placing our hands on different parts of the body, within a few moments energy will flow from one hand to the other.

Activity: Moving blocked energy

Either lie on your back on a bed or couch or sit back in an easy chair. Create an Eeman relaxation circuit by crossing your ankles over each other, putting your right hand with the palm up under your tailbone and using your left hand to cradle the occiput at the base of your skull (back of your head, at the top of your neck). Close your eyes and breathe slowly and deeply, for about one minute.

What did you notice?

Now think of a tense or upsetting situation in your life. Mentally review it and attune to its emotional feelings and somatic sensations in your body. Gently breathe, notice and follow the feelings and sensations as they move, shift and unwind. Do this for 2–10 minutes.

Jot down your experience on paper or in your journal.

There are many systems of hands-on (and hands-off) healing. These include acupressure, shiatsu, massage and therapeutic body work, reiki, healing touch, therapeutic touch, Quantum Touch, laying on of hands etc.; live seminars and certification courses, which are very worthwhile and from which you can learn much, are available for most of these systems. But none of these are absolutely necessary. Energy is intelligent and flows all by itself. Energy will flow to those organs and areas where it is most needed. If you listen to your own or another's body, they will teach you.

Case study: How a woman in a coma responded to intention

Energy healer and psychotherapist Crystal Hawk shares this story.

Several years ago a good friend asked me to see the mother of a friend. She was dying in a Toronto hospital of paralytic ileus, a condition which arises after an abdominal operation and which the medical profession had not been able to correct. I found her lying in the intensive care unit with about six lines attached. In this hospital each patient in intensive care had a nurse sitting at their feet watching the monitor.

I've found that intensive care nurses in Toronto hospitals are the ones doing Therapeutic Touch™ because they can immediately see the changes in their patient on the monitor. The patient was in a coma and had already suffered through two abdominal operations with no results.

I asked the nurse to watch the monitor for me as my back would be to it when I stood next to the patient. As I stood there looking at the patient and the six lines, I wondered what I could possibly do and I was feeling great compassion for this lady. I put my hands out to begin the session when the nurse cried out. She said, 'It's all fixed now. She's getting oxygen,' and I then did something resembling a TT session as best I could considering those six lines.

The next day the patient had been moved to a private room and when I entered she was sitting up in bed and said, 'I remember you. You came to see me yesterday,' which shows me once more that people in a coma are aware of their surroundings.

Energy healing may be enhanced by the following:

▶ **Deep breathing:** Breath is the doorway between the material and spiritual worlds. Many of the world's healing and spiritual traditions teach breathing practices. Conversely we literally 'hold' our issues in place by holding and constricting our breath. Breathe deeply and rhythmically, from your belly, while doing energy work with yourself or another.

▶ **Visualizing:** You can imagine or visualize light coming down into the top of the head, through the centre of the crown, into the body. Or give your attention to an area of tension and imagine flowing energy through it. Or imagine healing colours, such as golden light, silver, green or violet, gently flowing and filling all the tissues in the body.

▶ **Rocking:** We hold issues in our tissues, as chronic patterns of tension and contraction. Rocking and rhythmic movements, as used in forms of body work such as pulsing and trager work, can help release these holding patterns in the body. Find a practitioner who does pulsing or trager work, or have a friend rock your body gently while lying on a bed or massage table.

▶ **Toning:** The practice of toning, chanting and making healing sounds is ancient, going back to biblical times. Toning stimulates the thymus and opens the chest and heart. Toning can also create resonant frequencies which can release blockages in the mind and body.

▶ **Intention:** Energy follows attention, i.e. energy goes where our awareness goes. Our inner energies are sensitive to our intentions. When we have a healing intention for another or ourselves, our energies flow to support that intention.

Activity: Qi gong clapping

Qi gong (pronounced 'chi gong') is an ancient Chinese healthcare system for cultivating internal energy. As with the martial arts, there are many styles of qi gong and many practices within each style. Here is an effective and stimulating way to move your internal energy.

Stand up straight, preferably outside (weather permitting). Breathe several deep breaths, look around and connect with the beauty around you. With open, flat hands, begin clapping yourself from top of your body downwards, starting with the top, sides and back of the head, tapping gently on your face and chin, going down to your shoulders, arms, forearms and hands, down your chest, abdomen and lower back, clapping down each leg to your ankles and feet. Then clap slowly back up again to the top of your head. Clap rhythmically and vigorously – enough so that you feel it, but don't hurt or bruise yourself.

After you've gone back up to the sides, face and back of your head, stop, close your eyes, breathe and notice the pulsation of energy in your whole body-mind.

Qi, internal energy, often becomes dormant or sluggish (especially when we don't pay attention to it). Clapping your whole body in this way stimulates acupoints, 'wakes up' the qi, gets the energy moving and leaves you feeling more awake, connected and revitalized.

How do we remove blocks and boulders from our subtle energy system?

We can remove these blocks and boulders by mentally attuning to the blockage while stimulating our subtle energies. There are many ways to move energy, including deep breathing, massaging, drumming, rocking and tapping. Moving energy while attuning to the blockage releases the blocks and restores the free flow of energy, thereby dissipating the 'negative' emotions and the stress, symptoms and dis-ease that accompany them.

To learn more about releasing blocks, see Chapter 4.

Things to remember

The main points to remember from this chapter are:

✱ the Universe is one indivisible, dynamic whole in which energy and matter are so deeply entangled that it is impossible to consider them as independent elements

✱ who we are most essentially is something called 'soul' or 'spirit'. We are energetic beings bathed in fields of energy.

✱ virtually all forms of energy are invisible. We cannot see energy, but we can measure its effects with sensitive instrumentation.

✱ the body heals itself. When we remove the blockages and disruptions, our vital energies flow freely and our bodies heal themselves spontaneously.

✱ health is our natural state. It is natural and normal to feel alive, happy and healthy. When we feel unhappy or unhealthy, something is out of balance.

✱ energy healing may be enhanced by deep breathing, visualizing, rocking, toning and intention.

Breaking through blocks and walls

The key question isn't 'What fosters creativity?' It is 'Why in God's name isn't everyone creative?' Where was human potential lost? How was it crippled? I think therefore a good question might be not why do people create? But why do people not create or innovate?

Abraham Maslow

In this chapter you will learn:

▶ *the nature of resistance*
▶ *the freeze-immobility response*
▶ *different kinds of blocks*
▶ *the Blockbuster technique*
▶ *the magic of self-acceptance.*

As we look at the natural world, there is movement all around us. Winds and clouds, seas and storms, planets and stars and galaxies are engaged in ceaseless rhythmic activity. Our hearts beat, lungs breathe, stomachs digest and bladders eliminate easily and effortlessly. Molecules join to form tissues, atoms combine to form molecules, electrons flow to power our homes and factories and infinitesimally subtle wave-particles dance on subatomic levels. When we hear musicians performing, watch a ballet or observe figure skaters competing, we are moved to use words like 'grace' and 'ease' and 'harmony'. Everywhere we look, at the great Cosmic Dance within and without, there is rhythmic movement.

Our bodies are the stage for a symphony of rhythms and melodies. On a physical level there are polyphonic rhythms: the pulsing of our hearts, the breathing of our lungs, the pumping of the cerebrospinal system and the rhythmic expanding and contracting of our muscles. Our hearts and brains have magnetic fields, and every organ, tissue and cell has its own field. These subtle rhythms and fields vibrate and resonate together to play a magnificent symphony of health when they're well-orchestrated, and a cacophony of conflict and dis-ease when they're not.

Yet when it comes to human beings, something changes. We humans are unique in our ability to resist our natural rhythms. We get 'stuck in a rut', novelists get 'writer's block', artists lose inspiration, salesmen hit a plateau and athletes 'hit a wall'. We do things that we know are bad for us and we resist doing what we know is good for us. Many drink or drug or act out. We are conflicted and we often act against our own best interests. Sometimes we simply feel 'blocked'; sometimes we actively 'resist'; sometimes we 'shut down'; and sometimes we actively sabotage ourselves.

All blocks are rooted in fear. Like a turtle pulling back into its shell, we contract and pull into ourselves in an attempt to avoid pain and harm. Over many months and years these contractions get 'locked' in our bodies as chronic tension patterns, and become what psychologists Wilhelm Reich and Alexander Lowen referred to as 'character armour'. Once what is called 'resistance' has solidified into character armour, it can be more difficult to change.

Resistance is not necessarily bad. Without resistance, planes would not fly, cars and bikes would not have traction, and nuts, bolts and knots would not hold. Some of our greatest lessons come in the form of resistance. It is in challenging and working through resistance that we grow emotionally and spiritually. It is when the resistance becomes chronic and thwarts us from growing, flourishing and being all we can be that it becomes problematic.

Hitting the wall

You have a goal. You want to do something. If it's short and easy, you probably just do it. But let's say it's an ongoing behavioural challenge that you'll need to accomplish over time, like getting up earlier or losing weight. At first you start out feeling excited about having a new goal, taking steps and feeling proud of yourself. But at some point you begin having doubts and temptations:

'I don't know if I can do this.'

'It's really hard to lose weight.'

'I think I've got fat genes.'

'I've failed so many times before.'

And then the temptations creep in:

'I just don't feel like doing this now.'

'I need a little fun in my life.'

'One little piece of cake won't hurt.'

And then you hit the Wall of Emotion; you start feeling anxious, upset or overwhelmed, you get emotional, you can't think straight and then you'll do anything, including drink, drug, distract or sabotage, just to quell those horrid feelings. So then your goal falls by the wayside, you feel good temporarily, but then you start beating yourself up, the guilt, shame and self-punishment sets in and you retreat to the internet, a good novel or in front of the telly.

SANDRA'S SHUT DOWN

'Sandra' was a resource counsellor for grades K–2 in a US public school system. It was her job to handle the 'problem kids' and 'fix them'. One day she herded children from three different classes to her office, where she was expected to magically come up with a plan to remedy their defects on the spot. 'How am I supposed to help these kids? What am I supposed to do? I CAN'T DO THIS!' Feeling frustrated and overwhelmed, she felt herself shutting down.

What was happening to Sandra? We have already discussed the 'fight or flight' response. In response to a threat or danger, our adrenal glands secrete adrenaline and cortisol, our hearts start pumping faster, our blood pressure goes up, blood flows to our limbs and we get ready to fight or flee. But when neither fight nor flight are possible, our bodies default to the 'freeze-immobility' response. Like the proverbial deer caught in the headlights, we freeze and 'shut down', both mentally and physically, in response to a threat or danger. The freeze response is an instinctual response system designed to conserve energy and maintain survival functions during threat or crisis. It works well on those rare occasions when we're confronted by tigers and there's no way out; it becomes maladaptive when it's triggered every day.

It's important to recognize that when fight or flight are not possible, both the body and our rational brains shut down automatically and instinctively; rational thinking is impaired and there is no conscious choice involved or even possible. Many rape victims will often blame themselves for not fighting back or for not 'doing something'. The reality is that when we are immobilized by the freeze response, we are simply unable to do anything. People sometimes feel stuck or 'trapped' with abusive partners or bosses in homes, offices or classrooms where fight or flight are neither possible nor appropriate. With repeated experiences, these patterns of feeling 'stuck' and 'trapped' can become habitual reactions, which then get 'locked' into our bodies as chronic patterns of holding and contraction.

Key point

When we are immobilized by the freeze response, we are temporarily unable to do anything else.

When we freeze and 'shut down', the following things happen:

- muscles become immobilized
- we can't speak
- we go 'numb'
- we can't 'think straight'
- we feel 'stuck' or 'paralysed'.

We generally cannot challenge the freeze response while it's happening. Like the fight/flight response, it impairs our capacity to think clearly; confronted by danger we go into survival mode and literally 'cannot think straight'. But we can challenge the habitual freeze response after the fact: by breathing, attending to its somatic sensations in our bodies and by actively working through the freeze impulse by walking, running or tapping.

Identifying and breaking through blocks

The field of Energy Psychology has identified different kinds of blocks and the nature of resistance, and developed methods for overcoming them. These different blocks include switching, reversals, blocked access, freezing, dissociation and energy toxins.

One reason why therapy sometimes doesn't work and why blocks can be difficult to overcome is because these blocks are:

- mental: they consist of a 'negative' attitude or mental block
- emotional: there is a blocking emotion, usually fear, anxiety or numbness
- physical: they're 'locked' into physical patterns of tension and contraction
- energetic: they exist as disturbances in our energy fields.

Thus, to fully challenge and change these blocks, it is best to address these four levels simultaneously.

SWITCHING
Switching was first discovered in the field of applied kinesiology (muscle testing). Also called *neurologic disorganization*,

switching occurs when part of the brain shuts down or 'switches off'. Normally, all of our brain centres are connected and communicating harmoniously. But sometimes when we're under stress or overwhelmed, one or more parts of the brain 'switch off'. This happens commonly with people with learning disabilities, such as dyslexia and attention deficit, where the two hemispheres of the brain are not well-coordinated.

Some of the symptoms of switching include:

▶ 'switching' letters or numbers, as in dyslexia

▶ 'brain fog'

▶ not being able to remember people's names or phone numbers

▶ making mistakes

▶ losing your keys or pocketbook

▶ feeling uncoordinated or bumping into things.

Activity: Getting unswitched with the Cross-Crawl

This is a simple exercise for getting the right and left hemispheres working and communicating with each other. You can do this if you suspect you may be switched or at any time you feel the need to 'get your head together'.

Begin by standing and marching on the spot, swinging your knees high. While still marching, swing your arms so that you touch the outside of the left thigh with your right hand as the left knee rises, and the outside of the right thigh with your left hand as your right knee rises. Note that each hand crosses the midline of your body as you touch the outside of the opposite knee. Do this for about a minute; what do you notice now?

Another exercise for getting unswitched is called the Brain Buttons; it is described in Appendix 5.

REVERSALS

In his early work Roger Callahan noticed that tapping on emotional memories was effective only about 65–70 percent of the time. He reasoned that if there are natural laws governing tapping and if we are all hard-wired the same way, then it should work virtually every time. Using muscle testing, he discovered that some people would test 'weak' when saying 'I wish to be happy', and would test 'strong' when saying 'I wish to be miserable'. He realized that their intentions and energies were reversed; and so long as they were reversed, no progress was possible.

Our minds are very powerful. As Henry Ford noted, 'Whether you believe you can do a thing or not, you are right.' You are familiar with the power of the placebo effect: plain sugar pills are often effective 30–35 percent of the time; to prove effectiveness, pharmaceutical companies must demonstrate that their medications are more effective than placebos.

A reversal, also called psychological reversal, is a block to healing associated with a limiting belief or intention that is opposed to your conscious intention. Freezing is like trying to drive your car when it's stuck in neutral; reversals are like trying to drive your car when it's stuck in reverse. Reversals are objections to success; they are 'good reasons' why we are keeping the problem or symptom. There are many different kinds of reversals; they are a major reason why we sabotage ourselves and often fail to get what we want.

A reversal:

▶ is an *objection* to healing or success

▶ is subconscious *resistance* to change

▶ causes a *blockage* in the bio-electrical system

▶ involves *conflict* between one or more parts of self.

Key point

A psychological reversal is a block to healing associated with a limiting belief or intention that is opposed to your conscious intention.

Since Callahan's initial discovery, others have identified many kinds of reversals. The more common reversals include: wanting, possibility, safety, identity, self-worth and secondary gain.

Common reversals include:

Reversal	Limiting belief
Wanting	'I don't want to get over this issue.'
	'I want to keep this issue.'
Possibility	'I can't get over this.'
	'I will never get over this.'
Safety	'It's not safe for me to get over this.'
	'It's not safe for someone else to get over this.'
Identity	'I am...... .'
	'Being this way is part of who I am.'
Self-worth	'I don't deserve to get over this.'
	'I'm not worthy to...... .'
Secondary gain	'I'm getting something out of keeping this.'
Hypervigilance	'I have to stay vigilant and keep my guard up to survive.'
Feeling overwhelmed	'I can't handle this.'
	'This is too big, too dangerous, too overwhelming.'

Activity: Breaking through reversals – the Blockbuster technique

The Blockbuster is a very powerful technique for breaking through reversals, blocked access emotions and other blocks. It consists of three parts:

* acknowledging the block
* affirming self-acceptance
* tapping an acupoint.

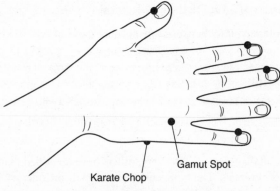

Figure 10: The Karate Chop, Gamut Spot and finger tapping points

We'll start with the tapping first. Find the Karate Chop acupoint, which is on the fleshy outside part of each hand where you would make a karate chop. You can tap the side of one hand with three or four fingers of the other hand; or you can tap both sides, by tapping the outer sides of both hands together at the Karate Chop spot. Tap gently and rhythmically at a comfortable pace.

Then recall a recent memory or issue where you felt 'stuck', and notice whether there is any fear or resistance to releasing it. Notice where in your body you're holding this and ask yourself whether there are any good reasons for holding on to it. Name and acknowledge the block while repeating this affirmation aloud and rhythmically tapping the Karate Chop point on one or both hands, four or five times: *'Even though I have this* [name the block], *I deeply and completely accept myself.'*

If you can't name or don't know what the block is, you can use an affirmation like this one: *'Even though I feel stuck and don't even know what it is, I deeply and completely accept myself.'*

What do you notice?

The block you're focusing on may or may not dissolve completely. You may also need to do the EFT tapping sequence in Chapter 5. Usually people will notice a lightening and both an emotional and energy shift, when using the Blockbuster technique.

Case study: Tapping away cigarette cravings

EFT master Lindsay Kenny of San Francisco shares this experience.

Tapping almost always brings unexpected surprises or results. I recently did a demo for a drug and alcohol rehab centre for women. I had eight new outpatients and only had an hour to work with them. They had already gone through the 30-day detox programme, so they were sober, but certainly not yet well.

I asked how many smoked, and seven of the eight did. All seven said they wanted to quit smoking and all had tried and failed. The non-smoker wanted to get rid of her craving for chocolate, so I had her tap along with the rest of us. Their 0–10 intensity levels ranged from 6 to 10 (with 10 being a very strong craving for a cigarette). I had the '10' stand at the front with me to do a demonstration while the rest tapped along from their seats.

Since addicts usually have *reversals* (subconscious resistance to change), I wanted to demonstrate that with muscle testing by having my 'demo lady' state that she very much wanted to stop smoking. Not surprisingly, her arm tested 'weak' on that statement, which meant she had a strong subconscious resistance to letting go of her smoking habit. I then had them all tap on the Karate Chop point while saying: *'Even though I really don't want to stop smoking, I want to love and accept myself.'* They all chuckled at this.

I muscle tested her again and she now tested 'strong'. I explained reversals, which they liked as an explanation for why they seemed to have a push-pull impulse within them and kept reverting to their old habits.

Next we all did the Blockbuster while tapping on the Karate Chop point, saying: *'Even though I have a strong craving for this cigarette right now, I want to accept myself anyway.'* I then had them focus on the statements *'This craving to smoke'* and *'I really want this cigarette,'* while doing two rounds of EFT. I then asked the demo lady what her desire to smoke was and she said 'Zero.'

That was a surprise for me, since it usually takes 2–4 rounds to eliminate a craving. 'OK,' I said, 'take a dry drag on this ciggie then.' But she said she couldn't; just the thought of it made her sick.

I admit I was a bit sceptical. But then the rest of the ladies said the same thing. They were all at a zero and had no desire to smoke! Really, this is quite unusual so quickly. So I tried to get them to smell a cigarette or take a dry drag, but none wanted to do it. The most sceptical lady said, 'Hand me that lighter and that cig and I'll light it up.' Her pals passed them down to her but she just couldn't make herself light up.

I also explained a very important element about craving-busting via tapping; tapping alone doesn't eliminate an addiction. Doing the procedure we did helps deal with the craving, making it easier than trying to resist something they really wanted.

These women were thrilled, realizing they had a tool to help them. One tattooed lady asked, 'Can we use this for, umm, stronger addictions?' 'Yes,' I said, 'that was the point of this. EFT is a way to manage cravings rather than just trying to use willpower.' It was as if they had just received the present of their dreams. It was a nice present for me too, to see these formerly unhappy, negative, downtrodden women with a glint of hope in their eyes and smiles on their faces.

Activity: Tapping away doubts

We sometimes doubt, put up walls or have resistance to doing a new technique like tapping. Get a pen and a piece of paper and write down a short list of why tapping may not work for you:

For example:

* Tapping is silly.
* People will think I'm weird.
* How could this possibly work?
* It's all placebo anyway.
* It might work for others, but...
* I'm too [stuck, old, wounded...]
* If I open up Pandora's box, I'll be overwhelmed
* I don't deserve to...
* I'm not worthy of...

Reread your list and put a mark (or a double or triple mark!) by those objections that have a strong emotional charge. Then do the Blockbuster technique on each one, remembering to acknowledge the belief and repeating the affirmation four or five times, while tapping.

BLOCKED ACCESS

Defusing the emotional charge of a memory or issue requires that we be able to attune to it. Remember the principle *what you can feel, you can heal*. Sometimes we cannot attune to these feelings and sensations because another feeling or emotion is blocking access to it. Many people have a fear of their own feelings. One common form of this is anticipatory anxiety, where even just thinking about something can trigger profound anxiety. The most common blocking emotions are fear, anxiety, terror, confusion, feeling overwhelmed and feeling numb.

We human beings will do almost anything to avoid ourselves. When feelings start to arise, we do the avoid-dance: we eat, drink, drug or distract to avoid our feelings and ourselves. We may have made the decision that whatever happened was so painful or terrible that 'I'll never go there again' and so we develop a phobia about our own feelings. Like guard dogs at the gates, growling and barking when anyone gets near, so our inner guard dogs 'growl' with fear and anxiety whenever we start to get close to our own inner experiences.

Key point

When feelings start to arise, we often do the avoid-dance; we eat, drink, drug or distract to avoid our feelings and ourselves.

Activity: Breaking through blocked access

Think of a situation where you have difficulty getting in touch with your feelings. Ask yourself, 'What other feeling might be getting in the way of my tuning into this memory?' You may notice fear, anxiety, numbness or something else.

Then tap the sides of your hands together (on the Karate Chop point) slowly and rhythmically, while repeating this statement four or five times: *'Even though I'm feeling this block* [name the block], *I deeply and completely accept myself.'*

What do you notice, mentally, emotionally and physically, now?

Note: If the block does not release completely, you may need to follow up with the EFT Basic Recipe in Chapter 5.

FREEZING

The psychologist Peter Levine spent several years researching the behaviour of animals in the wild. He found that wild animals that survive an attack (by freezing and shutting down) will afterwards engage in spontaneous body movements, such as shaking, trembling and stomping their feet. These spontaneous movements normalize the animals' muscular and nervous systems by allowing them to discharge the pent-up energy.

Levine developed a system of therapy called 'somatic experiencing', which involves attending to micro-sensations in the body and allowing the body to shake, shiver and discharge. Another way to release habitual freeze responses is by tapping on the felt experience of freezing and shutting down. Taking physical action challenges this response, energizes our sympathetic nervous system and gets us awake, moving and better able to confront the issue.

It is important to recognize that these blocks (what psychoanalysts call 'fixations') are not just mental and 'all in your head'. They are both physical – showing up as stress, tension, constriction and 'holding patterns' in our bodies – and energetic, involving the blockage of the free flow of subtle energies in the body. These blocks show up as patterns of stress-induced contraction in our bodies. We literally hold issues in our tissues. As these blocks are both physical and energetic, we need to address them both physically and energetically.

We can break through habituated freeze responses after the fact by using the Blockbuster technique along with the EFT Basic Recipe described in Chapter 5.

DISSOCIATION

Dissociation is a condition where a part of our consciousness separates or disconnects from our conscious awareness, resulting in breaks or gaps in awareness. We humans have the amazing ability to wall off parts of the psyche, to protect ourselves from overwhelming pain. Dissociation most often occurs in response to trauma. Denied and dissociated impulses are sometimes converted into physical symptoms. For details about working with symptoms, see Chapter 9. Mild forms of dissociation may be treated effectively using the methods described in this book. Clinical forms, such as dissociative identity disorder (DID) and multiple personality disorder (MPD), are beyond the scope of this book; if you suspect that you are experience dissociations, please see a qualified mental health practitioner.

ENERGY TOXINS

Energy toxins are substances that 'zap' our energy and will be discussed in Chapter 13.

Case study: The veteran who wouldn't do his homework

EFT master Mary Stafford of Tucson, Arizona, relates this story.

For the past three years I have participated in the Vets Stress Project, a research project studying the efficacy of EFT in treating veterans with PTSD, headed by Dr Dawson Church. The project starts with standardized psychological testing to assess PTSD and then three sessions of EFT, retesting, then three more sessions of EFT and then retesting. During the first session the veterans are taught how to use EFT for their traumatic experiences and then given homework consisting of making a list of their traumatic memories and then using EFT to clear one trauma a day in between sessions.

Most of the veterans I worked with did their homework, but 'Bill' never made his list or used EFT on his own between sessions. He had been physically abused by his father, had joined the military to escape his father's abuse and was carrying tons of anger about his father. During the third session he came in and reported, 'I think I've discovered why I won't do the homework. If I tap on those memories, I won't know who I am and I won't be able to instantly defend myself.' We tapped on and cleared these reversals and he began doing his tapping homework every day.

After the sixth session I retested him again and he scored in the 'normal' range, indicating that he no longer had PTSD. The day after the sixth session his wife called me and thanked me profusely and repeatedly, 'Mary, thank you, thank you, thank you. He is so much easier to be with now. He doesn't explode with anger at the slightest thing any more. He is like a totally different person now. Thank you, thank you, thank you.'

How does the Blockbuster work?

There is a magical power in naming and acknowledging things. So long as something is unknown and unnamed, it is mysterious and potentially fearful. When we acknowledge it by naming it, we begin to familiarize ourselves with it, have power over it and call it our own. What you can name, you can change.

Many ancient peoples intuitively knew this. The Hebrew name for God, Yahweh, was traditionally spelled with four consonants without vowels, to signify 'That which is unknown and unnameable'. It was considered blasphemous to speak or even to name 'That which is beyond names'. Even today many orthodox Jews spell the name of the divinity as 'G–d'.

There is a psychological technique called 'affect labelling', which is simply putting feelings into words. It has been known for a long time that putting feelings into words decreases their intensity, but it was not known why. Recent neuroimaging studies by Matthew Lieberman and colleagues at UCLA show that the simple act of putting feelings into words disrupts the activity of the amygdala (which reacts to fear and strong emotion) while increasing activity in the prefrontal cortex, the seat of rational thinking and decision making.

Many people feel afraid of accepting 'negativity', whether out there or in themselves. They don't want to accept or acknowledge it for fear of succumbing to it or 'giving it power'. Some of us hold on to self-judgment and self-criticism, believing that self-acceptance leads to complacency and that the whip is more powerful than the carrot. Yet, as the psychologist Carl Rogers noted, self-condemnation can keep us stuck while paradoxically, when we truly accept ourselves as we are, we begin to change.

Key point

When we can truly accept ourselves as we are, we begin to change.

We slice and dice the universe with our concepts and judgements. When we judge another or ourselves, we cut and separate ourselves from the underlying unity of all that is. Conversely, when we speak the truth, we realign ourselves with the world around us, and in so doing the energy shifts. There is deep wisdom in the biblical adage, 'Speak the truth and the truth will set you free'. When we speak two apparently conflicting 'truths', such as 'I'm upset with myself' and 'I deeply accept myself', our minds will generally resolve the conflict in the direction of the more truthful perception. Reconciling conflicted perceptions repairs the internal conflict dividing us, reconnects us with our roots and realigns us with the world around us.

The first step to breaking through blocks is to name, acknowledge and accept them and ourselves. What we resist, persists. Conversely, what we acknowledge and accept, shifts and softens. When we name, acknowledge and accept an issue, it removes the sense of judgement and separation, and helps us reconnect with the situation and ourselves in a new way. Physically tapping, just like tapping on a rusty pipe, can release the patterns of constriction that kept everything 'stuck' and blocked.

Key point

Just by naming, acknowledging and accepting our blocks and feelings, they start to shift and release.

To learn the EFT Basic Recipe for defusing memories and issues, see Chapter 5.

Things to remember

The main points to remember from this chapter are:

* all blocks are forms of fear. Like a turtle back pulling into its shell, we contract to avoid pain and harm.
* Energy Psychology has identified several different kinds of blocks, including blocked access, switching, reversals, freezing, dissociation and energy toxins
* when we are immobilized by the freeze response, we are temporarily unable to do anything else
* switching is a phenomenon where part of the brain shuts down or switches 'off'. Switching can be corrected with mind-body exercises such as the cross-crawl.
* a psychological reversal is a block to healing associated with a limiting belief or intention that is opposed to your conscious intentions
* just by naming, acknowledging and accepting our blocks and feelings, they start to shift and release
* when we can truly accept ourselves as we are, we begin to change.

How to tap

In every culture and in every medical tradition before ours, healing was accomplished by moving energy.

Albert Szent-Gyorgyi, Nobel laureate in Medicine

In this chapter you will learn:

▶ *the EFT Basic Recipe*
▶ *tapping point locations*
▶ *setting up the issue*
▶ *the importance of being specific*
▶ *the EFT Movie technique.*

EFT is easy to learn and use. It's so simple that even children can learn how to do it. The essence of EFT is to gently tap energy points on your hands, face and upper body while thinking about an upset. Each point is on a specific acupuncture meridian, which stimulates and balances both energy flow and emotions. You will be able to memorize the sequence of points in just a few minutes. After learning the points, I will show you how to begin freeing yourself from negative feelings and experiences.

Knowing where to tap

There's an old story about a factory that was having problems with its boiler. Several plumbers and heating technicians had been consulted, but none had been able to repair it. The manager was told of a master technician who was known far and wide for his expertise and so he called and made an appointment.

On the day of the appointment, the manager was surprised to see the master technician dressed in suit jacket and tie, rather than workman's clothes. Also he carried only a very small tool box. After examining the boiler, he opened up his toolbox and removed a pencil and tape measure. He made some careful measurements and made three marks with his pencil. He then replaced the pencil and tape measure in the box, removed a small hammer and then proceeded to tap the boiler at the precise locations he had marked. The boiler worked perfectly from then on.

A few days later, the manger received a bill for £1,000 from the technician. The manager felt angry, as the technician had spent only about 20 minutes working on the boiler. The manager wrote a letter expressing his upset and demanded an itemized statement.

The manager received a note and the itemized statement from the technician. The note said that he agreed with the manager that it would be 'unreasonable' to charge so much for just 'striking the boiler with a hammer'. Looking at the itemized statement, the manager read:

Tapping boiler with hammer	£10
Knowing where to tap	£990
TOTAL	£1,000

As this story suggests, it is important to know specifically where to tap. It is also important to follow these directions very carefully. If you've ever baked an angel's food cake, you know that you need to separate the egg whites from the yolks, beat them up separately and combine all the ingredients in a certain order. While there are now many meridian therapies and different variations of these, you will get better results initially if you follow these directions exactly.

We'll start with a description of where the tapping points are, follow with an overview of the EFT Basic Recipe and then explain each step.

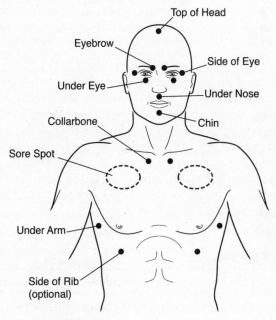

Figure 11: The EFT tapping points

Let's get familiar!

To get familiar with the tapping points, touch and then gently tap the following points 7–10 times on each point. Use two, three or four fingers as you tap.

Top of Head	Right on the crown of your head.
Eyebrow	At the inside edge (toward the midline) of either eyebrow.
Side of Eye	On the flat bone bordering the outside corner of either eye.
Under Eye	On the upper edge of the lower eye socket, right below the pupil of the eye.
Under Nose	On the midline, halfway between the bottom of the nose and the top of the upper lip.
Chin	On the midline in the middle of the crease, between your lower lip and the chin.
Collarbone	At the junction where the collarbone, breastbone (sternum) and first rib meet. Find the 'U' in the middle of the collarbone. Slide down one inch and then slide laterally across 1–2 inches, to a tender spot that's just outside the breastbone. The correct point is *below* the collarbone and in a small 'hollow' where the sternum drops off.
Under Arm	On the side of the body about four inches below the armpit. This point is exactly parallel with the nipple on men and approximately in the middle of the bra band on women. It will be tender when you find it.

Activity

Get a piece of paper and jot down your state of mind in 2–4 words, such as 'calm and curious', Rate the emotional intensity of your state of mind from 0–10. Then touch and hold each set of points in turn, starting with the Top of the Head point and finishing with the Under Arm point, while breathing slowly and deeply, one set of points per breath. After touching and breathing each set of points, jot down your state of mind again in 2–4 words.

What do you notice now?

Acupoints are psychoactive. They are portals into our inner energy system and affect us mentally, emotionally and physically.

Tip

When first learning EFT, think of three to five recent, low-intensity experiences (not your worst traumas) to tap and practise on. Meridian tapping can work with even horrific traumas, but when you're first learning the system, it's easier to begin with simple, recent memories.

The EFT Basic Recipe

1 Select a specific memory or experience.

2 Tune and rate its emotional intensity from 0–10.

3 Set-up: Tap the Karate Chop point on the side of the hands while repeating aloud three times, *'Even though I have this......, I deeply and completely accept myself.'*

4 Tap the sequence of points, with a reminder phrase.

5 Test: Tune and rate again.

6 Adjust: If not yet finished, return to step 3 and repeat the sequence as needed. For subsequent rounds, use this set-up: *'Even though I'm STILL feeling SOME of this......, I deeply and completely accept myself.'*

Here's a fuller description of each step.

1 Select a specific memory or experience

The key word in this sentence is 'specific'; it needs to be a *specific* memory with *specific* emotions and body sensations that happened at a *specific* time. This is sometimes described as 'the time when...'. Give the experience a short label (3–7 words), e.g. 'the time when the teacher shamed me', or 'the time when dad grounded me'. This short phrase will become your 'reminder phrase', which is repeated while you tap.

The mind can be like a drunken monkey, swinging on branches from one thought to another. The purpose of the reminder phrase is to keep you attuned to your felt experience while you're tapping.

2 Tune and rate the experience's emotional intensity

Tune into the experience, like you're tuning a radio dial. Focus your attention, 'raise the volume', and feel the feelings and sensations in your body. Just as musicians pluck a string and listen to hear whether the note is sharp or flat, so you listen and attune to your inner experience before balancing it by tapping. Notice where in your body you feel it and what it feels like. Then rate its intensity from 0–10, where 0 = no intensity and 10 = overwhelming.

3 Set-up

We 'set up the experience' for tapping by tapping the Karate Chop spot on the side of the hands while repeating the set-up affirmation three times. This set-up phrase has two parts:

▶ a brief, specific statement of the problem

▶ a statement of self-acceptance.

You've seen the set-up already, as the Blockbuster in Chapter 4. It goes like this:

'Even though I have this......, I deeply and completely accept myself.'

or

'Even though I'm feeling this......, I deeply and completely accept myself.'

Here are some examples of Set-up phrases:

▶ Set-up: Even though I felt embarrassed when Jill told my secret at the party, I deeply and completely accept myself. Reminder phrase: Embarrassed when Jill told my secret.

▶ Set-up: Even though I got really angry at the clerk in the grocery store, I deeply and completely accept myself. Reminder phrase: Angry at the clerk in the grocery.

▶ Set-up: Even though I felt upset with myself for being late for my appointment with my attorney, I deeply and completely accept myself.

Reminder phrase: Upset with myself for being late.

As mentioned before, this set-up (the Blockbuster) is the remedy for reversals. While it is not always necessary, it is designed to remove any psychological block that's in the way and only takes a few seconds to do.

4 Tap the sequence

Recall and feel the issue in your body while breathing deeply.

Then tap each point in the sequence below about 7–10 times, while recalling, feeling and repeating your set-up phrase once on each set of acupoints:

▶ Top of Head

▶ Eyebrow

▶ Side of Eye

▶ Under Eye

▶ Under Nose

▶ Chin

▶ Collarbone

▶ Under Arm.

Key point

Remember that *feeling is healing*. You can enhance your success by feeling and connecting with your felt experience, with feelings and sensations in your body, while tapping.

5 Test

What happened when you tapped? Did you notice a shift? Tune and rate the intensity again. The goal is to reduce the emotional intensity down to '1' or '0'.

If the intensity increased – which is good, as it shows you're in touch with more emotion or a deeper layer – use the 'Subsequent Set-up' (below) and repeat the sequence.

If the intensity did not shift or dropped only one point, get more specific. Look for a specific aspect to tap on, use the Subsequent Set-up and repeat the sequence.

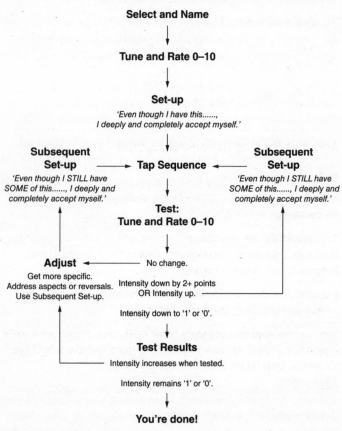

Figure 12: The EFT Basic Recipe

If the intensity dropped at least two points, use the Subsequent Set-up and repeat the sequence again.

6 Adjust

The goal is to reduce the emotional intensity down to '1' or '0'. If the emotional intensity rises or if it feels 'stuck', look for a specific aspect that is emotionally charged. Then repeat the sequence using the Subsequent Set-up and the more emotional or deeper layer or the more specific aspect.

Adjust your focus by getting more specific and adjust the set-up phrase by using the Subsequent Set-up while tapping the Karate Chop point as before and repeat the sequence.

The Subsequent Set-up is:

'Even though I'm STILL feeling SOME of this......, I deeply and completely accept myself.'

When the intensity goes down to '1' or '0', you're done. Congratulations! Thank yourself for a job well done.

Activity: Putting the pieces together

Now we're ready to put all the pieces together. **Select** a recent, mild upset. Give it a specific name (e.g. 'My partner ignored me') and **tune and rate** its intensity from 0–10. Choose a reminder phrase (e.g. 'Upset that my partner ignored me').

Then **repeat the set-up** phrase three times, while rhythmically tapping the Karate Chop point: *'Even though I'm feeling this......, I deeply and completely love and accept myself.'*

Example: *'Even though I'm feeling upset that my partner ignored me, I deeply and completely love and accept myself.'*

Then **tap the sequence of points** below 7–10 times on each point, while repeating your brief reminder phrase: Top of Head, Eyebrow, Side of Eye, Under Eye, Under Nose, Chin, Collarbone, Under Arm.

Then **test**. What did you notice? Rate the intensity 0–10 again.

If you're down to '1' or '0, you're done.

If not, **adjust** the aspects, get more specific, use your Subsequent Set-up phrase and repeat the sequence as needed until the upset has lost its emotional charge.

Some issues may have aspects or layers (see Chapter 6) and will require persistence. You may need to repeat the sequence several times and readjust and fine-tune your focus each time before the memory or issue releases completely.

Gary Craig enthusiastically urges us to 'Try it on everything!' EFT does not necessarily work on every issue for every person every time. But it is safe and painless and it only takes a few minutes to do 3–5 rounds of EFT to try it out.

Activity

Make a short list of five to seven recent upsets. Use the Basic Recipe on each upset, until its emotional charge is down to '1' or '0'.

Tips

Try it on everything! Try it on old memories, issues and negative habits, as well as on current stresses, irritations and the 'upset du jour'.

If you're feeling 'numb' or not able to feel anything, that 'feeling numb' is itself the block. Do 2–3 rounds of tapping on 'feeling numb' and notice what happens.

Gaining experience

The EFT Basic Recipe is simple and easy to use. Here are some of the kinds of things you can apply it to:

▶ recent upsets

▶ childhood memories and traumas

▶ aches, pains and symptoms

▶ achieving peak performance

▶ relationship issues.

I will discuss applying EFT to health, relationship and performance issues in future chapters. What is most important now is to gain experience by practising the Basic Recipe, first on yourself and then with friends or family members. When working with others or yourself, begin with recent, simple memories and then gradually work your way back to childhood and 'heavier' memories.

There's an old story about a violinist who comes out of the train station in New York, walks over to a cab driver and asks him, 'How do I get to Carnegie Hall?' The cabbie looks at him and says, 'Practise, man, practise.'

The same is true for each of us. EFT is an Art; if you ever have the opportunity to see one of the EFT masters working with a group, you will appreciate what a fine art it is. To begin to master the Art of EFT will require consistent practice, just like learning to play tennis or the piano. Every person is a little different and you will learn much by working with different people. Fortunately, even EFT newbies can sometimes achieve surprising results.

Case study

Hypnotherapist Rhonda Heyns from Albuquerque shares this story of 'Arnold', her first professional experience with EFT.

Arnold came into the office complaining of daily panic attacks. I had worked with him before with hypnosis, working to ease the memories of the traumatic events that had started the attacks. This had worked for a short time, but then they came back stronger than before. These attacks were now so bad that he would throw up and they would totally incapacitate him. I had just learned how to teach EFT to a client, so I decided that this was the time to try it.

When he walked into my office, he was well on his way to a full-blown panic attack. He could not get comfortable in his overstuffed chair, constantly squirming and looking more uncomfortable by the second. Very soon we could hear his stomach roiling as it was preparing for its daily nausea session. I quickly explained what EFT was, went over the basic tapping points, had him rate his discomfort (8–9) and began. The first round of tapping brought the symptoms down to '4'. We did a second round and this brought the discomfort down to '2'. At this time, I decided to see if there was a side effect to his panic attacks and asked him what else he felt while experiencing the attacks. His answer was 'frustration and helplessness'. We addressed these aspects as well, which brought the feelings of helplessness down to '2'. By this time, his stomach was silent and the squirming was greatly diminished.

I took him through one last round of tapping and then asked, 'What are you feeling now?' He sat very still, not moving at all and replied, 'Nothing. Just peace.' And then the tears started. They were tears of joy and we just sat there for a while and let them come. By the time he left, we were both smiling and grinning from ear to ear. He told me his mother had been trying to get him to try EFT for the past two years, but he had just brushed it off as 'a bunch of hooey'. Now he was kicking himself for not listening to her earlier!

I saw him again over a year later and when he walked into the office, I did not recognize him at first. He had filled out, put on muscle and looked great. He told me that since that day he had not thrown up once, not even when he had the flu. The panic attacks were gone as well and he had not had one since that day in my office.

Like any tool or technique, EFT does not always work the first time. You may need to address the different aspects and layers as they come up and you may need to repeat the sequence several times. Be persistent, get more specific and you'll find the emotional intensity diminishing, leaving you feeling lighter, clearer and more present.

Key point

EFT does not always work the first time. You may need to address different aspects and layers and you may need to repeat the sequence several times. Be persistent!

Defusing the emotional charge of simple memories is usually straightforward. You focus on the memory, rate it from 0–10, say your set-up phrase and tap tap tap! Usually the memory will desensitize rather easily. Eventually you will come across issues that are more challenging. The intensity may not come down, the person may feel 'stuck' or, as you encounter more aspects, the issue may seem to jump from one thing to another.

The EFT Movie technique

After you have used the EFT Basic Recipe on several memories and you're feeling comfortable with it, you can try the EFT Movie technique. This is used for an upset or trauma that happened over a period of time. In essence you create a movie of what happened and then watch your movie, making sure to stop the movie and tap tap tap! whenever you feel any discomfort.

Here are the steps:

1 Think of an upsetting experience and give it a movie title. If there were several events in the experience, see them as separate movie scenes. Select the first scene to work with; you'll be tapping on each scene in your movie separately.

2 If you start feeling very upset just thinking about the movie, first do some tapping on the movie as a whole. Use a set-up phrase such as, *'Even though just thinking about this movie feels upsetting, I deeply and completely accept myself.'* Tap on the movie as a whole until it's down to an intensity like '3' or '4' that you feel you can handle OK.

3 Run the first scene forward in your mind and rate its intensity from 0–10.

4 Do your set-up, *'Even though I have this...... movie, I deeply and completely accept myself.'*

5 Watch the first scene in your mind, and stop and tap whenever you feel any discomfort, tapping until the discomfort is down to '0'.

6 Rewind the movie back to the beginning, then run it forward, again stopping and tapping whenever you feel any discomfort, tapping until the intensity is down to '0'.

7 Repeat these steps with each scene in your movie, until you can watch the movie from start to finish without discomfort.

Remember to go for complete release. Some people stop when a scene still has a lower intensity on it. This can be a sign that there's another aspect just beneath the surface. Continue uncovering aspects and tapping on them until the whole movie is down to '0'. This may take several rounds or even several tapping sessions! Be persistent and your persistence will pay off.

Knowing the Basic Recipe comprises about 20 percent of EFT. Some people think that this is *all* there is to EFT and stop there. But to get really consistent results requires practice, learning the nuances and subtleties of working with human beings and learning to work with aspects, layers and roots. To learn about these, see Chapter 6.

Things to remember

The main points to remember from this chapter are:

✳ for best results, learn the tapping point locations accurately

✳ we 'set up the experience' for tapping by tapping the Karate Chop spot on the side of the hands, while repeating the set-up affirmation three times

✳ when first learning EFT, it's easier to begin with simple, recent memories

✳ remember that *feeling is healing*. You can enhance your success by feeling and attending to your felt experience, with feelings and sensations in the body, while tapping.

✳ EFT does not always work the first time. You may need to address reversals, aspects and layers and you may need to repeat the sequence several times. Be persistent.

6

Going deeper

> If psychological issues exist as energy fields, then they can
> be resolved much more easily than one might assume... it
> would then be merely a matter of altering the field.
>
> Fred Gallo, *Energy Psychology*

In this chapter you will learn:

- ▶ *the difference between memories and issues*
- ▶ *how to work with aspects, layers and tail-enders*
- ▶ *the tabletop metaphor*
- ▶ *how to uncover roots*
- ▶ *the power of skilful questioning.*

Case study

EFT trainer and coach Lorna Minewiser of Charlotte, North Carolina, relates this story.

I was holding an EFT practitioner mentoring meeting at a country club. There were big windows along one side of the room and someone walked by in a kilt, carrying bagpipes. 'Angela' said, 'I hope he's not going to play *Amazing Grace*! I'll be out of here!' I asked if she would like to let go of her reaction to *Amazing Grace* as the demonstration. She agreed and said that the song had been played at her grandfather's funeral when she was a teenager and since then she had had a reaction to it. We tapped one round on 'They played *Amazing Grace* at granddad's funeral.' What came up next was a belief; she thought that she was supposed to have to gone to see him before he died. She had held this belief that she was supposed to 'be there' for someone when they died and it was wrong if she wasn't.

After tapping on this, Angela realized that this same belief had been causing her much grief over her father's recent death. So we tapped on both this belief and on the grief and guilt she felt. The bagpipe player was still walking up and down in front of our window, but it no longer bothered her. There was a piano in the room and one of the other participants went over and played *Amazing Grace*; Angela had no reaction. Later that day I received an email from her. After she went home, she logged on to YouTube and played every version of *Amazing Grace* she could find and thoroughly enjoyed it. She also reported having an image of her younger self twirling around and feeling free (she is in a wheelchair).

Issues such as this are like tangled fishing lines, all knotted together. This story shows how rules and beliefs ('I was supposed to have gone to see him', 'I'm supposed to be there for people') can get tangled up with feelings (grief and guilt) and attached to a memory (grandfather's funeral) to form an issue. Feelings are the glue that keeps issues stuck together; when you tap on the originating memory with its attached emotions, the issue begins to release. Learning to unwind and unravel issues, by tapping on the different aspects and layers as they arise, is an important skill for success with EFT.

Key point

Issues are like tangled fishing lines, where rules, beliefs and decisions get tangled up with emotions and attached to specific memories to form an issue. Learning to unravel issues by tapping on aspects and layers is an important skill for EFT success.

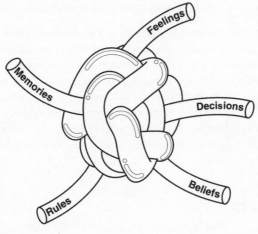

Figure 13

Gary Craig says that learning the Basic Recipe constitutes about 20 percent of the EFT healing 'treasure chest'. Some people will get results with it and feel satisfied. But to get the most from EFT and other forms of meridian tapping requires diving into the other 80 percent. Approximately 40 percent involves working with aspects and layers, 20 percent involves uncovering roots and going deeper, and the final 20 percent involves polishing and fine-tuning your technique. This chapter will discuss working with issues, aspects, pop-ups, layers, tail-enders and how to uncover the roots of an issue.

Key point

Feelings are the glue keeping issues 'stuck'. When you tap on an originating memory with its attached emotions, the issue begins to unravel and release.

Memories and issues

Memories are remembered events, single experiences that happened in the past. Although specific memories may be painful, it is fairly straightforward to release and desensitize them with EFT. You simply specify a memory, tune and rate it, say your set-up phrase and tap tap tap! while holding the memory in mind. And *voila!*, the memory releases.

Issues are more complex. An issue is a problematic pattern that is reflected in a person's thoughts, perceptions, emotions and behaviour. Issues are rooted in mental-emotional-physical states within which we think, perceive, feel and behave differently. Our issues are built up over many repetitions of a behaviour, where the behaviour is reinforced, creating a stable (or stuck) pattern. Just like beads forming a necklace, these patterns are rooted in specific memories, usually emotional and often traumatic in nature.

Aspects

Did you ever play the game of 'connecting the dots' as a child? There would be an apparently random ordering of dots on a page. You connect the dots with a pencil and the picture emerges.

Good EFT practice involves 'connecting the dots'. Sometimes we're not able to resolve an issue because we have not put all the pieces of the puzzle together. Some part of us is holding on (or holding out!) and keeping things disconnected. The different dots, little pieces of the puzzle, are called 'aspects'. You retrieve and connect the aspects and a picture emerges. When this picture emerges there is often an 'Aha!', a recognition, a sigh of relief and release.

Aspects are additional, important details that are necessary to resolve an issue. Until you find and uncover them, you can't complete the puzzle. Learning to uncover and identify aspects is essential to success with EFT and to eventual mastery of this healing art.

In tapping on a fear of spiders, someone may have an image of a spider. They think of it, tap, defuse the emotional charge and 'Ta daa!', it's done. Or maybe not. They were thinking of a sitting spider. When they think of a moving spider, the fear comes back. So, 'moving spider' is the next aspect to tap on. After tapping on 'moving spider', they may have a thought, 'It's ridiculous to have this fear! What's wrong with me, anyway?' This is the next aspect. When tapping, it's important to tap on all the aspects, all the relevant details connected with the issue.

Key point

It's important to uncover and tap on all the aspects of an issue to fully release and resolve it.

There are several signs indicating a new aspect.

▶ **Shifting to a new detail:** When a new detail pops up and has the person's attention, it's probably a new aspect to tap on. If you were focusing on 'what he said', and find yourself shifting to 'the look in his eyes', that will be another aspect.

▶ **Intensity won't go to '0':** If the intensity has not dropped to '0' after a few rounds of tapping, your client may have shifted to another aspect. It's common that as the intensity on the initial piece of the puzzle drops, another piece/aspect pops up. Also, you will not notice complete relief until all aspects have been uncovered and treated.

▶ **Intensity comes back:** If you think you've addressed an issue completely but then it comes back, whether a day or a month later, it's likely due to another aspect. Review the previous aspects, check their intensity and tap them down to '0'. Then find and uncover, using specific questions, any remaining aspects.

▶ **Intensity increases:** If the intensity increases or seems to get worse, it's because you've just uncovered another, more intense aspect. This is a good thing – it shows you're making progress and getting down to the roots. Tap and desensitize the more intense aspect and then go back and test the original aspect you were tapping on previously.

UNCOVERING ASPECTS

Aspects often just pop up by themselves. You tap and release one layer and the next aspect pops up. If no aspects are popping up, you can uncover them with skilful questioning. Simply ask questions such as:

▶ Is there anything else about this issue that still bothers me?

▶ Does this feel 100 percent complete now?

▶ If there were something else still upsetting about this, what might that be?

Another useful technique for uncovering aspects is using sentence completions. Select an issue you're feeling incomplete about and write a sentence such as *'I feel upset about......, because......'*. Write five to seven reasons why you feel upset about this and then tap on each one individually.

An alternative is to ask yourself, *'What else about this...... still feels upsetting to me?'* Notice what comes up in response to that question and tap on that. With a little digging and a little practice, aspects are easy to uncover and release.

How do you know when you've gotten all the aspects? Test yourself or your client in different ways. Think of the issue, mentally provoke it and try to get it back. You can imagine encountering the issue in the future and notice your reaction. If you can successfully challenge the issue without getting retriggered and you're still at '0', then you've gotten all the aspects and you're done.

Case study: Jane's rattlesnake encounter

One of the benefits of living in southern Arizona is getting to share this beautiful desert with some interesting creatures. Among these are rattlesnakes. While many people are afraid of them, rattlesnake bites are relatively rare, in part because these amazing creatures generally have the courtesy to rattle and warn you of their presence. Nonetheless many people feel frightened to death of them.

'Jane' came to my office following an encounter with a rattlesnake near her home. Even though she was never really in danger, the image of the snake haunted her during the day and in fearful dreams at night.

After hearing her story and doing a brief intake interview, I taught her the Basic Recipe. We tapped a couple of rounds, during which her fear went down from '9' to '5'. There was obviously something still there. So I asked her, 'What *aspect* of this encounter with the snake was most upsetting for you?' She thought a moment and answered, 'It's blue and green and slimy.' I noted that this was odd, because rattlesnakes are neither blue nor green, and Jane had not touched it so she could not know whether it was 'slimy'.

So we moved to our next round, tapping on 'blue and green and slimy'. Halfway through the round she started sobbing and stopped tapping. 'That's it,' she said. She sobbed a little more and then told me the story. When she was about four years old, she was playing with her friends, when she felt something in her pocket. She reached in and pulled out an enormous caterpillar, that was blue, green and slimy. She was so shocked and frightened that she soiled her pants. She ran home to her mother, who yelled at her and blamed her for soiling her clothes, compounding an already frightening experience.

We then tapped on the remaining aspects: the shock of finding the caterpillar; the guilt about pooping in her pants; the guilt and shame from her mother's admonishment; the anger with her mother, because Jane wanted to throw those pants away but her mother made her continue to wear them. By the time we finished about 45 minutes later, she was at peace. Following-up a couple of weeks later, she told me, 'I've been sitting on that experience all these years and I realize that my snake encounter was a shamanic experience and the snake came into my life to help me reconnect and heal that memory.'

Dealing with pesky pop-ups

Those of us who are citizens of cyberspace are familiar with pop-ups, those unwanted ads that annoyingly 'pop up' on your computer screen when you least want or expect them. There are pop-up blocker utilities that will block and stop these pop-ups, but what about the pop-ups in our minds? These are the little voices, also called 'tail-enders', that pop up and say things like 'You can't do that', 'What will other people think?', 'Who do you think you are?' etc.

Pop-ups are a form of psychological reversal. They are objections to success which keep us stuck, cause internal conflict and block us from achieving our goals and dreams. Also called 'automatic negative thoughts', or ANTs, they have a life of their own and tend to pop up when you're working on a goal or project.

Case study: Popping Mary's pop-ups

I recently worked with 'Mary', a happily married and middle-aged mother of two adult children. Although she had had a successful career as a counsellor, she wished to change careers and write. She loves writing, finds it easy to write and was close to completing her first book of inspirational stories. When she thought about publishing and marketing her book, however, she found herself attacked and besieged by pop-ups such as:

✲ 'My writing isn't good enough.'
✲ 'I'm not as smart as others.'
✲ 'My manuscript will be rejected by 20 publishers.'
✲ 'I think I have good ideas, *but*... .'

Whenever one of these negative beliefs popped up for her, it would dampen her enthusiasm and love for her writing and leave her feeling unhappy, unmotivated and hopeless. After listening to her story and getting a sense of her strengths and resources, I wrote all her pop-ups on a large whiteboard. We then reframed them and incorporated them into the following set-up statements:

✲ 'Even though A PART OF ME THINKS that my writing isn't good enough, the REST OF ME KNOWS that my writing is good enough for me!, the REST OF ME KNOWS that I've been writing for years and I have a lot to say!, and I'M CHOOSING TO share my ideas and insights so that others will enjoy them too.'

✲ 'Even though A PART OF ME THINKS that I'm not as smart as others, the REST OF ME KNOWS that there will always be people who are more and less intelligent than me, and I'M CHOOSING TO value and appreciate the smarts and intelligence I have.'

✲ 'Even though A PART OF ME THINKS that my manuscript will be rejected by 20 publishers, the REST OF ME KNOWS that many successful authors got numerous rejections before being accepted, the REST OF ME KNOWS that getting 'rejected' only brings me closer to my goal, and I'M CHOOSING TO submit my book, put it out there and see what happens.'

We then did several rounds of tapping on her doubts and fears, on her 'felt experience' in her body. By the time we finished she was feeling relaxed and confident. Mary continued tapping on her own and completed the first of several books.

Tapping through layers

One of the many myths about tapping is that all issues will magically disappear after just one round of tapping. This has led to unrealistic expectations, with people trying EFT and giving up after tapping 2–3 rounds and then saying that EFT doesn't work. Would you expect to ride a bike, drive a car or learn a language in just one try? Of course not! The same is true for meridian tapping. There is a powerful truth in a slogan from the Twelve-Step programmes: 'It works when you work it!'

Key point

It's a myth that all issues will disappear with just one round of tapping. Most issues will require persistence, uncovering reversals, working through aspects and treating layers with repeated rounds of tapping.

Issues usually involve treating several layers. Finding the next layer or aspect is easy. Tap on the presenting emotions and sensations and then after each subsequent round of tapping, 'check in' with yourself, notice any aspects or what is still 'left' from the previous round or what pops up next. Perhaps the intensity has increased or the tension has moved from the solar plexus up into the chest. Whatever you notice, whatever is different in this new moment of time, is the next layer. Therapy is a process of 'peeling the layers of the onion', so EFT often involves tapping through several layers until you get to the root of the issue. Let's take a look at how Marilyn resolved her fear of the future.

Case study: Marilyn's fear of the future

Marilyn was a confident, successful woman who had owned and managed several businesses in her life. Her husband had died four years earlier and she was looking forward to retirement. Yet she experienced a vague 'fear of the future'. This surprised her, as she thought of herself as being optimistic as well as a practical, 'no nonsense' businesswoman used to handling problems and challenges.

After a brief interview and reviewing the EFT Basic Recipe with her, we tapped one round on her 'fear of the future'. I checked in with her and she said, 'I'm feeling confused – this fear doesn't make any sense to me.' This was the next layer: confusion ('this fear doesn't make any sense'), so we tapped on her confusion. Then she reported feeling an intensification of the fear, as though 'something *really bad* is going to happen'. This was the next layer, so we tapped on 'something *really bad* is going to happen'. Halfway through this round she sat up and stopped tapping. 'I just had a memory. I'm about 11 years old, sitting in the back seat of our family car, my parents are in the front seat arguing and I realize that they're going to divorce. All these thoughts about the future are going through my mind: "What will happen to our family? Who will I live with? What school will I go to?".'

We did two more rounds of tapping, first on the initial memory of her parents arguing in the car, then on her thoughts and fears about the future. After that round, she thought about it and said, 'You know, I've had this fear of the future for years. But I'm 63 years old, I survived, I've had a family of my own, I'm retired and I've made it in life.' We tapped on her (positive) sense of relief and reassurance that 'I survived, I've had a family of my own, I'm retired and I've made it', after which she reported feeling more relief, reassurance and much stronger. She also had a realization: 'Now that I know where that came from, I don't need to feel afraid of the future any longer.'

Marilyn's worksheet

Experience	Rate (0–10)	Set-up and Tap Karate Chop points	Tap point and Reminder	Test (0–10)	Adjust and Aspects
Fear: vague anxiety 'I feel afraid of the future.'	8	'Even though I'm feeling afraid of the future, I deeply and completely love and accept myself.'	'Feeling afraid of the future'	5	'I'm 63 years old, and I'm a very strong, capable woman. This fear doesn't make sense.'
Confusion: 'This fear doesn't make any sense.'	6	'Even though this fear doesn't make any sense, I deeply and completely love and accept myself.'	'It doesn't make any sense.'	4	'It doesn't make any sense, but I still feel apprehensive...'
Apprehension: 'I feel apprehension that something really bad is going to happen.'	8	'Even though I'm feeling apprehension that something really bad is going to happen, I deeply and completely accept myself.'	'Fear that something really bad is going to happen...'	5	Memory: parents fighting in the car. 'I realized they were going to divorce.'

Upset: Memory of parents fighting, discussing divorce	10	'Even though I was upset and freaked out when my parents fought in the car, I deeply and completely accept myself.'	'Upset about my parents fighting and yelling in the car.'	6	'What will happen? Who will I live with? What school will I go to?'
Uncertainty: 'What will happen to our family? What will happen to me?'	7	'Even though I felt upset and uncertain about my parents divorcing, I deeply and completely accept myself.'	'Feeling uncertain about what will happen.'	3	'I'm 63 years old, I survived, I'm retired, and I've made it in life.'
Reassurance: 'Now it all makes sense why I've had this fear of the future for years.'	4	'Even though I used to have this fear of the future, I know it all makes sense now, and I deeply and completely accept myself.'	'Understanding, feeling safe and reassured now.'	0	'I'm OK now, I'm a very strong woman, and whatever happens, I can and will handle it.'

Getting down to the roots

Even though EFT works very quickly, some people are in as much of a hurry with their tapping as they are with everything else! They just want to feel better ASAP, so they will tap on the surface layer of a memory or issue, which then seems to release. They feel better and they go on their way.

Sooner or later, however, the issue is likely to be retriggered. This is like trying to weed your emotional garden using a grass trimmer. It looks fine for a little while, but then the weeds will start growing back. To fully release and clear an issue requires uncovering them and pulling them out by the roots. Uncovering and releasing the roots of issues is a huge topic; what follows can be only a brief introduction.

All issues are rooted in individual memories. Emotional roots are formative memories giving rise to the presenting problem. When tapping on the presenting problem, there may be a partial release, but you sense that something deeper is still there. Another sign is resistance. You start to work on a particular issue but as you start getting into it, you begin avoiding or distracting or putting up a 'smokescreen'. Something is blocking access: 'Don't go there – it's too dangerous!' Another indication of an underlying root or reversal is a symptom that doesn't change, no matter how much you tap on it.

There is a principle in psychotherapy that *we are never upset for the reason we think*. All issues are old issues. We project the shadows of the past onto the present without being aware we are doing so. This is one reason why it can be difficult to 'be fully present' or to 'live in the Now', because we are continually painting the present with the emotional colours of the past.

Key point

All issues are old issues. We project the shadows of past experiences onto the present, without being aware we are doing so.

To change and resolve an issue often requires reconnecting and re-engaging with one or more specific earlier memories, called 'originating traumas'. Fortunately, it is not necessary to recall and resolve every single trauma! Gary Craig uses the metaphor of a tabletop (an issue) with many legs holding it up (specific memories). When you tap on and collapse enough legs, the whole table collapses.

Figure 14

Key point

The tabletop metaphor – when you tap on and remove enough of the legs of the table, the whole table collapses.

The most direct way to uncover the roots of an issue is to ask:

▶ what does this remind me of?

▶ when did I experience (something like this) before?

▶ what is the cause, source or origin of this......?

When using this technique, notice how your body responds, with any emotional shifts or shivers. Remember that *feeling is healing*; listen to your own inner 'truth bell' that lets you know when you've found your truth.

Tip

Listen to your own inner 'truth bell' that lets you know when you've found your truth.

HYPNOTIC REGRESSION

Another method that many therapists use is hypnotic regression. The practitioner does a hypnotic induction and guides you into a trance state, which puts the conscious mind aside temporarily, allowing deeper access to the subconscious. You can use a similar method without having to go into trance. Simply close your eyes, feel and connect with the issue and then imagine going back in time, back in time, back in time, to the cause, origin or source of this issue... and notice what comes up. Sometimes one or more specific memories will arise, and sometimes not. But even when nothing comes up, pay attention to your body. Sensations, sounds, images or memory fragments may come up. You may sense a deeper feeling, a fine-tuning or refinement of the original issue, which you can then tap on.

Tip

One way of 'going deeper' is to listen to music that moves you. Listen to music that evokes a strong emotional reaction, notice where you feel it in your body and then tap on the emotions and sensations you feel.

THE TAIL-ENDER TECHNIQUE

One more way to find core issues is to use the Tail-ender technique. 'Tail-enders' are the (often unconscious) replies we make to positive affirmations. For example, a person may tell themselves, 'I am now making $100,000 a year' and their inner self-talk will reply, 'Yeah, right!'. The deeper issue is self-doubt, and perhaps disappointment because expectations have been disappointed in the past. Tapping on both these feelings, as well as on the 'earlier similar experiences' that gave rise to these feelings, will then release and collapse the feelings, and the issue along with it.

USEFUL QUESTIONS FOR GOING DEEPER

Another way to 'go deeper' and uncover the roots of an issue is by asking questions. Questions (like the question mark symbol itself) are like fishing hooks. We cast them out into the vast ocean of the subconscious mind and wait until they hook something.

▶ Where in my body do I feel this?

▶ Where did this come from?

▶ What do I tell myself when......?

▶ What am I telling myself about......?

▶ What does this remind me of?

▶ How old do I feel when......?

▶ When did I experience this...... before?

▶ What seems to be stopping/preventing me from......?

▶ What are the advantages of holding on to this issue? (What am I *getting out of* holding on to this issue?)

▶ What are the disadvantage(s) of giving up this issue? (What is holding on to this issue *costing* me?)

▶ What happened the last time I tried to...... (e.g. lose weight)?

▶ What was going on in my life in the 3–6 months *before* this symptom/condition first showed up?

▶ What will I have to give up, in order to get......?

These are powerful questions and it's usually not necessary to ask each one. Sometimes just asking one or two and listening to your body's response will be sufficient.

Case study: Trapped in my own car

I frequently drive to Albuquerque, New Mexico, to teach EFT. It's a seven-hour drive, about eight hours including lunch and stops. I noticed that initially I would enjoy the drive, feeling excited about travelling and the opportunity to share EFT etc., but within a couple of hours I'd start to feel upset, 'stuck', and trapped in the car. These feelings would persist even when I stopped to get out and stretch or have lunch. What was going on?

I tapped two or three rounds and it released only slightly. There was a deeper layer. So I asked myself, 'What is going on? What does this remind me of?' For a while I felt puzzled; then it came to me. When I was a child, our family sometimes went on long road trips. My parents sat in the front, while my sister Franny and I sat in back. My dad was an excellent driver, but was often uptight about getting to our destination on time, and so he'd get angry and yell if there were any interruptions. My sister and I, being kids, had a different agenda and we were frequently reprimanded for 'making too much noise'.

I also realized that I had internalized my father's strict, very conscientious-but-uptight approach to driving. I then did several rounds of tapping on my fear of dad, fear of dad yelling, feeling 'stuck' in the car, 'paying attention to the road' etc. Since then I no longer feel upset while driving and my road trips are much more enjoyable.

Tip

While it is possible to 'dig deep' and uncover roots by yourself, it's often easier to work with a partner or skilled practitioner.

And even deeper

Our two fundamental emotions are love and fear. Underlying all our issues there is usually some form of fear and/or a lack of love – for either another or oneself. We're either feeling afraid or feeling unloved or unlovable. Judgements are rooted in fear and block our experience of love and connection. So, ask yourself:

▶ what am I feeling afraid of, in this issue?

▶ who is withholding love, in this issue?

▶ how am I withholding love, in this issue?

Then plug the fear or lack of love into your set-up phrase, treat that as the issue and tap tap tap!

It can be very effective to identify the specific fear or lack of love and tap on those, and then to find a positive resource inside (e.g. courage, resilience, self-love) and tap tap tap! on this positive resource. Tapping on the positive will help to both strengthen and integrate that resource in your experience.

To learn more about tapping on the positive and other upgrades, see Chapter 7.

Things to remember

The main points to remember from this chapter are:

✻ learning the Basic Recipe constitutes about 20 percent of the EFT healing 'treasure chest'. To get the most from EFT requires going deeper and addressing aspects, layers and roots.

✻ issues are like tangled fishing lines, where rules, beliefs and decisions get tangled up with emotions and attached to specific memories to form an issue. Learning to unravel issues by tapping on aspects and layers is an important skill for success with EFT.

✻ feelings are the glue keeping issues 'stuck'. When you tap on an originating memory with its attached emotions, the issue begins to release.

✻ 'aspects' are additional, important details that are necessary to resolve an issue. It's important to uncover and tap on all the aspects of an issue to fully release and resolve it.

✻ it's a myth that all issues will disappear with just one round of tapping. Most issues will require persistence, uncovering reversals, working through aspects and treating layers with repeated rounds of tapping.

✻ you can 'go deeper' and find emotional roots by asking questions.

7

Fine-tuning your results

By mentally activating a psychological issue and stimulating a set of energy points, the neural connections governing that issue can be rewired in desired ways… . This tool which allows almost surgical precision in changing neurochemistry without causing side effects is unique within both psychotherapy and education.

The promise of Energy Psychology is profound.

David Feinstein, *The Promise of Energy Psychology*

In this chapter you will learn:

- ▶ *ways to fine-tune your results*
- ▶ *testing*
- ▶ *future pacing*
- ▶ *tapping scripts*
- ▶ *reversing reversals*
- ▶ *the PARTS set-up*
- ▶ *borrowing benefits*
- ▶ *positive tapping.*

Some people learn the Basic Recipe and think that this is all there is to EFT. Those folks are cheating themselves, because there is so much more to EFT than simple mechanical tapping. Anyone can tap! Fine-tuning your technique with the tips and ideas in this chapter will take your tapping practice to an even higher level.

Creating a safe space

When doing EFT with yourself or another, it's good practice, as with any kind of healing or personal growth work, to create a safe space. On the one hand, meridian tapping is very robust and flexible and people tap in all kinds of places and situations. On the other hand, you will likely get better results if the radio or television is not blaring and if you're not being interrupted by phone calls or texts. Therapists know the importance of creating a safe space for their clients. You can do the same for yourself. Set yourself up in a clean, quiet room or office, where you can feel safe being present with yourself or another while tapping.

Tapping with intention

Intention is not often discussed in EFT circles. You just think of an issue, tap on it and then it releases – or not! It may then require persistence in treating aspects and layers. Very often, tapping seems so bizarre that people expect it not to work and then feel surprised when it does.

Yet intentions are very powerful, especially when doing healing work. Sometimes the presence and intention of the healer, which is part of 'holding the space', helps carry the client over the waves of their fears and doubts. Our intentions are often implicit and unconscious, even to ourselves. By stating them explicitly and making them conscious, we can create a stronger motivation to heal and transform the issue at hand.

Sometimes our intention is simply to get release from pain. It may be to have a better relationship or to be a better person. Or it may be to resolve suffering for another through surrogate tapping, or to extend healing and happiness to all people. The more you can involve others, the greater will be your intention. Our intentions, like our words, carry weight and power.

The sound of two hands tapping

EFT and Thought Field Therapy (TFT) began with one-handed tapping and you will see Gary Craig teaching people to tap with one hand on his DVDs. However, as we hold 'issues in our tissues', many of these issues are located in one side of the body or the other. Also, all the meridian pathways, except the Central Vessel (running along the front of the body, from the pubic bone to the chin) and the Governing Vessel (running along the back, from the tailbone to under the nose), are bilateral and run on both sides of our bodies. Thus you may experience a deeper balancing effect by tapping on both sides with both hands.

Another very powerful therapy is Eye Movement Desensitization and Reprocessing (EMDR), developed by psychologist Francine Shapiro. The original versions of EMDR involved having people focus on an issue while following a therapist's hand movements laterally back and forth. EMDR's mechanism of action is believed to be bilateral hemispheric stimulation, i.e. that stimulating both hemispheres of the brain while focusing on an issue triggers the brain to process traumatic memories faster and more effectively. It has been discovered that the same bilateral effects can be achieved by listening to alternating auditory tones or with alternating kinesthetic stimulation – tapping!

You can harness the power of bilateral hemispheric stimulation by tapping with both hands alternately, left–right–left–right–left–right and so on, on the acupoints on both sides of the body. The only two points which are not bilateral are the Under Nose and Chin points; you can tap these two alternately, nose–chin–nose–chin–nose–chin and so on, with both hands.

Thousands of people have learned to tap with one hand only and single-handed tapping works well. I suggest you try both ways and see what works best for you. I find that, as with drumming and dancing, people feel more engaged and connected with the process when using both hands.

Amplify tapping with breathing

One of the ways we hold ourselves back is by breathing shallowly. This is one result of the freeze-immobility response, when we freeze, shut down and try to make ourselves as small as possible. Over many repetitions this has the effect of inhibiting our emotions, as our emotional expression (think of sighing, crying and yelling) is expressed or repressed through our breathing. When we inhibit our breathing, we are simultaneously inhibiting our life force and our creative expression in life. We hold ourselves back from living and loving and experiencing life fully. Conversely, as we release holding and constriction in our breathing, we become not only more alive but better able to express our careers, creativities and intentions in the world.

You can amplify the power of tapping by breathing while you tap. Deep breathing is a powerful practice in itself and is always to be recommended! Rather than counting mechanically, simply tap each set of points while inhaling and exhaling. This is a very easy rhythm to follow and harnesses the synergy of breathing and tapping together.

Activity: Experiencing the synergy of tapping and breathing

Think of an emotional upset you'd prefer to feel better about. Name it and create a reminder phrase. Attune to it in your body and rate its intensity from 0–10. After repeating your set-up phrase and tapping the Karate Chop points three times, tap each set of points, alternating right and left hands, while breathing slowly and deeply, one acupoint (both sides) per full inhalation and exhalation. Tap and breathe through the sequence like this and then check in with yourself afterwards.

What do you notice?

You may need to repeat the sequence if there are additional aspects, reversals etc. But notice any differences between two-handed tapping compared to one-handed tapping and see which feels better for you.

Mindfulness

Mindfulness meditation, also called insight meditation, has been gaining popularity as meditation practice, for stress release and as an adjunct to therapy. Research studies have found mindfulness to be effective in improving immune function, reducing blood pressure, reducing pain and stress, and enhancing cognitive function. While EFT is not meditation, mindfulness training can enhance tapping by focusing attention on the issue and on its felt experience in the body. In the insight meditation tradition there is a practice called 'noting'. While there is more to it than this bare description, the essence is simply to note and acknowledge each subtle somatic sensation as it arises, observing and noting it as it rises and falls, and then let it go, focusing on the next one (or the same one) as it arises and falls, and so on. Incorporating mindfulness techniques with tapping will assist you in going deeper and can enhance the efficacy and enjoyment of your tapping practice.

Activity: Mindful tapping

Think of an emotional experience to explore. Notice:

* where in your body is it?
* how big is it?
* are there any colours or textures associated with it?

Allow yourself a few moments to explore and taste and savour your felt experience. Sometimes your experience will start to shift, just by noticing and being present with it.

Then rate its intensity from 0–10 and tap slowly and mindfully while breathing, one inhalation and exhalation per set of tapping points. Notice how your felt experience shifts as you tap. After one round of tapping, stop, check in with yourself and attune to your felt experience again. How is it different now?

Repeat the rounds as needed, until the experience has released and defused.

Case study

EFT master Judy Byrne of London shares this story about 'Janice', a woman with multiple anxieties.

Janice was a 48-year-old solicitor who came to see me about her anxieties, including using lifts and tunnels, being in crowds and being shut in aircraft during flights. One practical consequence of this issue was that she felt she could not apply for jobs in central London, where there would be more challenging opportunities and prospects of better pay than near her home in a London suburb. She was sabotaging her own career prospects. Or was that just an unintended consequence?

Before she came, she had given a lot of thought to what might have been the origin of these broad and spreading anxieties. The only thing she could remember was that more than 20 years earlier she was in a crowd at a football match which was squashed between a metal fence on one side and police horses on the other for what she thought was about 20 minutes. She had only bruising, and the memory did not still feel emotional. But it was still vivid – usually a giveaway that a memory is traumatic and has not moved into long-term memory in the way non-traumatic 'digested' memories do. We did some tapping and it quickly went from low intensity to '0'.

Janice noticed some dramatic changes immediately. She told an employment agency she wanted a new job in central London and enjoyed going for interviews. But, as is so often the case, there had been subsequent traumas overlaid on the original one that had sensitized her to experiencing similar situations as traumatic. We tapped on other memories, including one of a fire alarm drill when an emergency exit had been accidentally blocked and of being stuck, twice, in a train that stopped in a tunnel under the Thames.

Janice realized that she regularly made pictures in her head of things that had not happened to her. Those anxious anticipation-of-disaster neural networks in her brain were being strengthened all the time, like well-exercised muscles. Challenging them by tapping on the feelings that gave rise to them began to unravel the networks.

Over the next few months Janice got a job that involved meetings all over central London and often in very high buildings. She started shopping in London's premier shopping street, Oxford Street, which she had previously considered off-limits for herself. She was unfazed by crowded lifts. She flew to Portugal and found herself actually looking forward to the return flight. And one day, when the train service was particularly bad, she actually walked through the 1,215 ft long foot tunnel 50 ft beneath the Thames – and texted all her friends to tell them she had done it. Then she walked back again in the other direction.

Testing your results

It is important when working towards a goal to test your work periodically. If you don't test your work, how will you know whether you're making progress? While driving we are continually watching the road and adjusting the wheel. Similarly, checking in and testing our results is necessary for getting the best results with EFT. Gary Craig compares testing to a compass that keeps you on course.

Treating an issue thoroughly involves finding all its aspects, even when they are hidden below the surface. Testing your work will assist you in finding and uncovering hidden aspects.

The 0–10 scale used in EFT is called the Subjective Units of Distress (SUD) scale. It is widely used in behavioural psychology to assess an individual's felt experience. It lets you know how much progress you've made and how much further you have to go.

In working with the SUD scale, you begin by rating the issue or experience from 0–10. Then after doing your set-up and one round of tapping, you check in again. As long as there is still some intensity, you know there are one or more aspects to deal with. When you think you've tapped on all the aspects, check yourself for intensity on both the last aspect you tapped on and the original issue. You can then use 'future pacing' about the issue (see below) to check how you might respond in the future.

When working with children, instead of asking them to rate issues from 0–10, you can ask them to show you with their hands 'how big' the feeling is.

Testing has several benefits:

▶ it allows people to sense and 'own' their progress

▶ it helps build rapport between the client and facilitator

▶ it gives you immediate, sensory feedback as to how much progress you've made

▶ when someone 'plateaus', it indicates it's time to look for another aspect.

IN-DEPTH TESTING

To really test your work, you may need to do 'the acid test' at some point. If someone has a fear of heights, go to a hotel or apartment building and (safely) look out the window to test it. If they're feeling upset with someone and now feel that they're 'past all that', have them contact the person and see how they respond in real life.

If you're working with another person, another way to test is through role-playing. After tapping, the facilitator will mimic the offender's voice, gestures etc., to try to get a reaction. Another method is using what Gary Craig calls 'vivid visualization'. You imagine going through the situation again, but this time turn up the sound, the colours, the brightness etc.; exaggerate all features and aspects of the incident, especially those that triggered you previously. If you can review the incident with no reaction, you're complete.

FUTURE PACING

Future pacing is a technique borrowed from Neuro-Linguistic Programming (NLP). It involves imagining yourself confronting an experience in the future. If you can see and imagine yourself in the same situation calmly, then you're complete.

Future pacing is another way of challenging and testing your work, by 'pacing' it in the future. It allows you to mentally rehearse the situation in the safety of your own mind, to 'take it for a test drive' and see what it feels like. You can also imagine possible aspects, by asking yourself, 'And how would I feel if...... were to happen?'.

Future pacing is a powerful technique which embeds and extends changes from the past and present into the future, leaving you feeling prepared and empowered.

To script or not to script

Tapping scripts are pre-prepared lists of set-up statements about an issue, such as weight loss or abundance. They have become very popular and may be found on numerous websites and books.

Gary Craig has pointed out the 'perils' of scripts, such as getting only partial results, and has called it a 'surface approach to a deeper problem'. He recommends customizing the process by working with aspects and getting down to the roots.

While I agree with Gary, I see tapping scripts as being like bicycle training wheels. They may be useful temporarily, while one is still learning the languaging of EFT, and can then be discarded as soon as you can customize and generate your own scripts.

The art of delivery

If you ever have the opportunity to watch one of the EFT masters work with a group, you will observe what a fine Art EFT can be. Part of this involves what Gary Craig calls 'the art of delivery', how smoothly and fluidly you deliver EFT to your family or clients. This also involves languaging EFT, the verbal patter, using the 'right' words.

The most commonly asked question I get after teaching EFT Level 1 is, 'How do I know what to say?' What you say is very simple: plug your own words and phrases back into the set-up phrase. When I'm working with someone, I will have either a clipboard or a large whiteboard. As they are describing their issue to me and in response to my questions, I jot down their responses. Then when we begin doing EFT, I use their exact phrases in the set-up phrase and the reminder phrase. A person's own words and phrases are like music to their ears; when they hear their own words coming back to them, they relax and feel acknowledged because they know they've been heard.

Key point

In creating set-up and reminder phrases, it is best to use your (or their) own exact words and phrases.

You are already familiar with the basic EFT set-up phrase: *'Even though I have this......, I deeply and completely accept myself.'* This phrase is very flexible and lends itself to endless variations. Karen Ledger in Vancouver, Canada, was working with a big burly veteran who would not go anywhere near 'love and acceptance'. They brainstormed and came up with an acceptable set-up phrase for him: *'Even though I have this blistering rage, we're gonna go and git 'er done!'*

Psychologist Patricia Carrington developed what she calls 'the choices method'. Instead of using acceptance at the end, she has her clients make a positive choice: *'Even though I have this......, I'm choosing to......'*. She finds that for many people, making a positive choice is more empowering than simply accepting oneself.

Self-acceptance is problematic for some. Some people baulk at self-acceptance, saying that they can't or don't (or won't!) accept and love themselves as they are. Many of us hold the idea that we 'could' and 'should' be 'better', more beautiful, more accomplished, more... . Others believe that they are 'unworthy', and 'undeserving' of love and acceptance. Please note that an unwillingness to accept oneself is a reversal and is another aspect to be treated.

One way out of the quagmire of unworthiness and self-hatred is to build a 'ramp' up to Self-Acceptance. It begins by recognizing that *'Even though I may not accept and love myself as I am just yet..., this is the direction I wish to move in.'* Building a semantic ramp up to the level of genuine self-acceptance starts moving us in this direction and helps us begin to experience what was previously forbidden territory.

We can ramp ourselves up to Self-Acceptance with these phrases:

▶ 'Even though I have......, I am WILLING to love and accept myself.'

▶ 'Even though I have......, I am WILLING TO LEARN to love and accept myself.'

▶ 'Even though I have......, I am WILLING TO BEGIN TO LEARN to love and accept myself.'

▶ 'Even though I have......, I am WILLING TO BEGIN TO CONSIDER THE POSSIBILITY that I could love and accept myself.'

As you can see, willingness works like a ramp, moving us up to the level of greater Love and Acceptance and Worthiness.

Full-hearted, 100 percent commitment is a powerful thing. But very few of us experience 100 percent commitment, especially when we're caught in an issue. More often, we are beset by fears and doubts, confusion and indecision. Fortunately, complete certainty and commitment are not necessary. All that is necessary is a little bit of willingness. When we are willing to go somewhere and experience something, we automatically begin moving in that direction; and that is enough.

Some people have great resistance to loving and accepting themselves. They may believe that they are sinners, that they 'deserve to be punished', or that they are unlovable. People who are spiritually oriented and believe in a god or divinity will usually be open to the idea that God loves them. Alternative set-ups can be phrased as follows:

▶ 'Even though I have......, I'm WILLING to remember that God loves and accepts me as I am.'

▶ 'Even though I have......, I'm WILLING TO BEGIN to remember that God loves and accepts me as I am.'

▶ 'Even though I have......, I'm WILLING TO OPEN UP to the possibility of God loving and accepting me as I am.'

I find that using these set-ups gets people 'over the hump', out of the stuckness of self-condemnation and unworthiness, and begins to move them in the direction of self-love and self-acceptance. When we can truly accept ourselves as we are, with all our faults and flaws, we begin to change.

Reversing reversals

As discussed in Chapter 4, a psychological reversal is a block to healing associated with a limiting belief or intention that is opposed to your conscious intentions. Reversals are blocks to success, whether in therapy, personal growth or any area of life. There is always a very good reason, often subconscious, why a person is holding on to an issue. The psychologist Bruce Ecker refers to this as the 'pro symptom position'. Reversals are reasons for holding on.

Issues become much easier to treat when you first address reversals, the objections to succeeding. Sometimes an issue will clear up simply by addressing and treating its reversals.

Key point

Issues are easier to treat when you first address any objections to success. Sometimes an issue will clear up simply by addressing and treating its reversals.

The generic set-up statement (the Blockbuster) is designed to challenge and remove reversals. Much of the time it works as it is; but sometimes, as when working with aspects, you may need to identify the specific block or objection and challenge it specifically. Here is a chart of common reversals.

Reversal	Limiting belief	Set-up phrase
Possibility	'I can't get over this.'	'Even though I think I can't get over this...'
	'It's not possible to get over this.'	'Even though I think it's not possible to get over this...'
Want	'I want to keep this issue.'	'Even though part of me wants to keep this issue...'
	'I don't want to get over this issue.'	'Even though I don't want to get over this issue...'
Safety	'It's not safe for me to get over this issue.'	'Even though I think it's not safe for me to get over this issue...'
	'It's not safe for others/for me to get over this issue.'	'Even though I think it's not safe for others/for me to get over this issue...'
Deserving	'I don't deserve to...'	'Even though a part of me thinks that I don't deserve to...'
	'I'm not worthy of...'	'Even though a part of me thinks that I'm not worthy of...'
Identity	'This is just the way I am.'	'Even though I think that this is just the way I am...'
	'Being this way is the way I am.'	'Even though part of me identifies with being this way...'
Secondary gain	'I'm getting something out of keeping this.'	'Even though I'm getting something out of this...'
	'I'm trying to get something by keeping this.'	'Even though I'm trying to get something by keeping this...'
Suffering	'I want to be miserable.'	'Even though a part of me wants to be miserable...'
	'I want to be ill.'	'Even though a part of me wants to be ill...'
Feeling overwhelmed	'I can't handle this.'	'Even though I think I can't handle this...'
	'This is too big, too dangerous, too overwhelming.'	'Even though this feels too big, too dangerous or too overwhelming...'

You can uncover hidden reversals simply by asking questions, such as:

▶ 'If there were something stopping you from......, what might that be?'

▶ 'What terrible thing might happen if you achieved this......?'

▶ 'What beliefs are you holding about this issue or yourself?'

▶ 'If there were some good reasons for keeping or holding this issue, what might they be?'

▶ 'What else do you think might be going on here?'

Key point

You can uncover hidden reversals simply by asking questions.

After uncovering the reversal, plug it into your set-up statement: *'Even though a part of me thinks that......, I deeply and completely accept myself.'*

An even more powerful way to challenge and change reversals is by using the Parts set-up, below.

The Parts set-up

Reversals are symptoms of inner conflicts. Part of us wants to heal, get better and succeed, and part of us wants to play, party, drink, drug or distract. Like an ostrich burying its head in the sand, a part of us seeks safety by hiding, ignoring and avoiding. While this may be appropriate avian or infantile behaviour, it's usually not the best strategy for solving our problems.

The first step toward healing and integrating these conflicting parts involves simply naming and acknowledging them. Remember, *what you can name, you can change*. A very clean way to separate the parts and get clear about this is to use what I call the Parts set-up. It goes like this: *'Even though A PART OF ME THINKS that......, the REST OF ME KNOWS that......, and I'M CHOOSING TO...... .'*

In the first space you insert the reversal, the objection to healing, which is a limiting or negative belief; in the second space you insert a positive, truthful fact which confronts and removes the limiting belief; and in the third space you insert a positive action you are choosing to take.

Case study: The lady who couldn't do anything 'right'

'Mary' believed that she 'couldn't do anything right'. This was not true, of course, but that was her belief. She only saw her flaws and was almost oblivious to the fact that she did many things well. Believing that she 'could not do anything right', she thought she would not be able to do EFT 'right'. This limiting belief was sabotaging her results.

So I had her custom-design her set-up phrases like this:

✵ 'Even though A PART OF ME THINKS that 'I can't do anything right' [limiting belief], the REST OF ME KNOWS that I do some things very well [positive, truthful fact], and I'M CHOOSING TO love and accept myself [positive action], whether I do things well or not.'

✵ 'Even though A PART OF ME THINKS that 'I can't do anything right', the REST OF ME KNOWS that I've held a responsible job for many years, and I'M CHOOSING TO focus on what I do well, rather than on what I don't.'

✵ 'Even though A PART OF ME THINKS that 'I can't do anything right', the REST OF ME KNOWS that 'I am intelligent, competent and capable', and I'M CHOOSING TO tap on myself, overcome this belief and get the results I want.'

After several rounds of tapping, Mary came to recognize that 95 percent of what she did, she did quite well. Realizing this, she said, was 'like dropping a huge burden', and her children reported that she became happier and easier to be around.

Here are three more examples of the Parts set-up at work:

▶ 'Even though A PART OF ME THINKS that this is too hard and I'll never get over this problem, the REST OF ME KNOWS that I've worked through many other issues in my life, and I'M CHOOSING TO buckle down and do whatever it takes to work through this.'

- 'Even though A PART OF ME THINKS that I've got "fat genes" and I just can't lose weight, the REST OF ME KNOWS that millions of people are successfully losing weight every day, and I'M CHOOSING TO work out, follow my programme and do my best with this.'

- 'Even though A PART OF ME THINKS that this tapping stuff is ridiculous and can't possibly work, the REST OF ME KNOWS that there are thousands of people doing it, so there must be something to it, and I'M CHOOSING TO check it out, tap on myself and see what happens.'

I will have my clients repeat the set-up three or four times, using the same psychological reversal/objection, but with different positive truths and choices in the second and third phrases. I find that a well-designed set-up, followed by tapping, is like a 'one–two punch' that will effectively knock out many issues easily. By directly acknowledging, confronting and removing the specific reversal, the presenting issue can be tapped away much more easily. Often the intensity level will decrease by 50 percent or more just by using this set-up. It is also very useful for cases where the intensity level goes down only 2–3 points and then plateaus there.

The Parts set-up is not a 'canned script'. It is a template for creating and customizing your own set-up phrases. Part of mastering the Art of EFT involves being able to improvise, be creative and create your own set-up phrases as needed. As you continue to tap every day, you will find your intuition and creativity expanding, developing rapport comes easily and you will find yourself saying 'the right thing' spontaneously.

Truth is the antidote for lies. We sometimes make excuses about why we 'can't' do something when we simply don't want to. These little white lies keep us small and prevent us from playing a larger role in Life. As mentioned before, comparing a falsehood and a truth side by side creates cognitive dissonance. The mind will attempt to resolve the conflict and usually does so by aligning with the more truthful statement. We can correct reversals (i.e. limiting beliefs) by comparing them side by side with unlimiting truths in the Parts set-up, as in the examples below.

Reversal/Limiting belief	Unlimiting truth
'Even though A PART OF ME THINKS that...'	'the REST OF ME KNOWS that...'
I feel afraid to confront this,	I am stronger than my fears and feelings,
I can't get over this issue,	I've worked through other issues,
it's not safe for me,	I'm not a child, I'm a strong mature adult now; I've survived, and I'll get through this too,
I don't deserve to have......,	I'm human, and all humans deserve......,
Dad should not have beaten me,	parents sometimes beat their children,
this will never change,	all things are changing, like clouds in the sky,
I'm getting something out of this,	I'll be able to get/have even more after I confront and work through......,

then complete the set-up by stating, 'and I'M CHOOSING TO...... .'

Borrowing benefits

Meridian tapping is a new and excitingly robust field and people are discovering new ways to tap and change every day. While leading seminars, Gary Craig discovered a phenomenon he calls 'borrowing benefits'. When working with a group, he would ask everyone to think of an issue, write it down and rate its intensity from 0–10, and put it aside. Then he'd call one person up front and have everyone tap along on that person's issue. After the person up front was finished, Gary would ask everyone to check their own issue again. Approximately 80 percent of the room would find that their issue had also diminished, if not totally released.

I find that EFT really lends itself to group work. Whenever I'm working with one person, I'll ask everyone else to write down an issue of their own and then have everyone tap along. Very often, people experience relief with their own issue, as well as having a good feeling that they were joining and helping the person they tapped with.

You can 'borrow benefits' by tapping with another person, tapping in a group or by logging on to YouTube and tapping along with one of the demonstrations. Your issue does not have to match the issue the other person is tapping on.

Key point

You can 'borrow benefits' by tapping with another person, tapping in a group or by logging on to YouTube and tapping along with one of the demonstrations.

Tip

Take a tapping break! If you're feeling groggy, fatigued or 'out of sorts', get away from your desk, breathe, stretch and do some gentle tapping. It's a great practice to take 3–5 short tapping breaks throughout your day.

Positive tapping

When we're in a funk, we forget. It's hard to see the forest when we're stuck under a log.

We forget and ignore the tremendous potentials we have within ourselves. Tapping not only removes inner blocks, it also removes outer blocks, the blocks to perceiving and feeling, so that we can begin to see and hear with new eyes and ears. When we do that, we literally see and experience a different world.

Business success coach Betsy Muller says that a lot of her work involves connecting clients with resources. In every community there are external resources – accountants, lawyers, marketing consultants, social media gurus – whose expertise we can tap. But equally as important is connecting people with their inner resources, the untapped potentials of their internal states: courage, creativity, intuition, equanimity, emotional intelligence. These resources are always there; we simply need to invoke and attune to them. We can consciously connect with our inner resources by first tapping out the negative and then tapping in the positive.

Activity: Tapping in the positive

1 Select a limiting belief you wish to change.
2 Attune to the experience in your body and rate its intensity from 0–10.
3 Plug your belief or experience into the Parts set-up, while tapping the Karate Chop point: *'Even though A PART OF ME THINKS that......, the REST OF ME KNOWS that......, and I'M CHOOSING TO.......'*
4 Tap one or more rounds as needed, to defuse the emotional charge of the belief or experience.
5 Think of a positive resource or experience you'd like to replace the negative with. (Positive resources can include courage, creativity,

balance, enthusiasm, love etc.). You can also insert a positive affirmation into the second part, *'THE REST OF ME NOW KNOWS that.......'*

6 Do alternate tapping, as follows. Starting at the Top of Head point, tap while saying out loud:

  ▷ Top of Head: *'A PART OF ME USED TO THINK that......'*
  ▷ Eyebrows: *'But now the REST OF ME KNOWS that......'*
  ▷ Sides of Eyes: *'A PART OF ME USED TO THINK that......'*
  ▷ Under Eyes: *'But now the REST OF ME KNOWS that......'*

And so forth, for 3–4 rounds.

7 Do 1–3 final rounds of alternate tapping, focusing on the positive, as follows:

  ▷ Top of Head: *'NOW THE REST OF ME KNOWS that......'*
  ▷ Eyebrows: *'And I'M CHOOSING TO......'*
  ▷ Sides of Eyes: *'NOW THE REST OF ME KNOWS that......'*
  ▷ Under Eyes: *'And I'M CHOOSING TO......'*

And so forth, through the sequence.

After completing tapping, check in with yourself: what do the negative and positive beliefs feel like now? Then thank yourself for a job well done!

Things to remember

The main points to remember from this chapter are:

✻ you can enhance the power of EFT by creating a safe space, tapping with intention, deep breathing, future pacing, integrating mindfulness and testing your results

✻ issues are easier to treat when you first address any reversals, which are 'objections to success'. Sometimes an issue will clear up simply by addressing and treating its reversals.

✻ you can uncover hidden reversals simply by asking questions

✻ in designing set-up and reminder phrases, it is best to use your (or your clients') own exact words and phrases

✻ the Parts Set-up is a useful template for challenging and correcting reversals

✻ all feedback is valuable, whether seemingly positive or negative. 'Negative' feedback is a course correction, guiding us back into balance.

8

Tapping and relationships

It is only with the heart that one can see rightly; what is essential is invisible to the eye.

Antoine de Sainte-Exupery, *The Little Prince*

In this chapter you will learn about:

▶ *relationships and happiness*
▶ *buttons and triggers*
▶ *undoing buttons with EFT*
▶ *improving communications with EFT*
▶ *overcoming blocks to intimacy*
▶ *tapping with children.*

At the seminars I teach I will often ask 'How many of you are in relationships?' Usually between half and two-thirds of the audience put up their hands, as they assume I mean a romantic relationship. We are all in relationship: with our parents and partners, our children, siblings, friends, family members, co-workers, employers and employees. We are related.

Relationships can be the source of our greatest happiness and sense of fulfilment. Those of us who have children can feel satisfaction in seeing our children and grandchildren growing and maturing, developing careers, finding partners and starting families of their own. It is in and through relationship that we come to see and know ourselves, to see what kind of people we really are. Relationships define us, as wife or husband, son or daughter, grandma or grandpa. It is in and through relationship that we experience love, bonding, connection and intimacy. In the words of an old Lakhota (Native American) blessing: *Aho Mitakwe Asin* ('All my relationships').

Yet relationships can also be the source of our greatest frustration and disappointment. We experience frustration when we try to change something or someone, who cannot or will not change (as we well know they should!). We experience dis-appointment when someone does not 'keep their appointment' with us, i.e. does not behave in the ways we want or expect them to. People should behave the way I say, because I know what's best! But, of course, life does not work that way.

Whenever we are upset, it's a common tendency to point a finger, see the problem as 'out there' and to blame the other for it. This is not to say that problems do not exist; the world is full of people who are lazy, stupid, corrupt or incompetent. But recall that we are never upset for the reason we think. My perceptions are *my* perceptions; they say as much about me and my history as they do about others. Both happiness and unhappiness are 'inside jobs'.

Some people have had bad experiences in relationship and feel reluctant to even contemplate starting another one. Most of us have been hurt and wounded in different ways; these are universal human experiences. It is in and through relationship that we were hurt and wounded, but it is also in and through relationship that we can learn and grow and heal. When we begin to use all our interactions and relationships, whether seemingly 'positive' or 'negative', as learning opportunities, we begin to make the transition from victimhood to self-mastery.

Key point

It is in and through relationship that we were hurt and wounded, but it is also in and through relationship that we can learn and grow and heal.

Push my button!

We all know people who push our buttons. Some of them are in our own families! Sometimes we try to change their behaviour, letting them know how much their behaviour bothers us, how rude or wrong or inconsiderate it is. Yet, the oblivious blockheads just keep doing what they do.

As much as we may want to change other people and the whole world, there is only one person I can change. But when I change myself, my world changes with me. This is, in part, because we perceive the world through the prisms of the past. While we cannot change the data of the past, the apparent facts of what happened, we can change our interpretation, the meaning we give it. When we change the meaning of our past, our present and future changes and opens up as well.

Key point

There is only one person I can change. But when I change myself, my world changes with me.

What we call buttons are triggers, triggering us into earlier traumas. When people 'push our buttons', we usually react mechanically and thoughtlessly, sometimes regretting our actions later. We are reacting out of defence, attempting to avoid our own hidden pain. But in the process of trying to avoid pain ourselves, we sometimes cause others pain, especially those we love. These buttons are old wounds, calling out for healing and transformation.

Case study: Lionel's anger with his ex

'Lionel' felt angry with his ex-wife, 'Reba', for years, both during their 22-year marriage and after it ended. As she was less educated and less refined than he was, her speech and social manners pushed his buttons and he felt critical of and embarrassed by her. He had tapped on his anger with her several times, with only a slight reduction in his anger.

Lionel's anger with Reba was at '8'. I guided him through a couple rounds of tapping and it only came down to '6'. So I asked him, 'Lionel, if there were a deeper layer underlying this anger, what might that be?' He thought for a moment and said, 'When Reba behaves inappropriately I feel upset and scared.' I waited a moment and then asked him, 'When you were a little boy, who scared you?'

Lionel had been raised in a very proper family, where his speech and behaviour were often criticized and corrected. Lionel was 'correcting' Reba both because it was an old 'familiar' habit, but also because he felt afraid of being criticized and experiencing that hurt again. He realized that he was pre-emptively judging and criticizing her, and others, in an attempt to ward off being judged and criticized himself. We tapped several times on his fear of being judged and attacked by others.

After a couple of rounds he burst out laughing! He said, 'All these years I've felt so afraid of being judged and criticized by others. But I just realized that *I'm* the judge, *I'm* the attacker, *I'm* the critic I've been afraid of all these years. I've been so afraid of being criticized because that's what I do, I criticize others and because I criticize myself...'. His voice trailed off as he began crying.

We tapped on his grief over the loss of love in his relationships, and also his fear of attacking and feeling attacked. Realizing that he was both the critic and the one being criticized was a shock to him, but simultaneously he realized that, as both sides were in him, it was in his power to confront and resolve these polarities. We tapped on both the impulse to criticize and find fault (fuelled by the fear of being attacked) and his fear of being attacked (by others and by himself), and the whole issue softened and dissolved. Although he and Reba are still separated, he understands the origins of his judgementalness now and they have a much gentler and more understanding relationship.

Activity: Defusing buttons with EFT

1 Think of someone or something that pushes your button. Watch it in your mind like a movie, notice your reactions, feel the sensations in your body and rate the intensity from 0–10.

   Repeat a set-up phrase three times and then tap tap tap! until the intensity decreases.

2 Ask yourself, 'What does this remind me of?', or 'When did I experience something like this before?', or 'Who used to treat me this way?'

   Notice what arises in your mind. Some earlier similar experiences will likely come to mind. Jot these down and then tap and desensitize each of these, one at a time.

   If no specific memories come up, just by asking these questions you may feel vague sensations, a sense of fear or anxiety ('I don't want to go there!'), or thoughts or images may come up. Accept whatever your inner mind gives you, whether it makes sense or not. Then treat these images or sensations as new aspects and tap and desensitize these, one at a time, until each one as well as the original button is no longer reactive.

3 Then future pace. Imagine this same person, or someone else, doing the same thing, pushing your button in the future. What do you notice? How do you react now? If there's any reaction, that's likely a new aspect to tap on. If not, thank yourself for doing more great work with EFT.

Communicating our needs

Communication is the heartbeat of a relationship. We may make love two or three times a week, but we communicate many times, in many ways, every day. Communications are non-verbal as well as verbal; we speak more eloquently with our actions than our words. We all have many ways of saying 'I love you', or 'You're important to me' or 'I'm glad you're here'.

It's important to remember that we cannot hear another when our button is pushed, when we're feeling reactive. We cannot hear each other when we're in fight, flight or freeze mode. We need to breathe, calm down, 'catch our breath' and come back to our senses before we can begin to hear another or ourselves. Meridian tapping is one way to do this.

Key point

We cannot hear another when our button is pushed, when we're reactive or in fight, flight or freeze mode. We need to breathe, calm down, 'catch our breath' and come back to our senses before we can begin to hear another or ourselves.

Activity: Releasing communication blocks

This is an exercise for couples. It may be used to work through a difficult topic. It may also be used with partners who are continually interrupting or with partners who hold back from speaking freely.

Pick a difficult topic to discuss, something you know is a 'touchy' issue. Think of the topic and jot down 4–5 key points you wish to communicate to your partner.

Partner 'A' begins, telling their partner her/his side of the topic. As soon as she/he feels any upset or discomfort, both people stop and tap tap tap! on the first person's discomfort. (Partner 'B' can either tap on his/her own discomfort or can 'borrow benefits' by tapping on their partner's issue.) Tap until the discomfort is released and desensitized. Then partner 'A' returns to the beginning and starts telling her/his side again, once again stopping any time she/he feels upset or discomfort. Repeat as needed until partner 'A' can tell her/his side freely without discomfort. When partner 'A' has finished, switch roles and partner 'B' discusses his/her side of the topic.

Doing this exercise once a week for eight weeks is guaranteed not only to improve your communication skills, but also to help heal and transform your relationship.

Tapping into projections

It can be very humbling to recognize that we do not see others as they are; we see them as we are. What we are seeing is our story about them, our projection. We can have both positive and negative projections; there are movie stars and political figures whom we idolize and some whom we demonize. In my field, some people refer to me as 'Dr Freedom', even though I do not have a PhD after my name. This is their projection, their expectation.

Years ago I had a Japanese housemate. She was rather sloppy and off in her own little world (or so I thought!) and I felt critical of her. At some point I recognized that what I was seeing about her was my projection. I also saw that I did *not* want to tap on this; I wanted to be 'right' about my judgements about her. I was reversed! Eventually I did tap on my judgements of her and later I was amazed to discover what an incredibly beautiful person she really was and is.

Key point

We do not see others as they are; we see them as we are. What we are seeing is our story about them, our projection.

We human beings often blame and project issues 'out there', while ignoring or avoiding them 'in here'. But even though we think we can separate 'inner' from 'outer', inner and outer are intimately connected, just as our minds and bodies are connected. The Universe is a great mirror, constantly reflecting and showing us ourselves. Whenever I see a block or problem 'out there', there is a corresponding block or problem, often in the form of a belief or judgement, 'in here'. When I tap on the block or issue 'in here', the problem 'out there' often shifts as well.

Key point

Inner and outer are intimately connected, just as our minds and bodies are connected. The Universe is a great mirror, constantly reflecting and showing us ourselves.

Communications become problematic when we project the past onto the present, as we are constantly doing, whether consciously or not. It can be difficult to 'be in the present moment' with another, when we're perceiving them as being 'just like' someone else! As mentioned previously, *we are never upset for the reason we think*. When we recognize how often we react mechanically and begin to 'connect the dots' between past and present, we can break the spell of the past and release ourselves from our perceptual prisons.

Activity: Recognizing and releasing projections

Think of someone you're feeling angry or upset with. As you're thinking of them, attune to the sensations in your body, rate these from 0–10, and do 1–2 rounds of tapping.

Then, again thinking of the person, complete the following sentences:

✶ [Person's name] reminds me of...... .
✶ [Person's name] is just like...... .
✶ [Person's name] makes me feel like...... .
✶ When I'm around [person's name], I start to feel...... .
✶ The ways that [person's name] is just like me are...... .

Notice what your body senses, where your mind takes you and which statements provoke a response. Doing this will give you several tapping targets, aspects with emotional intensity. Then, thinking of the person, attune to the sensations in your body, rate the intensity from 0–10, and do several rounds of tapping until the feelings defuse and release.

THE TURN AROUND TECHNIQUE

Another very useful method for working with projections is to use the Turn Around technique. For example, suppose you're feeling angry or upset with someone and have tapped on it, but it does not release completely. Complete these sentences:

▶ 'I feel angry/upset with......, because...... .'

▶ 'I don't like......, because...... .'

▶ 'I think...... should...... .'

▶ 'I want...... to...... .'

After filling this out, replace the other person's name with the word 'me' and read it again:

▶ 'I feel angry/upset with ME, because...... .'

▶ 'I don't like ME, because...... .'

This turns the projection around, back towards yourself. Then tap on the anger/upset with the other person and with yourself and your reasons for it and it will usually shift and release.

Overcoming blocks to intimacy

One of our greatest needs as human beings is intimate contact with another. Intimacy is not only physical and sexual; it includes emotional intimacy as well. We all have a deep need to touch and be touched, both physically and emotionally, to feel that we matter to someone. Yet sometimes we fear and resist the most what we want the most. We put up walls to defend and protect ourselves and end up as prisoners in our own castles. This can be especially true of men, who as children are taught to 'buck up' and 'be tough', and then are unable to let their walls down.

Many women and men have a deep fear of intimacy. It was in and through intimate contact with our parents and caregivers that we were first wounded. Years later, even though we may crave intimacy and connection now, those early memories of hurt, betrayal and abandonment still lurk in the recesses of our minds. To experience the kind of deep connection and intimacy we want, we need to feel safe; but to feel safe, we need to release the ghosts of fear, hurt, pain and abandonment.

The process of releasing blocks to intimacy is similar to releasing any other kind of block. Remember the principles *what you can name, you can change* and *what you can feel, you can heal*. Give the block a name. If you start to go numb or freeze or shut down, call it 'this numb feeling' or 'this shutting down reaction'. If you're not even sure what it is, you can call it 'this block' or 'this thing that happens'. Attune to it in your body, feel and notice its sensations and rate it from 0–10.

Now create a set-up phrase (examples are given below but it's best to create your own), then name and acknowledge the block while accepting yourself:

▶ 'Even though I have this block which I don't understand, I know I'm a good person, and I'm willing to deeply and completely accept myself.'

▶ 'Even though A PART OF ME starts to shut down when we get intimate, the REST OF ME KNOWS that I survived and it's safe now, and I'M CHOOSING TO open my mind, heart and body to all my sensations and experiences.'

▶ 'Even though A PART OF ME has fears about sex and intimacy and even though I was hurt by......, the REST OF ME KNOWS that I survived and I'm OK now, and I'M CHOOSING TO tap on this, release these old ghosts and love and accept myself every step of the way.'

Then tap tap tap! while attuning to the sensations of the block in your body. Tap through the aspects and layers as they come up.

Blocks to intimacy are rooted in earlier, painful experiences. Ask yourself (or your partner) 'What does this [block] remind you of?', or 'When did you first start shutting down like this?', or simply 'What's going on when...... [you start to shut down]?' You may or may not have specific memories, but listen to your body and your body memories will tell you what you need to know.

Sometimes the 'right' memory, the originating trauma, just pops out. Sometimes we cannot remember, or they may have occurred before the age of two and a half years, or while we were still in our mother's womb. Remember that memories are holographic; each memory in a chain contains all the information about every memory in that chain. By tapping on a representative memory which holds the energy of the hologram, you can simultaneously begin to release all related memories in that chain.

Key point

Memories are holographic, in the sense that each memory in a chain contains all the information about every memory in that chain.

Case study: Tapping for PTSD heals relationships

EFT trainer Lorna Minewiser shares the story of 'Elaine', which demonstrates the effects on present-day relationships of clearing early childhood trauma.

Elaine volunteered as a subject for the Vets Stress Research project, in which we use six sessions of EFT to reduce the symptoms of post-traumatic stress. She scored well above the cut-off score of 50 for PTSD on the civilian PTSD checklist. Her goals for our six sessions included dealing with old traumas, healing old and current relationships, dealing with the deaths of her parents and brother and with being adopted as an infant, and getting closer to her family, including her two adult sons.

When Elaine came in for her third session she felt very depressed. It was the beginning of the holiday season and she said that she was always depressed and sad during the holidays. We uncovered some painful beliefs about what should happen during the holidays and how family members should feel and act. She believed that she was not a good mother because her two sons did not get along. This led to uncovering and tapping on her beliefs about being adopted. She had also resisted visiting her hometown because of the painful memories, especially of her brother's death. We tapped on these during the fourth session.

When she came in for the fifth session she was very excited because the son who lived near her hometown had sent her plane tickets to visit him during the holidays. She was looking forward to visiting him and visiting her hometown. We did more releasing of the trauma of her brother's death. She mentioned that she was surprised at how much less it bothered her that her sons didn't get along.

Her final session was after her holiday trip. She said that she had a wonderful time. She was able to go past the place where her brother died. She was able to embrace family members. She had decided to 'back off trying to push the relationship' between her sons and was in a better relationship with each of them.

In her post-treatment interview she responded to the question 'What changes have you noticed as a result of doing these sessions?' with 'I don't worry as much and I accept the way things are and not as I want them to be. I've changed the way I look at life.' We tapped on a lot of different issues over the course of the six sessions. She has decided to train in EFT so she can use it in her work as a veterans' advocate. Oh, and her civilian PTSD score went from 63 (indicative of severe PTSD) to 32. Six months later it was at 28, which is well within the normal range.

Tapping with children

Tapping with children is fun and easy! Kids do not have the resistance and egos that adults have and are much more willing to try something, especially if it's physical and looks like fun. The tapping protocol and how you explain it needs to be appropriate to the child's age and maturity level. With very young children you can try tapping on them (gently) or simply holding them; they will usually calm right down. Kids from three to six years old can be 'wiggly', and may not have the coordination to find all the tapping points; making a game of having them tap on their faces and bodies works quite well. Older children can be shown the Basic Recipe (if they're open to it) and can tap for themselves.

Case study: Teddy bear tapping

Lynne Namka of Tucson, Arizona, the 'happy psychologist', shares this story.

He came on like gangbusters, running into my room without looking at me, and hurled himself onto the couch, grabbing the stuffed lion and yelling and making loud growling noises. This was my introduction to six-year-old 'Zane', who came with his highly perplexed mother, who said, 'None of my other children act this way, I'm overwhelmed.' Indeed, I noticed myself becoming overwhelmed with all the movement and confusion. I took a deep breath and started an internal silent round of EFT to keep myself centred.

I offered Zane my collection of stuffed animals that represent the different parts of the personality. He caught on quickly and discussed his different feelings as he took the crab and talked about his anger, and the happy face to talk about what he enjoyed. When he took the heart, he said that he loved his mother, father and family members. When I asked who loved him, he said 'Mom, for sure, but no one else.' 'Dad?' I inquired. 'No', he said, 'Dad doesn't love me. He doesn't like me.' Zane looked very sad.

His mother added that his father believed in stern, conditional love and let Zane know how displeased he was when Zane acted up. Which was most of the time recently.

I observed that Zane did not have the attention span to tap on himself and was resistant to having his mother or me touch him. He jumped around the room talking in a loud voice and told me of the fun things he did, such as wrestling with his brother, jumping on the furniture and using his 'booty' to bump into the kid behind him in line at school to knock him backwards. Self-esteem for Zane seemed to be about being overactive and attention-seeking, but this got him in trouble.

Trying to corral him, I had my Super Hero Bear (a teddy bear with a cape) 'fly' in to whisper in his ear about learning to let go of his sad and mad feelings. He listened well and accepted the limits about not jumping off my couch. I used Super Hero Bear to whisper in his ear:

* 'Even though I like to yell and be loud, I'm a pretty good kid.'
* 'Even though my loud voice gets me in trouble, I'm OK just as I am.'
* 'Even though I use my hands and "booty" to bother people, I'm OK.'

He laughed as I had made Super Hero Bear use its nose to tap on him using the EFT points and anywhere I could reach as he curled up. He especially loved being tapped on his back and under his arm, as that tickled.

* 'Even though I feel good when I jump on the furniture, I like myself.'
* 'Even though I feel bad about being scolded after I feel good about jumping, I'm OK just as I am.'
* 'Even though I like to play rough and that gets me in trouble, I'm still a good kid.'

He relaxed and yawned and asked for more. I asked his mother if this sudden relaxation was typical of him. She said she had never seen him calm down before!

I knew he could not come up with specific events himself with his short attention span. So I fed him set-up phrases around the painful idea that his dad did not love him. I had to work fast to keep the specific events present in his mind before his attention waned. Again Super Hero Bear did the tapping:

* 'Even though I feel bad when Dad is disappointed in me, I still like myself.'
* 'Even though I get mad when Dad yells at me, I know I'm trying to do the best I can.'
* 'Even though I get mad when I think Dad doesn't love me, when I'm bad I choose to love myself.'
* 'Even though I'm sad when Dad is not nice to me, I will be nice to myself.'

My theory was that the roughhousing and acting out revved Zane up, releasing endorphins in his brain. His feeling bad about himself was interrupted by the boisterous behaviour, which released adrenaline and other active neurotransmitters. Zane's issue was a form of behavioural hyperactivity, which stemmed from a need to seek self-esteem in the only way he knew how – by delighting in rambunctious behaviour.

Using EFT to address Zane's pain and hurt made a big difference in how he saw himself. A different little six-year-old walked out of the room than the one who came in hurling himself across the room. Feedback from his school says that he is less rambunctious in class and less combative with the other boys. An evaluation from a psychiatrist says he does not need to be on medication. There are issues still to be addressed. He is still impulsive and wiggly, and we continue to work on these issues using EFT and teddy bear tapping.

Things to remember

The main points to remember from this chapter are:

✳ it is in and through relationship that we were hurt and wounded, but it is also in and through relationship that we can learn and grow and heal

✳ there is only one person I can change. But when I change myself, my whole world changes with me.

✳ we cannot hear another when our button is pushed, when we're reactive or in fight, flight or freeze mode. We need to breathe, calm down, 'catch our breath' and come back to our senses before we can begin to hear another or ourselves.

✳ we do not see others as they are; we see them as we are. What we are seeing is our story about them, our projection.

✳ inner and outer are intimately connected, just as our minds and bodies are connected. The Universe is a mirror, constantly reflecting and showing us ourselves.

✳ memories are holographic, in the sense that each memory in a chain contains all the information about every memory in that chain

✳ EFT can easily be adapted to children of different ages.

9

Tapping into good health

The next big frontier in medicine is energy medicine. It's not the mechanistic part of the joints moving. It's not the chemistry of our body. It's understanding... how energy influences how we feel.

Dr Mehmet Oz

In this chapter you will learn:

▶ *how to release pain with meridian tapping*
▶ *how allergies can be learned*
▶ *surprising correlations between health conditions and traumas*
▶ *how to desensitize simple allergies with meridian tapping*
▶ *how to explore health issues with meridian tapping.*

To be honest, this chapter is a bit of a problem. Psychologists and mental health practitioners can't treat pain! Or allergies! Or health issues! And everyone knows that tapping cannot possibly affect physical health conditions!

What's going on here?

For centuries the body, mind and spirit have been viewed as separate, and treated accordingly. Doctors attend to our bodies, psychologists and counsellors attend to our minds, and priests, ministers, rabbis and imams tend to our souls. Even today many doctors ignore their patient's thoughts and feelings or, when these become 'problematic', refer them to a psychiatrist. Yet body, mind and spirit are but different aspects of a common underlying reality. *We hold issues in our tissues*; psychological issues show up as patterns of holding and contracting in our minds, bodies and biofields. We can heal our minds by touching and stimulating our bodies; and we can heal our bodies by dialoguing and communicating with our minds.

Key point

Psychological issues and problems are not just 'in our heads'. We hold issues in our tissues. When we release emotional issues by tapping, our bodies often shift and change as well.

Case study: Angela's issue in her tissue

I'm teaching a class in Philadelphia. 'Angela' has had a back pain for the previous seven or eight months. We do some tapping on it in class; the pain subsides slightly, but it's still there. I give her some suggestions about how to continue tapping on her own at home. Three weeks later I received an email from her.

'I kept tapping on the back pain every day, as you suggested. The pain had started when I pulled a muscle while playing tennis. One morning while tapping, I remembered something else; my dog had also been in tremendous pain and that same morning we made the decision to 'put him down'. That terrible decision was on my mind the whole time while I was playing tennis. I tapped on my grief and guilt about this and the pain cleared up and hasn't returned since.'

While EFT is not a panacea, it is a fast and effective way to 'tune ourselves up' and rebalance our inner energetic system. Just as the zero point field, a field of tremendous potential energy, underlies all physical existence, so our inner energy system underlies our physical bodies. When we touch and balance our inner energy system, very often the rest of our systems (mental, emotional, neurological, biochemical and structural) shift as well.

The riddle of pain

The physician and humanitarian Albert Schweitzer once wrote, 'Pain is a more terrible lord of mankind than even death itself.' Pain not only affects how we feel, it also shapes and affects our world-view and philosophy of life. Chronic pain is a complex phenomenon involving sensory, cognitive, affective and behavioural aspects. More recently it has become recognized that pain, once it becomes chronic, is a syndrome in itself requiring treatment.

Chronic pain costs our society many millions of pounds, euros and dollars every year and is a major source of revenue for the pharmaceutical industry. Pain management is a specialty in itself. Unfortunately, pain 'management' is not always successful. Patients often become addicted to their medications or require increasingly higher doses to manage their pain. Pharmaceuticals often leave patients feeling groggy, so many either self-medicate with alcohol or give up taking their meds so that they can 'have a life'. There are issues with medication side-effects and drug interactions, so many doctors find themselves switching medications and trying different combinations to manage their patients' pain levels.

Dr John Sarno is a professor of rehabilitation medicine at the New York University School of Medicine. Sarno is considered controversial in the medical profession because he has proposed a very radical idea: back pain is a symptom created by the subconscious mind to aid in the repression of unconscious emotional memories and issues. Whether controversial or not, Sarno has helped hundreds of people relieve their back pain without drugs or surgery, by dialoguing with their subconscious minds.

Because pain is a complex phenomenon, involving both physical and psychological components and because of the problems associated with medications, there is a greater openness over the past 20 years to holistic alternatives for managing pain. These alternatives include acupuncture, deep breathing, hypnosis, biofeedback, guided imagery and EFT.

As discussed in Chapter 3, in Chinese medicine, energy (chi) and vitality are synonymous. When our inner energies flow freely, we experience joy, aliveness and well-being. When the flow of our inner energies is blocked or disrupted, we experience pain, fatigue, frustration and dis-ease.

Acupuncture can be very effective at releasing blockages in the meridian pathways. But for those of us who don't carry needles around with them, rapid pain relief is always available – at our fingertips.

Treating minor pain with EFT

The easiest way to release pain with meridian tapping is to just tap on it! Focus on the pain or discomfort, rate its intensity from 0–10, notice whereabouts in your body you're feeling it and tap tap tap! Very often the pain will release or diminish after 2–3 rounds of tapping.

If there is still some discomfort, tap on your feelings about having the pain. You may feel resentful about it, disappointed in yourself or angry at someone else ('Why me, God?') Tap on its associated feelings and as they release, the discomfort often releases as well.

If the pain does not release after doing this, there is likely an underlying emotional issue. You will need to put on your thinking cap, ask some probing questions and 'dig deeper' to find the underlying issue.

The colour of pain

EFT masters Paul and Val Lynch teach an interesting variation called 'the colour of pain'. The essence of the technique involves attuning to a pain or discomfort and noticing:

▶ what colour is it?

▶ how large is it?

▶ what shape does it have?

▶ what texture does it have?

▶ does it have a taste or smell?

▶ is it attached to an emotion?

Sometimes the pain will start to shift or release just by describing it.

Then after attuning to its colourful characteristics, tap tap tap! as usual. After each round, check in with its colour, size, shape, texture and taste/smell. Usually, these will change after each round of tapping. Following the colour of pain gives you another way of assessing progress as the colours shift and change.

A related variation is called 'chasing the pain'. Sometimes the pain will start to shift and move in your body, in response to tapping. So just like tracking an animal, keep following and tapping the pain as it moves and shifts, until it releases.

Case story: Tapping an angry pain away

I'm teaching an EFT Level 1 seminar in Anchorage, Alaska. After teaching the EFT Basic Recipe and tapping on some recent memories, I ask whether anyone in the group is experiencing pain. Two ladies, 'Karen' and 'Cecilia', raise their hands. Karen has had lower back pain for the past eight months; Cecilia has had chronic sciatic pain down her right leg for the past three years. I lead the group through a couple of rounds of tapping; their discomfort diminishes slightly but is still there. So I asked them, 'If there were an emotion associated with your pain, what might that be?' Karen mentions sadness, feeling abandoned; she relates it to an experience when she was 10 years old, going to the doctor by herself. Cecilia connects her sciatic pain with feeling angry with herself. We do another 2–3 rounds of tapping on their related emotions. Karen tells us her back pain is completely gone, along with the sadness. Cecilia picks up her right leg, extends her knee forward and twists her leg to the left and then the right. She reports, 'This is amazing; I could not even try to do this before, without flinching or experiencing major discomfort.'

Treating chronic pain with EFT

If the pain does not diminish following 2–3 rounds of tapping, you may need to put on your thinking cap. Take some time to read and ask yourself the following questions slowly. Notice which questions 'grab' you, or trigger an emotional or somatic reaction or an 'Aha!'.

These questions are designed to uncover aspects and give you targets to tap on. Please note that it is not necessary to ask or answer every single question. Some of these may apply to you and some will not. What is important is to listen to your body and pay close attention to those questions which 'ring your truth bell'.

▶ Where in your body are you experiencing discomfort?

▶ Describe your felt experience, the body sensations, of the discomfort.

▶ When did this first begin? What else was going on in your life at that time?

▶ What triggers it? What makes it better? What makes it worse?

▶ If there were some good reasons for having or keeping this pain, what might they be?

▶ If this pain were a message from your body, what might it be communicating?

▶ If this pain were trying to get you to do something, what might it be wanting you to do?

▶ What meaning does this pain have for you?

Answering these questions will provide valuable clues to the origin and source of the pain.

After uncovering aspects and tapping targets, you can treat the pain with meridian tapping. Simply tapping on the sensation may relieve the pain, sometimes temporarily and sometimes permanently. Usually it will at least cause a marked diminution of the pain.

Years ago I worked with a man who had fibromyalgia; his muscle pain was 'always a 10'. After learning EFT, he found he could reduce his pain level from '10' to '4' within two minutes and the pain relief would last four to five hours. This was not a cure, of course; but tapping is quick, effective and always available.

Key point

Pain is a symptom that something is 'wrong' or out of balance. If you are having chronic pain that cannot be relieved by tapping or simple medications, please consult a healthcare professional.

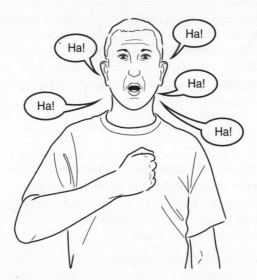

Figure 15: The thymus thump

Activity: The thymus thump

The thymus is the immune system's 'surveillance' gland. The thymus produces white blood cells, also called T-cells, which are critical for our adaptive immune system. After puberty the thymus begins to atrophy and is slowly replaced by fat tissue. However, we need to have a healthy immune system throughout our lifespan. One way to keep your immune system strong is to practise thymus thumping.

Make a gentle fist and place it at the centre of your sternum (the breastbone in the centre of your upper chest). Either breathe deeply or make loud 'Ha, ha, ha' sounds as you exhale and thump your chest for about 30 seconds.

Thumping your thymus can:

- stimulate your energy
- boost your immune system
- increase your strength and vitality.

Tapping for allergies

An allergy is an overreaction of the immune system. Allergic reactions occur when a person's immune system overreacts to normally harmless substances in the environment. Conventional medicine has used the biochemical model to explain and treat allergies, i.e. that the excessive activation of certain white blood cells results in an inflammatory reaction. People may develop allergies to common substances such as dust, mould, pollen and fragrances, to medications and to common foods such as milk, wheat, corn and soy.

Symptoms of allergies can include sinus and respiratory reactions, head and muscle aches, coughs and colds, eye irritation, dizziness, digestive issues, redness, hives and inflammatory reactions. Note also that seemingly 'psychological' issues, such as anxiety, depression and learning disabilities, can be caused by allergies.

Dr Sandi Radomski is a naturopathic doctor who has treated allergies extensively in her practice. She has developed a comprehensive system for treating allergies called 'allergy antidotes', which is based on Roger Callahan's work with

Thought Field Therapy. Seeking to understand those cases for which TFT failed to eliminate symptoms or in which negative symptoms reoccurred, Roger Callahan discovered that certain people undergo psychological reversal and treatment failure when exposed to substances to which they are sensitive. Callahan called these substances 'energy toxins' since they weaken the body's energy system (see also Chapter 13).

In the course of her studies, Sandi Radomski recognized that allergies are learned reactions. Her work is based, in part, on research by Dr Robert Ader, a prominent psychologist and academic who coined the term *psychoneuroimmunology* to describe the study of how our thoughts and emotions affect our immune systems. Ader conducted a series of studies in which his research team gave mice an immune suppressant drug in a saccharine solution. One month later, they gave the mice the saccharine solution only. They found that simply by tasting a saccharine solution which had been associated with the immune suppressant in only *one* previous experience, the functioning of the mice's immune systems again became depressed. The immune suppression had been conditioned to the taste of saccharine, just as one traumatic experience can become imprinted with specific stimuli, including the tastes and odours of foods and flowers.

Key point

Allergies can be learned, just as behaviours can be conditioned, by just one experience. Simple allergies can be cleared using energy techniques such as meridian tapping.

It is beyond the scope of this book to attempt to fully describe and present Dr Radomski's work; further information may be found at www.allergyantidotes.com.

Readers who have severe allergies or multiple chemical sensitivities should consult an allergy doctor or someone skilled in Nambudripad Allergy Elimination Technique (NAET). However, common allergies can often be eliminated with meridian tapping.

Case study: Julia's experience

A few weeks after my Level 1 training with John Freedom I attended a group tapping session organized by Susan Barrera. I went with the seemingly impossible goal in mind of getting rid of my lifelong allergy to dogs, which had always resulted in asthma within 15 minutes of being anywhere near them; it was so severe that I have had to go to the emergency room several times, when inhalers did not work.

Susan explained that sometimes our issues aren't about the obvious, but are instead about some idea or core belief that underlies the symptoms. The next day at home I tapped and tapped and tapped using the helping phrases, 'May I see that which I'm not seeing. May I see my blind spots around dogs! May I understand this judgement.'

The entire session took over two hours. I was determined to rid myself from this seemingly uncontrollable response to dog allergies. As my perceptions and perspectives changed while I tapped, I began to have flashbacks of scenes where I was with dogs and feeling like I was suffocating from asthma.

I tapped on phrases like, 'I can't breathe', 'I'm suffocating', 'I have no control of this situation', 'Nobody cares', 'I am invisible here', 'I have no voice'. I tapped on each phrase until there was no charge remaining. I had pen and paper to write down every image and word that popped into my head and to write down every sensation I felt in my body. At one point I actually broke out in hives on my neck and hands the way I would after petting a dog or being licked by a dog.

Suddenly I experienced the following vivid memory: I was sitting in the back seat of my friend's jeep, windows rolled down, with two of her children, aged five and three, and two large, hairy dogs. In the front seat was my friend's 10-month-old baby. It was an old jeep and there were no seatbelts in the back. The dogs were jumping back and forth freely. The three-year-old in the back with me was crying and inconsolable. The tape player blared some snappy children's song and my friend and the five-year-old were singing at the top of their lungs. I was miserable. I could not sing, I could not breathe and I could not holler at my friend and tell her that I was afraid we might crash with all the chaos in the car, nor could I tell her what a wreck her life was.

All of a sudden, time stood still as I tapped. I saw and felt the dogs' utter unconditional love that they freely gave to my friend and her children while they licked smiling and crying faces alike without any judgement.

They did not care one bit about the condition of their owner's life. All they knew was that they were loved and were the cause of great joy.

Then I experienced the pure unconditional love that my friend was able to freely receive from the dogs. I discovered that I was harshly judging myself unworthy of the unconditional love of a dog and anyone else who wanted to share it with me, including God. I experienced some very powerful and unusual physical sensations that indicated something significant was shifting in my body. Every cell in my body seemed to be vibrating.

I had the opportunity to put my 'healing' to the test over the next three weekends where I spent longer and longer lengths of time with different dogs and their owners in their homes. One afternoon I rode in a car for 20 minutes with two big, hairy dogs, one of whom was in my lap the entire time and I didn't even sneeze or rub an eye! Absolutely amazing! I declared myself completely free from dog allergies at the EFT Level 2 training last weekend, when I spent two whole days in a home with a dog where the training took place.

Activity: Tapping for allergies

1 Identify the specific substance you are reacting to. If you are not sure what the offending substance is, you may consult a physician for comprehensive allergen testing or consult a health practitioner who is skilful with muscle testing. Another way to identify potential allergens is by using the pulse test (see Appendix 9).

2 Rate from 0–10 your imagined reaction, how strongly you think you might react if you were to expose yourself to the substance.

3 Do 2–3 rounds of EFT. Use your own set-up phrases, customized from phrases such as:
   ▷ 'Even though a part of me is reacting to this......, I know this may be a learned reaction and I'm choosing to feel strong, balanced and healthy.'
   ▷ 'Even though a part of me is feeling fearful about this......, I know it's safe for many other people and perhaps it could be safe for me, too.'
   ▷ 'Even though a part of me is interpreting this...... as being dangerous, I know that it's OK for others and perhaps it could be safe and OK for me as well.'

4 After tapping, check in with yourself. Notice how you feel about the substance now, and whether you feel a shift. Then, when you're ready, gently test your results by exposing yourself to the substance in a way that's *safe and respectful* for yourself.

Connections between trauma and dis-ease

Psychological traumas are not just psychological. In the early 1990s, a team led by Dr Vincent Felitti and Dr Robert Anda investigated the link between emotional trauma and disease. Felliti and Anda interviewed their patients about what they called 'adverse childhood experiences', or ACEs. ACEs are early life traumas such as abuse, alcoholism, neglect etc. The researchers gave each adverse experience a numerical score; having more ACEs translated into a higher score. ACE traumas were found to be correlated with cancer, heart disease, hypertension, diabetes, hepatitis, obesity, smoking, suicide attempts and other common adult ailments. The higher the ACE score an individual had inherited from childhood, the greater the risk of that person getting one or more of these illnesses.

As Dawson Church reports in the *Energy Psychology Journal*:

> The study followed 17,421 participants over a period of many years. It was performed by Kaiser Permanente, a large health maintenance organization in San Diego, and the US Center for Disease Control. One shocking feature of the study was the mean age of the participants: 57. The adverse experiences had occurred about 50 years before the study data was collected, yet the results were now showing up as disease half a century later. Time was not, as Shakespeare wrote, 'the great healer'.

> The ACE study presented a wake-up call to medicine. It showed that *the roots of disease were planted in childhood and that many were emotional rather than physical*. Medical research usually examines cancer and other diseases as though they are purely biological disorders, looking for genes that are more highly expressed, molecules that are atypical and drugs capable of interacting with those molecules. It treats the human body as a biological machine, while ignoring the emotional aspects of human experience.

> Doctors Anda and Felliti became quite passionate about the error of this approach, comparing physicians to firefighters directing their hoses toward the smoke above a blaze, while

the fire that causes the smoke rages unchecked. The findings of the ACE study have been reinforced by other research studies showing that adult and childhood emotional trauma affects gene expression, brain development and predisposition to a variety of specific diseases. (my italic)

Key point

Many physical conditions have their roots in trauma. Adverse childhood experiences were found to be correlated with cancer, heart disease, hypertension, diabetes, hepatitis, obesity, smoking, suicide attempts and other common adult ailments.

Tapping into better health

Tapping affects us both physically and psychologically because of the mind-body connection; what we think and feel is affected by our physical state of health or dis-ease, and our physical health or dis-ease is affected by our mental-emotional states. The ACE study found a direct and graded correlation between adverse childhood experiences (i.e. traumas) and health conditions later in life. We are affected not only by childhood trauma; it is estimated that upwards of 85 percent of all conditions that cause people to visit primary care doctors are stress-related.

There are receptors for 'emotional' neurotransmitters, such as dopamine, serotonin and epinephrine in our immune system; and conversely, there are receptors for immunotransmitters in our brains. What we think and feel has a direct, immediate effect on our immune systems. Stress, anxiety and depression, as well as continual triggering of the fight, flight and freeze responses, suppress our immune systems. Thus, balancing our emotions with meridian tapping is one of the most effective interventions we can make to enhance our mental, emotional and physical well-being.

Key point

What we think and feel has a direct, immediate effect on our immune systems. Balancing our emotions with meridian tapping is an effective intervention to enhance our mental, emotional and physical well-being.

While research on the use of meridian tapping for health conditions is in its infancy, we hear many reports of health conditions improving with meridian tapping, including aches and pains, asthma, arthritis, sleep apnoea, fibromyalgia, psoriasis and chronic fatigue. This is especially the case with stress-related conditions. We've also heard reports of people 'nipping colds in the bud' by tapping as soon as they start getting cold symptoms.

I must emphasize that EFT is *not* a cure for cancer or for any medical condition. If you have a serious illness or symptoms that persist, please see a healthcare professional. However, as many illnesses are linked with earlier traumas, tapping on these traumas can sometimes have a profound impact on our health.

Key point

EFT is not a cure for cancer or for any other health condition. If you have a serious illness or symptoms that persist, please see a healthcare professional.

You can explore the mind-body connection yourself by asking yourself questions, listening to the wisdom of your body and doing meridian tapping.

Case study

I am teaching an EFT Level 3 training seminar at a hypnotherapy school in Albuquerque, New Mexico. One topic we cover in Level 3 training is how to work with health issues. I've asked the school's director for a volunteer for a demonstration. She brings in a young woman, 'Claire'. The only thing I know about her is what the director tells me: 'This woman has a lot of problems.'

Claire came out and avoids eye contact with me and everyone else. She speaks in a very subdued voice. Upon dialoguing with her, she mentions several issues: chronic anxiety interspersed with depression, insomnia and psoriasis. I chose to work with the psoriasis; with physical conditions, sometimes there's an obvious shift and sometimes not. She describes her skin as feeling 'hot and angry'. We do 2–3 preliminary rounds of tapping and she reports that her skin is 'feeling cooler'.

When I ask her to describe her felt experience of her symptoms, she says her skin is hot, itchy, embarrassing and unpredictable. She says she stays home a lot, because she feels embarrassed and 'never knows when it's going to break out'. I ask her to close her eyes and attune to the felt sensations in her skin, and then ask her, 'When you tune into these sensations, about how old do you feel?' '15,' she replies. 'What was going on in your life, when you were about 15,' I ask. Claire thinks for a moment, then looks down and starts coughing. When she composes herself, she says, 'My mom was an alcoholic, so our home life was unpredictable. I could never bring friends over, because I was so embarrassed. My mom and my brother used to fight all the time and then he killed himself and I blamed myself for it.' There was one other telling detail; she said she never knew 'when a fight was going to break out'.

We did several rounds of tapping: on her mother's drinking, her mother and brother fighting, chaos in the home, feeling ashamed and embarrassed, and never knowing when a fight would break out. When I finished working with her about an hour later, she looked like a different person; she was smiling, making eye contact and engaged with me and the group. As this was a hypnotherapy school, I asked one of the other students to follow up with her.

Two weeks later I received this note from the hypnotherapist: 'First of all I want you to know there has been a remarkable change regarding her psoriasis since her session with you. Her hands look completely clear and there is just a slight pinkish mark where the psoriasis was on her arm. It continues to fade away and that area is not itchy or annoying her in any way whatsoever. She doesn't have the itchy sensation any more and no need to scratch. She stopped taking the shots she was giving herself daily soon after her session with you so that she would know if it was the shots or the EFT that was making the difference. John, the difference is really more than remarkable. You would never know by looking at her hands or arm that she had ever had psoriasis.'

After two follow-up sessions, 'Claire' reported that her psoriasis was 95 percent gone.

Activity: Tapping for health symptoms

1   Select a symptom or health condition you'd like to explore and unwind. Write the name of the condition, if you know it, on a piece of paper. Then jot down a list of its symptoms, how it shows up in

your body. Select one symptom to focus on and give it a name for your reminder phrase.

2 Close your eyes, breathe gently and attune to the felt sensations of the symptom in your body. What do you notice? Rate its intensity from 0–10.

3 Create a set-up phrase and repeat it three times while tapping the Karate Chop point on either or both hands. Use a phrase such as:
  ▷ 'Even though A PART OF ME has this symptom, the REST OF ME KNOWS that I'm basically healthy, and I'M CHOOSING TO......'
  ▷ 'Even though A PART OF ME is experiencing......, the REST OF ME KNOWS that symptoms and illnesses come and go, and I'M CHOOSING TO accept myself and my body as they are.'
  ▷ 'Even though A PART OF ME is experiencing...... and even though I don't want to experience this......, the REST OF ME KNOWS that my body is communicating to me, and I'M CHOOSING TO listen to my body, get the message and take good care of myself.'

4 Do 2–3 rounds of tapping on your felt experience of the symptom.

5 Check in with yourself: what do you notice now? Was there a shift of any kind? If not, ask yourself the questions for unwinding symptoms one at a time. It is not necessary to ask and answer every question. Ask each question slowly, listen to your body, notice any questions that elicit a reaction inside you or that 'ring your truth bell', and write down your answers.

6 Each answer you write down is a potential aspect. Notice which aspects have an emotional charge or 'rang your truth bell'. Then do several rounds of EFT, focusing on one aspect at a time while you go through the steps of attuning, rating, the set-up phrase and tapping the sequence of points. Notice any shifts or 'Aha's.

7 Complete your tapping, jot down any shifts or 'Aha's, jot down any remaining aspects to tap on later and give thanks for the good work you've just completed.

QUESTIONS FOR UNWINDING SYMPTOMS

To explore the symptoms someone is experiencing, try asking the following questions.

▶ Describe the felt experience, the body sensations, of this condition.

- When did this first begin? What else was going on in your life at that time?

- What triggers it? What makes it better? What makes it worse?

- If there were some good reasons for having or keeping this pain, what might they be?

- If this symptom was trying to tell you something about your life, what might it be communicating?

- If this symptom was trying to get you to do something, what might that be?

- If this pain was a symbol or metaphor representing something else, what might that be?

- What meaning does this pain have for you?

Things to remember

The main points to remember from this chapter are:

* psychological issues and problems are not just 'in our heads'. We hold issues in our tissues. When we release emotional issues by tapping, our bodies often shift and change as well.

* we can heal our minds by touching our bodies; and we can heal our bodies by dialoguing with our minds

* health is our natural state of being. It is natural to feel happy, healthy, alive and energetic. When we are not healthy, something is out of balance.

* you can often release minor aches and pains simply by tapping on them

* allergies can be learned, just as behaviours can be conditioned, by just one experience. Simple allergies can be cleared using energy techniques such as meridian tapping.

* many physical conditions have their roots in trauma. Adverse childhood experiences were found to be correlated with numerous adult health conditions.

* what we think and feel has a direct, immediate effect on our immune systems. Balancing our emotions with meridian tapping is an effective intervention to enhance our mental, emotional and physical well-being.

Tapping for trauma

Although the world is full of suffering, it is full also of the overcoming of it.

Helen Keller

In this chapter you will learn:

▶ *the nature of trauma*
▶ *how trauma affects all of us*
▶ *the Tearless Trauma technique*
▶ *the Tell The Story technique*
▶ *about trauma versus post-traumatic stress disorder (PTSD)*
▶ *the symptoms of PTSD.*

The word *trauma* comes from the same word in Greek, meaning 'wound'. For many years, trauma referred to physical wounds and traumas. It was not until the late 19th century that the term expanded in meaning to include psychological wounding.

Trauma is an injury to the psyche. The traumatic event may be a single experience or a series of events that completely overwhelm a person's ability to cope or integrate the experience. Psychological trauma may or may not accompany physical trauma. Traumas may be caused by a variety of events, such as accidents, catastrophic events, domestic violence, verbal and sexual abuse, life-threatening medical emergencies etc. While the external causes vary, the inner themes experienced by individuals often include a sense of terror, violation, betrayal, feeling overwhelmed and helplessness.

Key point

Trauma is an injury to the psyche. The traumatic event may be a single experience or a series of events that completely overwhelm a person's ability to cope or integrate the experience.

It's important to distinguish between 'Trauma' with a capital 'T', as in PTSD, and 'trauma' with a small 't'; we all experience small-'t' traumas throughout our lives, in the forms of accidents, sports injuries, verbal abuse, medical procedures etc.

The experience of trauma can be highly subjective; what is traumatic to one person may be almost inconsequential to another. In 'The precarious present' (2006), Dr Robert Scaer wrote:

> 'A trauma is any negative life event occurring in a state of relative helplessness – a car accident, the sudden death of a loved one, a frightening medical procedure, a significant experience of rejection – can produce the same neurophysiological changes in the brain as do combat, rape or abuse. What makes a negative life event traumatizing isn't the life-threatening nature of the event, but rather the degree of helplessness it engenders and one's history of prior trauma.'

Traumas tend to 'stamp' and form imprints on our psyches, so that subsequent painful experiences are perceived and experienced in the same way as the originating trauma. Memories are holographic, in that each memory holds the 'hologram', the defining pattern of the whole. When you tap on one specific memory, it sometimes releases the whole chain of related memories simultaneously. These subsequent experiences are like the beads of a necklace, reminders and reflections of the original bead that started the chain.

Key point

When you tap on one specific memory, it sometimes releases the whole chain of related memories simultaneously.

Fortunately, it is fairly easy to desensitize small to medium traumas with EFT. Simply identify the memory, give it a name to use as your reminder phrase, attune and rate its intensity and then tap tap tap! until its intensity has decreased to '1' or '0'.

Note: While EFT can be very effective in treating trauma, be aware of your knowledge and capabilities. It's fine to use tapping for common or garden varieties of traumas. For severe trauma and PTSD, please see a healthcare professional who works with EFT.

Activity

Make a list of 3–5 emotional upsets or minor traumas from throughout your life. Rate the emotional intensity of each one from 0–10 as you experience it now. Starting with the upset with least intensity, use the Basic Recipe to release and defuse its emotional charge.

Usually you will find its intensity diminishing with 1–3 rounds of tapping. If it does not readily diminish, look for a blocking belief, a reversal such as 'It's too scary, too dangerous, too overwhelming', and look for and tap on aspects.

Tip

When working with traumas, tap on only one, two or three memories at one sitting. Do not try to tap all your traumas away in one day!

The Tearless Trauma technique

The Tearless Trauma technique is intended for experiences that feel too upsetting to address directly. It is best to use when dealing with severely traumatic events like sexual abuse, physical abuse, war memories etc. It allows you to defuse the experience globally without diving directly into it.

Here are the steps:

1 Identify a specific trauma from the past and give it a title.

2 Take a guess as to the intensity you might feel *if* you were to actively imagine the event and write it down. (This guess is usually very close to the true number and it minimizes the intensity of the emotional pain. By making a guess about its intensity, you are distancing yourself from the event, which significantly reduces the possibility of extreme emotional pain.)

3 Do a round of tapping on your guess of what the pain might feel like, but not the direct experience itself. Use very general set-up statements, such as:

   ▷ 'Even though I'm guessing this movie might upset me……'

   ▷ 'Even though I can't even think about what happened……'

   ▷ 'Even though it feels too horrific and overwhelming to even imagine……'

4 After that round, guess at the intensity again and compare it to the first guess. It will likely be greatly reduced.

5 Keep tapping and guessing at the intensity after each round.

6 When the intensity is down to '3' or less, try actively imagining what happened. If the intensity is down to '0' when you actively imagine it, you're done! If not, follow up with the EFT Movie technique or the Tell The Story technique.

The Tell The Story technique

The Tell The Story is one of the most important EFT techniques you will learn. It requires two people and is both simple and useful. You tell the story of some upset or trauma from the beginning to the end, but stopping and tapping any time you feel any discomfort. Because you're telling the details of the story, it guides you to be specific. Each stopping place is an aspect and so you're both being specific and covering all the aspects at the same time.

Here are the steps:

1 First, select an upsetting event and give it a movie title.

2 Ask your partner how they feel about telling the story. If their intensity is '5' or greater, have them 'take the edge off' by doing some global tapping:

   ▷ 'Even though I feel nervous about telling this story........'

   ▷ 'Even though I don't want to do this......'

   ▷ 'Even though I'm afraid that something might happen......'

   ▷ 'Even though just thinking about it is scary......'

3 Give your partner instructions. First, select a safe starting place and a safe ending place (just before and just after the upset). Then tell your partner they will be telling the story of what happened from the safe starting place to the safe ending place. Any time they begin feeling any discomfort, they are to immediately stop and begin tapping on that aspect. After tapping on and defusing that aspect, they return to the safe starting place and tell the story again, stopping immediately when there is any discomfort. Also, you as the facilitator may stop the story and ask your partner to tap whenever you notice they're having feelings.

Stopping to tap is critical to the success of this procedure. Many people try to suppress, ignore or deny their feelings and just 'push through it'. Remember that *feeling is healing*; it is only through noticing, stopping, feeling and tapping that the trauma will be defused.

Each stopping point is an aspect of the issue. Remind them to be specific and to tap on each aspect separately as it comes up. They should tap until the aspect is down to '1' or '0', and then begin telling the story again to find the next aspect. Repeat as needed until they can tell the story as easily and nonchalantly as driving to the mall.

The Tell The Story technique has several benefits.

▶ It gives people the opportunity to talk and tell their story and thus feel heard and validated.

▶ It creates a sense of rapport between the two partners.

▶ Aspects are found easily, whenever the person notices discomfort.

▶ It allows the issue to unfold and unwind gently.

▶ You check in and test the intensity at each stopping place, so you both know how you are progressing.

Activity

Find a friend or someone in your family and ask them to practise the Tell The Story technique with you. This will work best if you can switch roles so that both people have the opportunity to give and receive.

Case study: How Serena released a painful memory

'Serena' asked me to assist her in releasing a very painful memory. Forty years ago she and her favourite brother, 'Jack', had been out drinking at a party in Boston. She asked him to drive her home after the party. They got to Serena's home safely, but Jack had an accident and was killed driving back to his own home. Serena blamed herself; she felt that if she had not asked him to drive her home when they'd both been drinking he still might be alive today. She could not tell the story, or even think about Jack, without crying.

I gave her instructions for the Tell The Story technique and she began telling me the story, beginning with the two of them having a good time at the party. Whenever she started to get tearful or upset, I gently stopped her and we both tapped: on her grief, missing Jack, on her guilt, on how much she loved and appreciated him etc. By the time we finished 90 minutes later, she felt much more accepting and peaceful.

I saw Serena a week later and she asked me to 'check her out'. I had her tell me the entire story again. She told me the story and after finishing it said to me, 'This is amazing – I've never been able to talk about that night without feeling that overwhelming sense of grief, guilt and regret.'

EFT for PTSD

I'm working with Sally. Whenever she works overtime at her job as a lab technician, she 'goes crazy'; she yells at her roommate, lashes out with anger, throws and breaks furniture. These are all symptoms of post-traumatic stress. It's easy to follow the trail back to growing up feeling chronically unsafe with an alcoholic mother and an abusive stepfather. We do four sessions together and are making good progress, when she sends me an email: 'I need to stop working with you', she says. 'I'm mentally ill.'

Sally is an intelligent, responsible woman who holds a steady job and is in a stable relationship. While she has some very real issues, she is better off than many. When she tells me that she's 'mentally ill', what she's really saying is, 'I'm broken, I can't be fixed and it's hopeless.'

Pessimistic attitudes like these are widespread. For many years, experts in the US Veterans Administration and the British Ministry of Defence have considered PTSD to be 'incurable'. Many of my clients have told me things like, 'It's hopeless', 'I'm broken', or 'I'm damaged goods'.

What I told Sally, and what I want to tell the whole world, is that *trauma is treatable.* Treating trauma using meridian therapies is one of the great breakthroughs in psychotherapy in the 21st century and we should be seeing this on the front page of every psychological journal and personal growth magazine. As you read the stories of the brave men and women who have successfully overcome their traumas in this chapter, be aware that these are a tiny sample of hundreds of similar success stories. More scientifically minded readers will find research references in Appendix 2.

Key point

Trauma is treatable. There are effective treatments for trauma, including EFT, Thought Field Therapy (TFT), Eye Movement Desensitization and Reprocessing (EMDR), and Coherence Therapy.

For one who has not experienced it, the experience of PTSD can seem inconceivable. Chronic anxiety and hypervigilance, intrusive memories flashing into the consciousness randomly, waking up from a sound sleep to fight off imaginary enemies, and use of alcohol, drugs, anything to mask the pain are but a few of the symptoms of PTSD. Phrases such as 'I still feel terrified', 'I feel lost' or 'I feel like part of me is missing' can only begin to describe the deep sense of soul loss that many experience.

Most people associate PTSD with battle-scarred soldiers – and military combat is the most common cause in men – but any overwhelming life experience can trigger PTSD, especially if it feels unpredictable and uncontrollable. PTSD can affect those who personally experienced a disaster, those who witnessed it and even the professionals who clean up afterwards, such as emergency workers and law enforcement officers.

In 2008 the Rand Institute issued a report entitled *The Invisible Wounds of War*. The report stated that approx 18 percent of American veterans returning from Iraq and Afghanistan experience PTSD and another 15 percent will have Traumatic Brain Injury; thousands more suffer from alcoholism, addictions, domestic violence and relationship issues, and war-related health issues. The divorce rate for veterans in the US is three times higher than the rate for civilians. Whether you've served in the military or not, the repercussions of these international conflicts continue to reverberate throughout our world and, directly or indirectly, affect all of us.

There are three categories of PTSD symptoms: re-experiencing symptoms, avoidance symptoms and hyperarousal symptoms.

Re-experiencing symptoms include:

- intrusive, upsetting memories of the event
- flashbacks
- nightmares
- intense physical reactions, e.g. pounding heart, rapid breathing, nausea, muscle tension, sweating.

Avoidance symptoms include:

- staying away from places, events or objects that remind one of the experience

- feeling emotionally numb

- feeling strong guilt, depression or worry

- losing interest in activities that were enjoyable in the past.

Hyperarousal symptoms include:

- being easily startled

- feeling tense or 'on edge'

- having difficulty falling or staying asleep

- having angry outbursts

- hypervigilance.

Treating PTSD with meridian tapping is beyond the scope of this book. This is a specialized area and is best left to competent mental health practitioners. Be aware that most PTSD involves complex trauma, i.e. the most recent traumas are layered on a foundation of childhood trauma. Thorough treatment involves a process of creating safety, building trust and rapport, identifying, desensitizing and reintegrating earlier traumas and re-establishing relationships with the outer world.

Case study

EFT practitioner Susan Hannibal shares this story about a veteran, 'Sgt Joshua', with 'incurable' PTSD.

Sgt Joshua, a veteran of three tours of Iraq, was referred to me by his doctor at Fort Bragg, North Carolina. He was about to be discharged from the Army on health grounds with 'incurable' PTSD and chronic insomnia, and was taking a daily cocktail of psychotropic drugs. The day he came to my office, he was sceptical, anxious and irritable. I briefly explained EFT and how it works, then did a quick demonstration with him on 'this anxiety'. He reported a sense of relaxation spreading through his body with one round of tapping.

Since treatment of combat veterans always needs to address actual or perceived threats to survival, helplessness and feeling overwhelmed, I always begin by asking about their childhood, as that information will dictate how I begin the process of unravelling their layers of war trauma. Studies have shown that growing up in a war zone in one's home reduces emotional resilience and increases the risk of developing PTSD as well as life-threatening illness in adulthood. Sgt Joshua stated he had had a happy, stable childhood with no major traumas. So I asked him, 'In those three tours, what is the worst thing that ever happened?' He stated the worst thing was a long and bloody firefight in the first tour when his squad was ambushed by dozens of insurgents firing automatic rifles and rocket-propelled grenades. Three soldiers were killed and the unit had to fight for their lives.

We started with the EFT Movie technique: 'If that memory was a movie, what would be the title?' He called it 'Hell'. We started tapping: 'I thought they were going to kill me. Iraq – I thought I'd never get out of there alive. The ambush – all of a sudden they were everywhere.' As we tapped, I began the narrative in a general way, touching on threats to survival, the 'kill zone', the constant anxiety, not being able to relax enough to sleep well for fear of a rocket or mortar attack, and the imprinted shock and trauma of what he heard and felt during the ambush. Sometimes a client will be too traumatized initially to narrate as they tap, so I will sometimes speak for them until they can. As the emotional charge lessens, they are usually able to talk as they tap, as Sgt Joshua did.

About 45 minutes into the session, we took a break. He reported that the charge on the ambush was down to about '4/5' from '10+'. We continued tapping several more rounds. At the end, when I asked what number on the 0–10 scale that 'Hell' memory was now, he shrugged his shoulders, moved his head from side to side and said, 'I don't know, I feel really calm about it now, I think it's gone. I can remember what happened but I don't feel anything bad about it.'

I asked about the second worst thing that happened in Iraq, which was one of the other three repetitive nightmares/flashbacks. He related that he drove over a trip wire for an improvised explosive device (IED) in an unarmoured Humvee and when he looked down there were two artillery shells in the ground 'about as close to me as you are sitting right now'. Then he said the memory was 'funny'.

A client laughing or reflecting in an amused manner about a previously intense memory after EFT treatment is common. Sometimes, to test, I will say, 'How can you laugh about this? You were crying your eyes out a few minutes ago,' and they will insist that 'It's funny now.' Perhaps serotonin or some other feel-good chemical flooding the brain is producing the healing. The night of this session, he slept for 10 hours without the repetitive nightmares and flashbacks that had been tormenting him for months. After a second session, which cleaned up some remaining anxiety, he was taken off his medications and returned to active duty. I followed up with his doctor a year later and he was still on active duty with no further symptoms.

Tip

It's best to use a graded approach. Make a list of traumas and upsets over the course of your life. Rate their intensity from 0–10 and list them from 'lightest' to 'heaviest' in intensity. Then begin tapping and desensitizing lighter memories first, gradually working your way up to the 'heavier' ones.

Research on meridian tapping for PTSD

In 2008 Gary Craig and Dawson Church conducted an informal study of EFT for PTSD (I say 'informal', because there was no control group). Nine veterans and two wives were evaluated for PTSD 30 days before the study began, at the beginning and end of the study, 30 days after the study and one year later. The study had interesting inclusion criteria; Craig asked people to send 'the worst cases you can find'. The subjects received treatment with EFT for two to three hours a day over five days. After treatment, statistically significant improvements were found on the assessments. The group no longer scored positive for PTSD, the severity and breadth of their psychological distress had decreased significantly, and most of their improvements were stable at the one-year follow-up.

Dry statistics can not meaningfully convey the depth of healing these brave men and women experienced. A 10-minute video that includes pre- and post-treatment interviews can be viewed at www.vetcases.com.

Randomized controlled studies (RCTs) are considered to be the 'gold standard' in research. In an RCT conducted by Dawson

Church and colleagues, 59 veterans with PTSD were randomly assigned to a treatment or control condition; 54 of the initial participants completed the study. Each subject received six hour-long EFT sessions. The initial mean score on the PTSD assessment was 61.4 for the treatment group and 66.6 for the comparison group; scores above 50 are indicative of PTSD. After six sessions of EFT the average score for the treated veterans was 34.6 (in the normal range), while scores for the untreated veterans were unchanged. The untreated group was then offered treatment. After treating both groups, 86 percent no longer experienced PTSD. The other noteworthy aspect about this study is that most of the sessions were conducted over the phone.

In the first standardized study of acupoint tapping for PTSD, psychologist Carolyn Sakai and colleagues worked with survivors of the 1994 Rwandan genocide. They were now teenagers living in orphanages, and had witnessed their parents and other family members being brutally murdered. The teenagers experienced classic PTSD symptoms, including flashbacks, nightmares, bedwetting, withdrawal and aggression. Out of 400 children, the study focused on 50 identified by their caregivers as having the greatest difficulties.

All 50 scored high on assessments for PTSD. They were given a *single* Thought Field Therapy session of 60 minutes or less, combined with about six minutes learning two relaxation techniques, conducted with a translator. The scores of 47 out of the 50 teenagers fell dramatically (into the normal range) following this brief intervention; more importantly, their symptoms either diminished markedly or were eliminated entirely. They began to laugh and play like normal kids and the atmosphere at the orphanage changed dramatically. These gains remained stable when the teenagers were re-evaluated one year later.

Case study: A survivor of the 1994 Rwandan genocide

Sakai describes the experience of one of the study's participants, a 15-year-old girl who was aged three at the time of the genocide:

She'd been hiding with her family and other villagers inside the local church. The church was stormed by men with machetes, who started a massacre. The girl's father told her and other children to run and not to look back for any reason. She obeyed and was running as fast as she could, but then she heard her father 'screaming like a crazy man'. She remembered what her father had said, but his screams were so compelling that she did turn back and, in horror, watched as a group of men with machetes murdered him.

A day didn't pass in the ensuing 12 years without her experiencing flashbacks to that scene. Her sleep was plagued by nightmares tracing to the memory. In her treatment session, I asked her to bring the flashbacks to mind and to imitate me as I tapped on a selected set of acupuncture points while she told the story of the flashbacks. After a few minutes, her heart-wrenching sobbing and depressed affect suddenly transformed into smiles. When I asked her what happened, she reported having accessed fond memories. For the first time, she could remember her father and family playing together. She said that until then she had no childhood memories from before the genocide.

We might have stopped there, but instead I directed her back to what happened in the church. The interpreter shot me a look, as if to ask, 'Why are you bringing it back up again when she was doing fine?' But I was going for a complete treatment. The girl started crying again. She told of seeing other people being killed. She reflected that she was alive because of her father's quick thinking, distracting the men's attention while telling the children to run.

The girl cried again when she re-experienced the horrors she witnessed while hiding outside with another young child – the two of them were the only survivors from their entire village. Again, the tapping allowed her to have the memory without having to relive the terror of the experience.

After about 15 or 20 minutes addressing one scene after another, the girl smiled and began to talk about her family. Her mother didn't allow the children to eat sweet fruits because they weren't good for their teeth. But her father would sneak them home in his pockets and, when her mother wasn't looking, he'd give them to the children. She was laughing wholeheartedly as she relayed this and the translator and I were laughing with her.

We then went on to work through a number of additional scenes. Finally, when she was asked 'What comes up now as you remember what happened at the church', she reflected, without tears, that she could still remember what happened, but that it was no longer vivid like it was still happening. It had now faded into the distance, like something from long ago. Then she started to talk about other fond memories. Her depressed countenance and posture were no longer evident.

Over the following days, she described how, for the first time, she had no flashbacks or nightmares and was able to sleep well. She looked cheerful and told me how elated she was about having happy memories about her family. Her test scores had gone from well above the PTSD cut-off to well below it after this single treatment session and remained there at the follow-up assessment a year later.

Things to remember

The main points to remember from this chapter are:

* trauma is an injury to the psyche. The traumatic event may be a single experience or a series of events that completely overwhelm a person's ability to cope or integrate the experience.
* when you tap on one specific memory, it can sometimes release a whole chain of related memories simultaneously
* when working with traumas, tap on only one, two or three memories at one sitting. Do not try to tap all your traumas away in one day!
* trauma is treatable. There are effective treatments for trauma, including EFT, TFT, EMDR and Coherence Therapy.
* randomized controlled trials (RCTs) have demonstrated the efficacy of EFT in treating PTSD.

Tapping for career and self-esteem

There is no value judgment more important to man – no factor more decisive in his psychological development and motivation – than the estimate he passes on himself.
Nathaniel Branden, *The Psychology of Self-Esteem*

In this chapter you will learn:

▶ *how our self-esteem is correlated with optimism*

▶ *how to enhance self-esteem with EFT*

▶ *how to remove blocks to success with EFT*

▶ *how to set and achieve goals with the SMART goal system*

▶ *how EFT can enhance achieving your goals.*

Many years ago the Dalai Lama met with a group of western psychotherapists and the topic of low self-esteem came up. He asked them (through his translator) what it was, and they explained it to him as 'not liking yourself' or 'feeling bad about yourself'. Reportedly the Dalai Lama was shocked, as there is no equivalent term for this in Tibetan.

'Not liking ourselves' stems from our self-judgments. To continue the Nathaniel Branden quotation above: 'This estimate is ordinarily experienced by him, not in the form of a conscious, verbalized judgment, but in the form of a feeling, that can be hard to isolate and identify because he experiences it constantly; it is part of every other feeling, it is involved in his every emotional response.'

Martin Seligman, the 'father of positive psychology', has studied the correlations between optimism, character strengths and self-esteem. Numerous studies show that optimistic people are more successful, physically healthier, live longer and are happier. Optimism is correlated with greater achievement, superior physical and emotional health and lower stress levels. High self-esteem correlates with both optimism and resilience. Acquiring healthy self-esteem is more than saying affirmations or thinking 'I'm a great person', it involves setting and achieving goals that both stretch our limits and build our confidence.

Self-esteem affects not only how we feel about ourselves, but every aspect of our lives, perhaps especially our careers. Our careers represent years of intention, effort and hard work. As with all human endeavours, there are inevitable ups and downs, challenges and opportunities, successes and disappointments. Just as there is an 'inner game' in sports, so more people are paying attention to the 'inner energy game' in their careers. In this chapter I'll be sharing stories and techniques for improving your game and achieving greater success, prosperity and happiness.

Key point

Self-esteem affects not only how we feel about ourselves, but every aspect of our lives, especially our careers.

Tapping into higher self-esteem

The Australian psychologist Steve Wells conducted a unique experiment with himself, where he tapped on himself every day for 30 days. Here Steve describes what he did and what happened.

Around three months ago I set out on a 30-day Self-Acceptance Trial. For 30 days I decided to target my own issues of non-acceptance of self as the primary issue and apply EFT to this. The results have been astounding. In fact, so beneficial has this been that I decided some weeks ago to continue the programme indefinitely.

Earlier this year I noticed a lot of my clients were having trouble with self-acceptance. Usually this came to light when I asked them to make the set-up statement. Some clients would become upset and refuse to say the self-accepting part of the statement. How could they say they accept themselves when they very clearly did not?

'Even though I don't accept myself because of this problem, I fully and completely accept myself.' 'Even though I'm a terrible person (and this problem proves it), I fully and completely accept myself.' Many clients are able to move on at this point and successfully address the problem in question. There is something very powerful in acknowledging the negative parts of self and bringing them into the light.

I was going through a period where I wasn't really accepting myself. Basically I felt I had stalled. I wanted to move forward in my life but seemed to be making little progress. Instead of doing the things I knew I needed to do, I was wasting many hours playing computer games. I had also stalled in my exercise programme. My business wasn't moving forward in the ways I knew it could. I felt like a terrible father to my children, not able to give them the attention they deserved. And I felt terrible about me.

My first decision was to apply EFT to all the things I didn't accept about myself. I began to list them:

'Even though I played chess/video games on the computer tonight and that has stuffed up my neck, shoulders and back for another evening, I fully and completely accept myself.'

'Even though I am a bad boy for playing when I should have been working, I fully and completely accept myself.'

'Even though I am never going to be successful if I keep taking myself backwards like this, I fully and completely accept myself.'

I followed the thread of my thoughts as other irrational and related self-defeating beliefs came up and then proceeded to tap on these. For example,

'Even though I am probably not going to keep this (30-day trial) up, I fully and completely accept myself.'

'Even though I will just have another mediocre year and not achieve real, lasting success, wealth and happiness and joy, I fully and completely accept myself.'

'Even though I will end up losing my family if I become too successful, I fully and completely accept myself.'

As I did the EFT on these irrational thoughts I noticed my thinking actually becoming more and more rational. It was not a case of denying problems but instead of being empowered to address them head on. I continued on, addressing other negative and limiting beliefs that have blocked my success, including beliefs about confidence ('I'm not confident enough'), spirituality ('If I become really successful I might lose my soul'), money and self-worth ('How much I charge is a reflection of my self-worth; I can't charge more because I'm not worth it').

Another interesting experience during this experiment was that in most cases as I tapped on the fact that I was putting things off or doing things other than what I should be doing, I became more willing and able to do the things I had been putting off. Hmmm. Self-acceptance could be the cure for procrastination!

At one point this idea came to me: 'Deal with the faults of others as gently as your own.' When I read this I realized, 'Wow, I don't deal with my faults gently at all!' So I tapped on.

'Even though I am tough on myself…'

'Even though I won't allow myself to have faults or make mistakes…'

I followed my thinking through several associations such as: 'Making mistakes is important if I am to learn the right way. Because I have been so upset about making mistakes and down on myself for them, I have been less prepared to take the risks necessary to achieve big things.'

I realized this was another way of being down on myself, so I tapped on:

'I accept myself even though I haven't been prepared to take risks due to my fear of making a mistake.'

'I accept myself even though I have not achieved enough yet due to my fear of making mistakes.'

All of a sudden I was transported back in my mind to my Year 6 classroom where the motto was 'If you're going to do something, do it properly'. I then recalled a critical incident in that classroom when I had received 49.5 out of 50 for the weekly test – the highest mark anyone had achieved all year – and yet I copped a lot of criticism from both the teacher and my parents for falling short by making a silly mistake. I reviewed this incident in my mind and tapped on the parts that held negative emotional intensity. I also applied tapping to the following thoughts:

'Even though I made a silly mistake…'

'Even though their criticism hurt…'

'Even though I must do things properly or else…'

I realized that the truth was I didn't accept myself at all. I decided this was the issue that needed to be met head-on, not all the reasons I'd been amassing not to accept myself.

As I was tapping, I realized that underlying my non-self-acceptance was a fear that accepting myself was bad and would lead me down the path of ego. I also believed that if I accepted myself for all the things I had been doing that were wrong, then I might not fix them; I might just continue to procrastinate and do things that were not really good for me. At a deeper level I also believed I was unacceptable to God.

So I tapped on these beliefs in both positive and negative form. I applied EFT to each negative belief by putting it into the set-up statement and repeating the full statement at every tapping point. As I tapped on each statement, I paid attention to the thoughts and feelings that came up with it and applied EFT to any negative and related beliefs that were elicited.

After this I was able to go back to my work and became quite productive. As my fear of making mistakes had been relieved, I found myself no longer self-editing or self-critical to the same degree. Over the next few weeks I realized that I was able to achieve more in my work because I was no longer as fearful of making mistakes.

Overcoming blocks to success

To be 'on top of our game' in every aspect of life is challenging. Even when we are doing well, it can be valuable to review our progress, notice any bumps or glitches or areas that could benefit from fine-tuning and give these our conscious attention.

The first step is to conduct a rigorous self-inventory, noticing specifically what may be blocking you in your career – or in finding one. If you find this difficult, ask your partner or a close friend; other people can often see us much more clearly than we see ourselves.

Here are some of the more common blocks to success:

▶ **Fears:** These include fear of failure, of making mistakes, of being criticized, of not being 'good enough' and of success. Fear often discourages people from even trying or 'putting themselves out there'.

▷ **Limiting beliefs and messages:** These are beliefs such as 'Money doesn't grow on trees', 'No pain, no gain', 'You can't have everything you want', or 'You have to work *hard* to be successful'. These may include beliefs about rich people, such as the idea that some people are 'filthy rich', implying that having money is dishonest or dishonourable. Many of these beliefs are messages we heard repeatedly from our parents, caregivers or teachers as we grew up.

▷ **Mental states:** These include mental-emotional states such as anxiety, confusion, resentment, discouragement and moods. These states are like clouds of negativity hovering over our heads, clouding our perceptions and preventing us from thinking, seeing and feeling clearly.

▷ **Family rules:** There may be family rules, such as 'It's not nice to be superior', 'Women should not make more money than their husbands' or 'It's not OK to stand out and call attention to yourself'.

▷ **Self-worth:** Many people have issues with self-worth, feeling that they either don't deserve something good or that they deserve whatever bad is coming to them! Our basic programming and self-image are formed by the time we are five years old, at the time when we are smallest and most vulnerable. We internalize how our caregivers treat us and then live from that self-concept for the rest of our lives, unless we review and revise it.

▷ **Comfort zones:** Sometimes we stay where we are and don't risk 'rocking the boat' simply because it's comfortable to do so. Underlying the desire to stay in our comfort zone is often a fear of taking a risk. Staying in our comfort zone can keep us 'playing small', especially when we know we can play in a larger arena.

▷ **Self-sabotage:** This include desires to hurt or punish ourselves or to take revenge on ourselves, sometimes to spite others. An intelligent child may fail at school or later in her/his career just to spite her/his parents. We may think that we're 'getting back at them' or 'getting even', even though we're hurting ourselves in the process.

All of these blocks can be tapped and transformed with EFT. Remember, *what you can name, you can change*; and *what you can feel, you can heal.*

Case study: Jane taps her way to a musical career

Notice here how psychologist Martina Becher of Siegen, Germany, skilfully assists 'Jane' to overcome her fears about starting a new career.

Jane was a 40-year-old social worker who worked for a charity caring for disabled young people. Over the years her job started to wear her down, since it meant working long hours with difficult clients and their distressed parents. Her workload had grown over the years and as a result Jane had developed tinnitus and burn-out syndrome. She knew that sooner or later she would have to give up her job and find something more in line with her own personality. Jane thought she needed the security of a steady income and that leaving the charity would mean poverty.

In her wildest dreams Jane saw herself as a successful music teacher and musician but she never dared to turn her passion into her own job description because she felt that she would be unable to find students. Another issue was that she felt she was not good enough to live the life of her dreams.

Using EFT we managed to clear the belief that it wouldn't be right for her to leave her clients and her feelings of being a bad person if she left those who so desperately needed her assistance and help. After that cleared, Jane allowed herself to imagine what it would feel like to run her own school of music and immediately ran into another block: how could she deserve to be so happy if her younger sister was suffering from grave depression?

This subject brought up memories of childhood abuse. Jane still believed that she was responsible for her sister's suffering because she had not protected her sister from her father. Worse still, Jane feared that she herself might have done her little sister some kind of harm in younger years. Using EFT again we spent quite a number of sessions around the subject of her responsibility for her sister, which crystallized in the sentence 'I can never be happy as long as my sister is unhappy because I am responsible for her, no matter what.'

Walking EFT, as I call it, is one of my specialities – I just take my clients for a long walk in the nearby forest where we tap along on their issues.

So Jane and I took some rather long walks in different parts of the forest, tapping on her belief that she didn't deserve happiness because she felt that she was guilty and consequently a very bad person.

As this belief released, Jane's spirits lifted. Her fears of ruining herself if she dared to leave her job and start her own business diminished and she became optimistic that indeed things might work out well. A few months later Jane was very, very happy. She started her own school of music and also has a career as a female drummer with three to four gigs a month.

Activity: Tapping away blocks to success

1 Make a list of possible blocks to success. You can ask yourself:
  ▷ 'What seems to stop me from achieving......?'
  ▷ 'What (fears, doubts, feelings...) come up when I start moving towards......?'
2 Review your list of blocks to success and select one that has an emotional charge – one that causes you to wince or groan internally, just thinking about it. Give it a short name to use in your reminder phrase. Remember, *what you can name, you can change*.
3 Find it in your body, attune to its sensations, rate it from 0–10. Then speak your set-up phrase(s) three times, while tapping the Karate Chop point. Create set-up phrases such as:
  ▷ 'Even though I have this block......'
  ▷ 'Even though I feel afraid to take a risk, ...'
  ▷ 'Even though I don't want to leave my comfort zone, ...'
4 Tap tap tap! on the block, following it 'down the rabbit hole' as more aspects and layers arise. It's a good idea to use a tapping worksheet (see Appendix 3) to stay focused and keep yourself on track while working through aspects and layers.
5 Optional: think of a compelling, positive reason or resource why you will succeed. Then do 2–3 rounds of tapping on this reason or resource for success.
6 Thank yourself for a job well done!

Changing the world

A few months ago I was reading an interview with the British author Sophie Kinsella, who was discussing her novel *Mini Shopaholic*.

The interviewer asked her, 'What's the allure of shopping? Why do people get so excited about shopping?' Kinsella answered, 'I think it's the feeling that your life will be transformed with this one little purchase.' While we can smile at the naivety of this, there is a deep truth here; many of us try to fix ourselves and our lives through what has been called 'retail therapy'.

What Kinsella was talking about is *trying to fix the inside by changing the outside*. We may think that 'the problem' is in my wife or husband or lover, my parents, my boss, my job. We may change partners or jobs or where we're living. Women get makeovers, and businesspeople and politicians hire image consultants. But changing the whole world will not begin to address the inner pain and unmet needs that are still aching and festering inside. Real change comes from within.

We have been inundated over the past 30 years with books, CDs and films about positive thinking, creative imagery, the 'Law of Attraction' etc. Self-help gurus talk about the importance of keeping a 'Positive Mental Attitude' and thinking 'positively'. They advise us to ignore negativity, to not focus on it, so as to not 'give it power'. The problem is that ignoring problems does not get rid of them. They still fester in the cellars of our minds, periodically and unpredictably bubbling up in the forms of moods, bad dreams, anxiety and depression.

EFT addresses this age-old problem of negativity head on. *Tapping transmutes negativity*. If all the different forms of negativity are functions of disrupted energy flow, they can be harmonized by energetic tuning and balancing. While the exact mechanisms of how tapping works are still unknown, the fact remains that many forms of pain, distress and 'negativity' can be easily resolved with meridian tapping.

Moreover, 'outside' and 'inside' are intimately connected; they are two sides of the same coin. How we feel affects our perceptions, our performance and how others see us. How we feel affects our experience, both inner and outer. When we take the time to tune in and rebalance our inner energies, circumstances around us often shift and realign as well. When we change ourselves, our world changes with us.

Case study: A financial adviser who procrastinated for years

EFT master Jaqui Crooks of Leicester shares this story about 'Frank'.

Frank, a very successful financial adviser, came to me because he wanted to deal with procrastination. Although successful, he knew that, with a little effort, he could be much more successful and he couldn't understand why he wasn't making the effort.

We tapped as we discussed possible aspects and his thoughts about the downside of being successful and the upside of staying where he was. We cleared the obvious things, such as that he wouldn't be able to play golf if he worked harder, which logically he knew wasn't true. The issue that came up was the fear of other people's resentment if he earned more, because he knew he could do it easily while the people around him struggled. They already resented the fact that he had time in his life for holidays and golf.

Using his feelings as a guide, I asked him to go back to an earlier time in his life when he had the same feelings. He recalled being a young teenager, when all his friends had paper rounds and they had to be out every day delivering papers, whatever the weather, for £2 a week. He decided to ask a friend of his dad's for a job and ended up working four hours on a Saturday, for £2 a week, in an office! His friends weren't happy with him – they didn't think it was fair that he earned so much so easily, and on top of that his father told him off for asking his friend for a job!

He realized that he'd been thinking that, to be more successful, he would have to be able to show that he'd worked really hard in order for other people not to be resentful of his success, so he'd been sabotaging his efforts. In our second session, he realized that he had the same resentment of others who were more successful than him. We tapped to clear that so that he could admire them and see them as role models, and in being successful himself, he could be a role model for others.

After his first session he landed the biggest client of his entire career. After his second session, he was offered a partnership with one of the high flyers he'd been resenting. After tapping on and releasing his fears and considerations, he began allowing things to flow to him easily and celebrating that he could do that.

Setting and achieving goals and outcomes

Setting and achieving goals is one of the most powerful ways we can express ourselves in the world. Achieving our goals not only gives us the satisfaction of accomplishment, it also helps us develop mastery of whatever skills we're learning, while building self-confidence in the process. Setting and achieving goals develops other powerful skills as well, including the abilities to imagine and visualize, plan ahead, take responsibility, develop initiative, develop teamwork, manage time, money and resources etc. Setting and achieving our goals helps us to grow and mature into capable, confident and resourceful human beings.

Key point

Setting and achieving goals is one of the most powerful ways we can express ourselves in the world. Achieving our goals not only gives us the satisfaction of accomplishment, it also helps us develop mastery of our skills while building self-confidence in the process.

Goals are 'dreams with deadlines'. Yet, very often people fail to achieve their goals. This is sometimes because the goals are not well-defined or well-planned. They may lack the resources (time, money, energy etc) to carry them out. Sometimes there is inner conflict, a resistance or reversal, or the person will sabotage herself or himself. Sometimes it is because there is interference; an earlier, similar memory or limiting belief which acts like a hidden landmine, blowing up when we start moving towards achieving the goal.

All of these issues can be corrected. Goals and outcomes can be well-formed and set up to succeed (rather than set up to fail) by writing them up as SMART goals. Internal resistance and inner conflicts are reversals and can be treated using the reversal corrections. Tapping on the resistance, along with monitoring your progress and persistence, greatly increases the likelihood that you will accomplish your individual goals, as well as the quality of Life you envision.

SUCCEEDING WITH SMART GOALS

The SMART goal system is a method of setting your goals up for success rather than failure. People sometimes fail to reach their goals because these are vague, poorly thought out and/or lack the resources, energy or time necessary to accomplish them. The SMART goal system guides you through the steps of creating and organizing a workable plan for achieving your goals and outcomes.

SMART is an acronym for Specific, Measurable, Achievable and Agreed to, Realistic and Resourced, and Time phased. These criteria guide you to set goals that are specific, measurable and achievable.

Specific: Goals are different from hopes, dreams and wishes. A goal is something you are committing to; in order to know exactly what you're committing yourself to, it needs to be specific. Getting specific forces you to think things through and get clear about what you're committing to, how much it will cost you (in terms of time and money), how long it will take and whether it's worth it to you.

Begin by crafting a concise statement of your goal. It should include who (anyone besides yourself?), what (the goal), when (the deadline) and how (steps and means to accomplishing it).

▶ *Example of a vague goal statement:* 'My goal is to earn a higher salary.'

▶ *Example of a specific goal statement:* 'My goal is to make a minimum of £60,000 by...... [date] by taking professional development courses on leadership, applying for leadership positions within my company and talking to my supervisors so they are aware of my goal.'

Measurable: Goals need to be measurable so you can assess your progress weekly or monthly. You need to have a way of measuring your progress: Am I getting closer? Am I on track? Is what I'm doing working or do I need to modify my strategy? Keep the metrics simple. For example, the specific goal statement above could be measured by keeping a monthly earnings record and every month comparing it with your goal to keep on track.

Achievable and Agreed to: The goal needs to be under your control and achievable by *you*. Additionally, it needs to be 'agreed to'.

You need to have the support or 'buy-in' from your significant others. This buy-in may come from a supervisor or your spouse or children. If your goal is to double your income next year and your employer is not open to that, it's probably not going to happen – at least, not in that job! If your goal is to lose weight and your partner keeps bringing home chips, cookies and ice cream, there will be issues, not the least of which is the lack of support from him or her.

Realistic and Resourced: With all goals it's important to check the ecology – how will this goal affect other areas of my life? If your goal is to double your income but that requires many more hours on the job or on the road, this will impact your relationship. Will your partner and children be in alignment and support you on this?

SMART goals are also well-resourced, checking you have all the resources to achieve them. It's not necessary that you have all the resources yourself – having a rich uncle or sugar daddy, or at least a dependable line of credit, will help – but it is necessary to have access to these resources.

Time phased: Goals are dreams with deadlines. To be achieved in a timely way, goals need a timeline and a deadline. After setting a realistic deadline, break the goal down into manageable steps. Then create a monthly or weekly timeline, setting dates for accomplishing each step towards the goal. Setting a timeline will allow you to 'work backward' and set mini-deadlines to measure your progress and to ensure that you're on schedule.

Activity: Goal-setting and achieving with EFT

1 Think of a goal you'd like to achieve, something that is important to you. Write up your goal as a SMART goal. Create a short reminder phrase for the goal, e.g. 'losing 20 pounds by [date]'.

2 Read your goal to yourself. What comes up inside you as you read it? Attune to your body sensations and feelings, and rate the intensity from 0–10.

3 Repeat a set-up phrase three times while tapping the Karate Chop point. Use a set-up such as,

> ▷ 'Even though I'm not sure I can......, I deeply and completely accept myself.'
> ▷ 'Even though I have doubts about......, I deeply and completely accept myself.'
> ▷ 'Even though I feel afraid of......, I deeply and completely accept myself.'

4 Tap on the goal and its body sensations and emotions, tapping and treating aspects as necessary.

5 Ask yourself:

> ▷ 'What beliefs do I hold about this achieving this goal?'
> ▷ 'What seems to stop me from achieving this goal, right now?'
> ▷ 'What doubts and fears do I have concerning achieving this goal?'

6 Jot down any limiting fears, doubts or beliefs.

7 Select a limiting fear or doubt and then tap tap tap! Get specific and work through aspects and layers as needed.

8 Reread your goal as if it is an already accomplished fact: *'It is now* [date] *and I feel grateful that I've achieved......'.* How believable does it feel to you now? Rate its believability from 0–10, where '10' = already achieved and completely believable. Tap tap tap! to raise its believability, if necessary.

9 Give thanks for the shifts and changes you've experienced.

Remember, tapping by itself will not achieve your goal! You will need to create a plan of action, schedule your time and *do whatever it takes* over a period of time to accomplish it.

Case study: Women balancing a career and relationship

EFT coach Alina Frank of Seattle, Washington, shares this.

Many women in our culture limit themselves and doubt that they can have a wildly successful career and an equally successful love life. 'Lucy' was at the top of her game in the publishing world. She had just been offered a partnership at her firm when suddenly she developed fibromyalgia and chronic fatigue. A friend suggested EFT to her and she came in to work on the physical aspects of her condition. When I asked her what areas of her life were stressful she quickly told me about her fiancé, a CEO with a very demanding work life. His home life had gradually become Lucy's responsibility and she managed practically every aspect of it. Lucy took care of the bills, the housekeeping, the dogs, the cooking, appointments, running errands etc. Just prior to Lucy being offered her promotion, her fiancé had told her that he'd need even more of her time due to his company's restructuring. She had not told him about the possibility of her promotion. Part of her wanted to expand, receive recognition and make more money, but her fears of rocking the boat had internalized and left her body in near paralysis.

Over the next month we tapped on her resistance to change, her fears of upsetting her fiancé and her concerns about possibly making more money than him. While her body healed itself with the release of her blocked emotions, her mind made peace with her desire for a more expansive life than she'd been leading. By the time our work was complete, Lucy had received not one but two raises and had established workable household agreements that supported both her and her partner.

Things to remember

The main points to remember from this chapter are:

* self-esteem affects not only how we feel about ourselves, but every aspect of our lives, especially our careers
* we can tap into higher self-esteem by tapping away the negative beliefs and judgments that cause low self-esteem
* SMART goals are Specific, Measurable, Achievable and Agreed to, Realistic and Resourced, and Time phased. These criteria help to set goals that are specific, measurable and achievable.
* after defining our goals with the SMART goal system, we can then release the blocks to their success with meridian tapping
* setting and achieving goals is one of the most powerful ways we can express ourselves in the world. Achieving our goals not only gives us the satisfaction of accomplishment, it also helps us develop mastery, while building self-confidence.

12

Tapping for peak performance

Poor performances have more to do with blocked energy in your body than they have to do with lack of willpower or negative attitudes.

Greg Warburton, peak performance coach

In this chapter you will learn:

► *the importance of the mental game in performance*

► *how energy training improves your performance*

► *how to tap into 'the zone'*

► *how to release your breathing with EFT*

► *how to enhance performance with EFT.*

In 1972 Timothy Gallwey wrote *The Inner Game of Tennis*. At the time it was both a bestseller and a revelation to tennis players and other athletes, demonstrating how our mental game is just as important as our physical game. Now some athletes and peak performance coaches are working with a new 'inner game': our internal energy system. They are reporting increased focus and clarity, increased flexibility, better stamina and endurance and enhanced performance on and off the playing field. This chapter will take you 'behind the scenes' and show you how the new 'inner game of energy' can enhance your performance in all areas of life.

Athletes can range from sceptical to superstitious and don't necessarily believe in 'energy'. In a television interview the Oregon State University baseball pitcher Jorge Reyes said:

> I'm a really superstitious guy and I started off doing it as a superstition and then I felt good when I was pitching so I kept doing it... when I tap it's supposed to calm me down and keep me in control and give me a little extra energy so I won't be tired when I go back out. I don't think I can remember all the points. I just know I do it because I think it works for me. It's supposed to centre your body and give you energy and I thought I could take any help I can get.

This interview was conducted after Reyes led the OSU Beavers to their second consecutive national championship in 2007. That season Reyes and other members of the team received training in energy methods from peak performance coach Greg Warburton.

Yogi Berra was a catcher for the New York Yankees and later a coach for the Yankees and the New York Mets. Besides being a great catcher and coach, he was known for his 'Yogi-isms', short, pithy-but-profound observations on life. Yogi was famous for saying things like, 'It ain't over till it's over', and 'It's déjà vu all over again'. Speaking of baseball, Yogi once observed, 'Ninety percent of the game is half-mental.' This, of course, is true for all forms of performance.

For years many coaches ignored mental training entirely, other than giving pep talks. Others have stressed positive thinking or use visualization methods. Athletes were often advised to 'manage their mental game' or to 'reduce their stress' without being told *how* to do it. Energy training is handling the 'how', by giving athletes practical tools they can use before, during and after practice.

Energy training can:

▶ boost energy

▶ increase stamina

▶ improve workout performances

▶ speed up recovery from physical injury

▶ improve flexibility and range of motion

▶ release mental and emotional blocks to peak performance

▶ break through comfort zones and training plateaus

▶ improve the ability to relax and sleep

▶ manage adjusting to travel issues, e.g. jet lag, new ballparks, changes in weather and environment etc.

In addition to meridian tapping, there are other exercises for stimulating and balancing our energies; see Appendix 5.

Tapping into the zone

Tim Kremer is a professional sports coach and president of The Spirit of Golf organization. When athletes are engaged in their sport, their focus is usually 'out there': on the ball, on the other team, on the opponent. Kremer advises his athletes to focus on the inside and 'get the inside right first'. Getting the inside 'right' means aligning your thoughts and feelings with your motivations so they're working together, not against each other. When the inside is 'right', the outside falls effortlessly into place.

Feelings don't lie. We may not like them and we may judge them for being 'negative', but they are immediate, real-time feedback showing us where our energy is at. Emotions are *e-motions*, energies in motion, motivating us to take action. When we're feeling anxious or angry or upset, our e-motions are moving us away from our goal. There is conflict between what we want to achieve and what we feel inside. Going inside first and reconnecting our thoughts, emotions and energies by tapping is an effective way of balancing and harmonizing our inner energies so we can perform at our best.

In this regard, Greg Warburton advises his students to practise rigorous self-honesty. This involves careful self-observation and telling the truth about one's thoughts and feelings. A lot of sportsmen and women do the macho thing and pretend to be 'tough' and unflappable even when they're feeling sick or experiencing 'butterflies'. They try to 'push through' by ignoring and denying what they're feeling. Getting the inside 'right' begins with telling the truth about what we're feeling and experiencing. When we attune, acknowledge and accept the truth of our experience, whether 'positive' or 'negative', it shifts and realigns with our conscious thoughts and intentions.

Kremer also advises his clients to 'Be Here Now'. 'Be Here Now'? That sounds more like advice for meditators than for jocks! Athletes are often so focused on 'Who's going to win?' or 'Who's ahead right now?' or 'Damn, that was a really bad shot' that they're not able to be fully present with what's happening. They can be so focused on the goal that they miss the game. Kremer teaches them to just 'be here now': just *this* shot, just *this* putt, just *this* catch. When we're able to let go of everything else and be fully present in this little moment, time and space seem to expand, we go into 'the zone', and we're better able to focus on the task at hand, be that putting or pitching.

Not surprisingly, both Kremer and Warburton teach their athletes EFT. Tapping is a quick, effective mind-body technique for connecting inner and outer, emotion and intention, and fine-tuning our energies moment to moment.

Case study

Peak performance coach Stacey Vornbrock from Scottsdale, Arizona, talks about her work with athletes.

I have been pioneering the use of EFT with injuries and range of motion (ROM) issues since 2003 with remarkable results. My results have consistently shown an increase of 20 percent in greater range of motion. Sometimes we've been able to effect an increase in ROM of 60 percent or greater. (An increase of 10 percent ROM is considered excellent in the industry.)

Several years ago, a local company that works with athletes heard about my work and contacted me. They use sensors and a very high tech program to measure golf and baseball swings and motion of every kind. I met with their athletic trainer, Marilyn. I told her that I could get fabulous results with increasing range of motion. She asked me to work with three subjects and provided me with verifiable measurements of their results.

The first client was 'John', an athlete who was in his mid-thirties and had been in a car accident about two months prior. He had injured his neck and shoulders. Marilyn had been working with him for one month with no results. At the end of our first session John had an increase in ROM of 67 percent and by the end of our second session his symptoms were gone.

The second was 'Aaron', a 15-year-old young man who played baseball. Marilyn was stretching his hamstrings and he was wincing. He had no injuries, just very tight hamstrings. It had taken her two months to obtain a 20 degree increase in ROM in his hamstrings. I was able to increase his ROM from 20 degrees to 45 degrees (an increase of 25 degrees). That was over a 200 percent increase in ROM. She was speechless!

The third client was 'Julie', a 16-year-old who played softball and baseball. She had torn her anterior cruciate ligament (ACL), the ligament that helps hold the knee together, and had surgery for that. Julie missed a critical week or two of rehabilitation after the surgery and months later she couldn't straighten her knee. She needed to straighten it to do the exercises that strengthen the muscles above her knee and hold it in place.

Marilyn had worked with Julie for two months with no results. She was ready to recommend further surgery because she thought that the problem was scar tissue deep in her knee. Marilyn wanted to know if

Releasing your breath with EFT

Although we often take it for granted, breathing is vital for both our bodies and minds. Breathing deeply oxygenates our blood and brain, opens our lungs, chest, heart and mind and fills the body-mind with *prana* (energy). In many spiritual traditions, e.g. Sufiism, Buddhism, Hinduism and Hawaiian Huna, breathing is considered the 'doorway' between matter and Spirit. The most basic forms of Buddhist meditation begin with breathing meditation, following the breath. Our words 'respiration', 'inspiration', 'expiration', 'spirit' and 'spirituality' all share a common root in the Latin *spirare*, meaning 'to breathe'. In English the word 'inspiration' has a dual meaning, both 'to inhale' and 'to be stimulated to creative activity or moral fervour', while 'being inspired' means 'to be filled with Spirit'. In Hebrew, the word *ruach* refers to breath, wind and spirit.

Yet many of us breathe rather shallowly and unconsciously. This may derive, in part, from an automatic reaction to hold our breath when we are attacked or confronted. When the freeze response is triggered, we freeze and hold their breaths. Deep breathing is also related to feeling; the more deeply we breathe, the more deeply we feel. This is why therapeutic breathwork, such as rebirthing and holotropic breathwork, can be so powerful.

There are various breathing practices, such as hatha yoga, 'belly breathing', the 'breath of fire', the Sufi 'hu' breath etc., which one can do to open up the chest and lungs and breathe more deeply. Another way to free and release your breath is by using EFT.

We hold our entire emotional history in our breath. The memories of our birth, times we were attacked or frightened, times we yelled or sobbed or whimpered are imprinted in the rhythm of our breathing. By attuning to subtleties in our breathing rhythm, we can begin to free and release our breathing and ourselves.

Activity: The EFT breath release

1   While breathing normally and naturally, notice how deeply and freely you are breathing. Notice any places where the breathing 'hangs up' or where the breathing feels tight or constricted.

2   Rate the ease and depth of your breathing from 0–10 (with 10 = fully free, deep and easy).

3   Do 3–4 rounds of tapping while focusing on your (normal) breathing. Use set-up phrases such as:
   ▷ 'Even though my breathing is shallow......'
   ▷ 'Even though I don't breathe as deeply as I'd like......'
   ▷ 'Even though I've stifled and squelched myself for years by not allowing myself to breathe fully and freely......'
   ▷ 'Even though I've shut down my breathing and my creative life expression......'

4   After each round of tapping, rate the ease and depth of your breathing again. Notice any thoughts, images, memories, feelings or sensations that arise. Then do subsequent rounds on additional aspects and layers as needed.

Do the EFT breath release every day for three weeks. It will not only change your breathing, it will change your life.

Case study: EFT and the art of archery

'Terry' is an amazing athlete who competes in women's archery. When she first started competing she tapped on issues such as:

Self-doubt
✱ 'Even though I doubt my ability......'
✱ 'Even though I still don't think I am good enough......'
✱ 'Even though I am shooting with these experts......'
✱ 'Even though I don't think I can keep up......, I deeply and completely love and accept myself......'

Her technique
✱ 'Even though I don't always hold my bow in exactly the right place......'
✱ 'Even though I don't always line my peep up just right......'
✱ 'Even though I sometimes shoot too quickly......'
✱ 'Even though I drop my bow too quickly......'

✳ 'Even though my arm gets tired......'

✳ I deeply and completely love and accept myself......'

And feeling sick with a stomach flu at a competition:

✳ 'Even though I started this shoot off poorly......'

✳ 'Even though I am shooting with some of the best archers in the country......'

✳ 'Even though I am having trouble focusing......'

✳ 'Even though it is getting very hot......'

✳ 'Even though my first round wasn't very good and I was SICK......'

At one point in her career, Terry made an appointment with me. 'What seems to be the issue?' I asked. 'I'm rushing my shots,' she said. 'I want to be able to relax and take my time, but I'm pushing myself to hurry up and then I make bad shots.' In women's archery, the women line up in a queue and then one at a time each woman shoots at the same target. I asked her why she was rushing her shots. Terry said that she 'shouldn't keep the other ladies waiting.'

We tapped a couple of rounds on 'feeling rushed' and 'keeping the other ladies waiting'. The intensity went down, but there was something still there. So I asked her, 'Terry, when you were a little girl, who used to rush you?' She thought a moment and then her head dropped as she looked at the floor. 'It was my stepdad,' she said. 'He was always making me rush, telling me to hurry up.'

I asked her to recall three memories of her stepdad rushing her. Then we did our set-up phrase:

✳ 'Even though my stepdad rushed me, I know that was then and this is now, I'M THE ADULT NOW and I can take as long as I darn well please!'

✳ 'Even though he was always telling me to hurry, I know that I can take my sweet time, because I'm such a sweet lady and I'm choosing to LOVE, ACCEPT AND RESPECT MYSELF AS I AM, with every shot I take.'

✳ 'Even though he was always rushing me and even though I rush myself now, I know I shoot better when I take my time and I'm choosing to take as much time as I need, now.'

We then tapped on 'feeling rushed', her memories with her stepdad etc. By the time we finished she was relaxed and giggling again. After this she felt fine about 'taking her sweet time', and this raised her performance up to another level.

Terry began shooting competitively in 2007 and has won numerous medals since then. She has won state championships in New Mexico and Nevada and won the gold medal at the Rocky Mountain State Games (US Western regional competition) in 2010, 2011 and 2012. While she is talented and works very hard at her sport, she also credits EFT for helping her with her mental game.

Activity: Enhancing performance with EFT

We can all improve our game in life, whether we play sports or the piano or anything else. Perfection is an ideal that is rarely achieved. Striving for perfection gives us an ideal to work towards and a sense of satisfaction when we make progress towards it. No matter how old we are or how well we play, we can always do better.

1 Select a specific aspect of performance you'd like to improve.
2 Ask yourself, 'What is getting in the way of my performing as well as I know I can?' You may know the answer already, as a block or doubt. It may be a fear or anxiety. You may be having trouble with your tennis serve, or you may start out strongly but start to 'cave in' or 'lose it' at some point. Find your weak spot and name it. Remember: *what you can name, you can change.*
3 As you mentally review the block, notice where you sense it in your body. Rate its intensity from 0–10.
4 Name the block and put it in your set-up phrase. Tap the Karate Chop points while repeating your set-up phrase three times. Use phrases such as:
   ▷ 'Even though A PART OF ME DOUBTS that I can perform better, the REST OF ME KNOWS that I have almost unlimited potential, and I'M CHOOSING TO open my eyes, mind and heart to becoming the best I can be.'
   ▷ 'Even though A PART OF ME FEELS like I was kicked in the gut, the REST OF ME KNOWS that all athletes face physical challenges, and I'M CHOOSING TO tap on this, move through it and see what happens.'
   ▷ 'Even though A PART OF ME holds back from doing my best, the REST OF ME KNOWS that my example encourages others to do their best, and I'M CHOOSING TO do my best, put myself out there and accept whatever happens.'

5 Tap the sequence of points, using your reminder phrase, while focusing on the block.
6 After each round, check in with yourself, notice the intensity and tap on additional aspects and layers until the block feels 'flat'.
7 Ask yourself, 'What feeling or behaviour would I like to experience instead of......?'
8 Do 3–4 rounds of tapping on the new positive feeling, resource or behaviour you wish to install. Change your set-up phrase as follows:
    ▷ 'Even though A PART OF ME USED TO DOUBT that......, the REST OF ME KNOWS that......, and I'M CHOOSING TO......'
9 'Future pace' the new positive behaviour by mentally rehearsing what you will see, hear, feel, experience and tell yourself in the future. Do this several times, until the sequence including your new behaviour feels easy, natural and effortless.

Case study: The wrestler who doubted himself

Peak performance coach Greg Warburton reports: 'During the 2010 wrestling season, one of the wrestling coaches at Oregon State University recommended that five of their starters contact me to focus on mental training. Out of the five, one man, 'Chuck', contacted me. I began work with Chuck on his mental training, teaching him my 'Mental Mastery System for Peak Performance', which includes energy warm-up techniques and EFT.

From the beginning, Chuck felt frustrated about his self-criticism and 'negativity' about his wrestling performance but didn't know what to do about it. He was trying to 'stay positive' by fighting the negativity and it wasn't working. A lot of athletes struggle with their emotions because they're trying to 'keep positive' and don't want to admit to feeling fear, doubts etc.

I taught Chuck to practise rigorous self-honesty, to notice his thoughts and feelings and accept them, no matter how 'negative' they seem to be. I teach my athletes to 'Feel the feelings, not fight the feelings'. We started by having him tell himself the truth, that he was feeling frustrated and 'negative'. The words he used were, 'I cuss myself out.' We tapped on *'Even though I feel frustrated and cuss myself out, the truth is that's what I'm doing in this moment and I deeply accept myself anyway.'*

We then tapped on frustration, criticizing himself, 'cussing myself out' etc. Tapping in this way ended Chuck's emotional battle with himself, so he then had more energy and focus for his competitions.

At the start of the season Chuck was ranked in the top 20 nationally. However, he doubted that he was 'good enough' and didn't think he should be ranked so highly. We tapped on his fears and doubts and he went from doubting his abilities to being, in his own words, 'super-confident'.

Chuck practised his mental training techniques along with his physical training, even tapping during competitions. The next season he qualified for the NCAA championships and in 2011 he won the national championship in his weight class. He won six matches in a row, defeating five All-American wrestlers and the 2010 national champion to win the championship. OSU is a nationally ranked team, but Hanke is the first OSU wrestler to win a national championship. In February 2012, Chuck competed in his first international competition in the Ukraine and went 3–1 to win the silver medal.

Research on EFT and sports performance

Research in this area is in its infancy. In 2009 Dawson Church evaluated the effects of EFT on men's and women's college basketball. The experimental group received a single 15-minute EFT session, while a performance-matched group received a placebo intervention (a pep talk). Performance was measured on free throws and vertical jump height before and after the interventions. Those players who received 15 minutes of EFT improved their performance on free throws an average of 20.8 percent, while the performance of the players receiving the pep talk actually declined.

In another study, the psychologists Tam and Mair Llewelyn worked with women who were members of the Keepmoat Stadium Ladies, a group of soccer players at the Keepmoat Stadium in Doncaster, UK. A total of 26 players took part from the open and under-16 teams.

The test involved taking two sets of five dead-ball kicks at goal from a distance of 13.5 metres. The goal was the standard five-a-side goal (5.0 metres wide by 1.2 metres high). There was no goalkeeper, but only kicks which entered in the two outer thirds of the available goal area were counted as scoring. Those which entered the centre third of the goal were considered as would have been saved by the 'goalkeeper'. After the first ten kicks the players were given a short coaching session and then 10 more kicks were to be taken. The trial was to assess whether the coaching sessions served to make an improvement in performance, not to assess the performance of the individual players.

The two active (EFT) groups showed an increase in scoring rate of 40 percent and 45 percent, whereas the control group suffered a decrease of 4 percent. In a follow-up report six months later, the Llewelyns reported: 'Both teams we worked with are currently top of their divisions and the under-16s have won every single one of their matches since they learned EFT. They are now so far ahead that none of the other teams can catch up, so they will win the league cup. They have scored 147 goals (a record for one season) and their 'striker' (main goal scorer) has scored 57 herself – another record.

And finally, sports performance pioneer Stacey Vornbrock says that the most important thing is to play your sport from a place of joy, which supports your body and promotes better motor skills, oxygenation and improved decision making and vision, to name but a few benefits. Tap to release any negative emotions of fear, doubt and anxiety so you can reclaim why you began playing your sport in the first place – to have fun!

> EFT helps take their heads out of the way so they can do what they have trained their bodies to do.
> Dan Spencer, 2007 Pitching Coach of the Year, NCAA

Things to remember

The main points to remember from this chapter are:

* ninety percent of all performance is half-mental
* EFT is a mind-body technique that can help you improve your 'mental game'
* EFT can be used to boost energy, increase stamina, improve range of motion, break through plateaus, manage travel issues etc
* athletes perform better when they feel their feelings, rather than fight their feelings
* research studies are demonstrating the efficacy of EFT for peak performance.

Energetic self-care

We need to be the change we wish to see in the world.
Mahatma Gandhi

In this chapter you will learn:

▶ *the importance of personal self-care*
▶ *working with a tapping 'buddy'*
▶ *how to do covert tapping*
▶ *tips for successful tapping*
▶ *how to tap away jet lag*
▶ *unleashing intuition with meridian tapping*
▶ *troubleshooting when EFT seems to not work*
▶ *the Personal Peace Procedure.*

A healthy life is a life in balance. We all want our families and friends to live well, to be happy and healthy and to take care of themselves. We want and wish the best for them. But what about ourselves? Do we care for ourselves in the ways our loved ones wish we would?

Taking good care of ourselves involves more than eating well, exercising and getting enough sleep. It also involves managing our workloads and our stress levels. It involves time for fun and recreation and cultivating loving, supportive relationships. It also involves emotional self-care. Just as musicians will tune their instruments several times a day, so we need to tune our human instruments, our bodies, emotions and energies throughout the day.

We bathe, brush our teeth and practise personal hygiene every day. We can practise mental and emotional hygiene as well. Stress not only affects our health; it also affects our families, friends and all our relationships. When we are hurting or seething inside, we may deny, ignore or minimize it, but those close to us can sense it and 'feel the vibes'. Meridian tapping is an effective tool for daily 'mental flossing', for releasing the 'upsets du jour', so we can be the resilient, resourceful and loving people we know we are.

Energetic self-care is a missing piece of the personal healthcare puzzle. For years we've been conditioned to see ourselves as bodies, to think of ourselves as 'things' and to see our bodies as machines that need to be fuelled and maintained. As discussed in Chapter 3, we are energetic beings in an energetic universe. When we begin thinking of ourselves as energetic or spiritual beings connected with others by fields of energy, how we live our lives begins to shift as well.

As you have seen, meridian tapping can have profound effects on our mental, emotional and physical well-being. It affects us spiritually as well. My experience is that as we release our blocks and traumas, we become more gentle and loving, more capable and compassionate. Our hearts open and our hearts and minds begin working together as friends. We feel more connected and engaged, with our families and friends and with the greater human community of which we are a part.

Tapping as a tool for personal transformation

Managing our stress is one of the most important things we can do to improve our health and happiness. There are many excellent methods for reducing and managing stress, including biofeedback, meditation, yoga, t'ai chi and qi gong and self-hypnosis. All of these methods require a significant amount of time, whereas meridian tapping is a one-minute practice. Part of the power of EFT is its specificity; it targets specific stresses in your body and mind. By tapping on yourself every day, you can rapidly resolve emotional distress, and gently bring yourself back into balance.

I belong to a group of energy healing practitioners in Tucson, Arizona. Someone in our circle once said, 'If you practise Eye Movement Desensitization and Reprocessing, it will change your practice. But if you practise EFT, it will change your life.' This is my personal experience, and the experience of thousands of other EFT practitioners. Tapping is not just a 'quick fix' or a neat tool to use on our clients; tapping is a potent tool for personal transformation, for healing ourselves, our families and our world.

Key point

Tapping is not just a 'quick fix' or a neat tool to use on others; tapping is a potent tool for personal transformation, for healing ourselves, our families and our world.

Things you can do:

▶ try it on everything!

▶ start a tapping journal

▶ tap tap tap! on yourself, every day

▶ tell others how tapping is helping you

▶ share tapping with your friends and family

▶ pay it forward – help others, as you have been helped

- get additional EFT training at EFT Gatherings and Workshops
- encourage your family and friends to seek out tapping practitioners.

One of the most powerful things you can do is to develop a tapping practice of your own. None of us are perfect; we all have issues and 'buttons'. I know there are many times in my life I've reacted out of old patterns and behaved in ways I'm not proud of. We don't have to live and behave (or put up with) the way things have always been. We now have the technology to release these stuck patterns, reinvent ourselves and live our lives differently.

Case study: How Jamie overcame her fear of math

'Jamie' was an attractive woman in her late forties. She had returned to college as an adult student to get her degree, but was having difficulty with math. I taught her EFT in one of my evening classes. She got home that night about 9.30 p.m. and wondered, 'I wonder if this EFT stuff could help me with my math homework?' At that point, she was two months behind in her assignments and in danger of flunking out. She made herself a cup of tea and tapped on her fears about math: getting it 'right', feeling 'stupid', not making mistakes etc. After 15 minutes of tapping, she decided she would 'try to do just one assignment'. She got into 'feeling excited' about doing her math, began working on one problem after another and the next thing she noticed, she told me later, it was 3 a.m. and she had completed four assignments!

Jamie continued tapping whenever any fear or anxiety around math got triggered. She got all her back assignments done and completed the course with a 'B'.

Developing a tapping practice

For best results with EFT or any personal growth technique, it's important to practise it every day. We define ourselves, in part, by what we do every day. We spend our money and our time on what we value. When we devote our time to something, whether that's working, talking with friends or watching videos, we are subconsciously telling ourselves that that is valuable to us. Things that are 'very important' we put at the top of our lists or mark as 'priority' at the start of our day. All the money in the world cannot buy health; our mental, emotional and physical health should be at the top of our lists.

Key point

For best results with EFT or any personal growth technique, it's important to practise it every day.

If you're planning to work on an issue, it's best to set aside 20–30 minutes; it may not take that long, but there may be aspects and layers. The people I know who are dedicated tappers will often devote an hour or more to their tapping practice. If you're going to use tapping for managing stress, 5–10 minutes may be sufficient. Think of a potentially quiet time during your day: before breakfast, during your lunch hour, during the mid-afternoon tea or coffee break. Some people like to tap after they come home but before dinner, to clear out the stress of the day so they can be more present with themselves and their families.

The important thing is to find a time that works for you and write it in your schedule or calendar. I've learned to treat my daily tapping appointment with myself with the same respect as my appointments with others. The first client I see every morning is the one I see in the mirror. When I take care of that one first, by tapping and writing my journal, I am then able to be more fully present and compassionate with others.

Key point

Find a time for your daily tapping practice that works for you and put it in your schedule or calendar.

A great way to develop a tapping practice is to **get a tapping buddy**. Find a friend or family member with whom you can be emotionally honest. Schedule time once or twice a week to meet in person or by phone. Discuss your tapping practices, support and encourage each other, then spend 20–30 minutes tapping on an issue with your partner before switching roles. Tapping with a buddy will not only increase your commitment, it will give you valuable practice in learning to guide and facilitate others.

One advantage of meridian tapping is that wherever you go, your fingertips go with you. I once had a client whose husband was an executive in the travel industry. They were having a business dinner with another couple when the other woman said something that 'pushed her button'. My client was feeling very upset but did not want to spoil the evening. She went to the ladies' room, tapped on herself for five minutes or so and was able to return and enjoy the dinner.

While I do not recommend tapping while driving (although I will confess to having done it many times!), I can recommend **tapping at red lights**. Most red lights in the US are about a minute long; EFT is a one-minute practice. Having been a taxi driver in Boston and New York, I had developed some, let us say, curious driving habits, not the least of which was feeling impatient at red lights. For several months I tapped whenever I felt impatient sitting at a red light. Now not only am I a safer driver, my driving is more relaxed and enjoyable for myself as well as my passengers.

I also like to tap while I'm waiting in a queue, at the bank, grocery or airport. To avoid calling attention to myself, I practise **covert tapping**. Rather than tap each set of points, I'll gently massage each set of points, while breathing and attuning to any impatience or discomfort. It may be entirely subjective, but I find that when I release my impatience the queue seems to move more quickly. At the very least I feel more centred and comfortable and I'm a much nicer person to deal with. In meetings you can simply tap, rub or hold your finger points and no one will be the wiser.

Another way to do covert tapping is to practise **mental tapping**. You attune to a stress or discomfort, rate it from 0–10 and then mentally visualize and feel yourself tapping the points without physically doing so. This is subtle and may take some practice. Doing mental tapping will develop your ability to focus and concentrate and some people actually prefer this to physical tapping. Remember that energy follows intention; simply by focusing your attention (and intention) on both the issue and the acupoints, the energy will flow where it's needed.

You can also **tap into the healing power of forgiveness**. True forgiveness involves a shift in perception, a change of mind and heart. It involves much more than just saying 'I forgive you'. We can easily mouth the words without the feeling being there. One reason we are often unable to forgive is because we have been hurt; that hurt and pain is still there, unresolved. Another reason is fear; we may even be willing to forgive for now, BUT... . Thus there are hidden barriers blocking the ability to forgive, rooted in past painful experiences.

The person we need to forgive the most is ourselves. Whenever we have anger or resentment towards another, it's because they are mirroring something in ourselves that we don't want to see or don't want to be. The outer is a mirror of the inner. Tapping releases the blocks to healing as well as old painful memories. You can tap into the healing power of forgiveness simply by inserting it into your set-up phrase: *'Even though this......* *happened and even though I'm feeling very angry or upset* *about it, I'm willing to love, accept and forgive myself.'*

If you're not too frazzled to focus at the end of your day, a wonderful way to complete your day is **bedtime tapping**. Mentally review your day, think of what worked and what didn't work, the high and low points and any stresses. Then take five minutes to gently tap tap tap! on any remaining stresses, so that you're not taking them to bed with you. (This is fun to do with a partner and can be a prelude to something else!)

Tapping into deeper sleep

Millions suffer from insomnia and sleep disturbances. Sometimes this is caused by a mind that is 'racing', or the person is 'keyed up' and unable to slow down. To relax your mind and body and balance your energies, simply focus on and name your felt experience – for example, 'these racing thoughts' or 'this nervous energy' – while tapping before bedtime. If you find yourself worrying about some issue, use a set-up phrase such as, 'Even though A PART OF ME FEELS worried about this......, the REST OF ME KNOWS that I'll be better able to handle it after a good night's rest, and I'M CHOOSING TO relax and enjoy this time in bed, whether I fall asleep right away or later.'

Even more relaxing than tapping is **Touch and Breathe (TAB)**. This is described more fully in Chapter 14, but the essence is simply to touch and hold each set of points while focusing on the tension or nervousness. Another option is **Mental EFT**. Instead of visualizing and 'counting sheep', you visualize and imagine tapping each set of points, while focusing on the stress and anxiety. As the stress starts to release and unwind, you may find yourself drifting off as well.

Alcoholism and addictions and...

We are all too familiar with the problems associated with alcoholism and addictions. While drinking can be a social lubricant and help us loosen up and connect with others, in excess it disconnects us from others and ourselves. Our children are exposed to a plethora of drugs which were unknown and unthinkable only a few years ago. There have been few research studies on the effects of many 'recreational' drugs and no one knows the effects when they are combined with other drugs, alcohol or medications, especially long term.

We are also seeing the rise of what have been called 'soft addictions'. These are habits such as shopping, overeating, television and videos, texting and surfing, as well as sex and relationship addiction, habits which keep us from living the lives we want. For many, the habit becomes their 'dirty little secret', a source of hidden guilt and shame, yet having a secret (and sometimes fatal) attraction. These habits cost us time and money, numb our minds and feelings, and drain our energy and our lives. Their cost to society is incalculable. Their cost to us is the loss of expressing and fulfilling our full and precious potential.

Addictions can be difficult to treat, with many alcoholics and addicts going in and out of the treatment 'revolving door'. Treating addictions is far beyond the scope of this book, but EFT can be very effective for dealing with cravings.

Case study

Psychotherapist Meryl Beck from Cleveland, Ohio, used meridian tapping to help 'Joyce' free herself from compulsive overeating.

I have worked with Twelve-Step Recovery people and people with disordered eating for more than 20 years. Learning energy techniques completely changed the way I work with clients and shortens the amount of time needed in therapy. Joyce came to see me because she was a compulsive overeater. Although slim as a youngster, her weight ballooned in adulthood. In our initial interview, I asked her what was going on in her life just before she put on the extra weight. She had an 'Aha!' realization; she had just gone through a nasty divorce and her weight ballooned.

During that first session we used meridian tapping. I had her think about the divorce and her intensity was '6', with a combination of hurt, anger and sadness. After one round of tapping, she was at '4'. After the second round, she was at '1'. We then did another round replacing each of the feelings with a word of her choosing, which was 'love'. After our session she reported feeling centred and also very energized.

The following session Joyce came in and reported that she wasn't happy about her eating in the past week. She said that she had purchased a cake for her daughter's birthday and every time she passed it she took a swipe of the icing. Later, when cleaning up, she admitted to 'edging' – taking a small slice of cake around the edge – and doing it over and over again.

I asked her, 'What are you telling yourself right now about the cake and the way you ate it?' She said, 'I can't believe I did that. What's wrong with me? I am never going to lose weight!' I then asked her, 'And when you hear yourself saying that, what feeling do you have?' Without missing a beat she yelled out, 'I am so angry with myself!' The level of anger was '10'. We did a round of tapping and the anger went down to '6'. Upon completing a second round, the anger level had dropped to '2' and she said, 'Now I am feeling really sad and disappointed because I did that to myself.' Again, we used EFT with the sadness at '8'. After two rounds of tapping it was down to '1'.

I asked her to once more visualize herself edging the cake and now she said she felt guilty, ashamed and regretful. Reporting that her feelings were at '7', we tapped, which took the feelings down to '1'. She commented that she really liked the forgiveness piece and that it helped her release the remaining feelings.

I continued to see Joyce every week and she reported using meridian tapping whenever she had uncomfortable feelings or when she had a craving. After three months, she had lost 10 pounds and reported that the binges and cravings were almost gone. She discontinued therapy, saying that although she knew she still had issues to work on, now she had the tools to use and a belief in herself that she could effectively use meridian tapping on her own.

Tapping away cravings

A craving is an intense, abnormal desire for a food or substance. Cravings are self-soothing behaviours; they are ways we use to soothe ourselves, numb our pain and fill the 'holes in our souls'. People who use drugs talk about wanting to 'get high', but really they're trying to avoid feeling down. What drives the craving, the need to self-medicate, is what we are trying to avoid, whether that's stress, anxiety or emotional pain. It's not what we're eating; it's what's eating us. What causes these stuck alarms, these unresolved pains and feelings, is trauma – adverse childhood experiences.

Key point

It's not what we're eating, it's what's eating us. Underlying our cravings and addictions are adverse childhood experiences (ACEs).

As the ACE study reported in Chapter 10 noted, there is a direct connection between adult diseases, including addictions, and childhood trauma. Meridian tapping, skilfully used, can be a highly effective treatment for trauma. To release and clear cravings involves tapping first on the craving, then on the underlying stress, anxiety or pain that is driving it, and then on its emotional roots, the underlying traumas. As you tap on these underlying roots and release the pain that is driving the addiction, the cravings diminish as well.

Case study: Anger was eating her alive

Business success coach Betsy Muller of Cleveland, Ohio, shares this story about 'Mary'.

Mary scheduled several private sessions with me after attending a short EFT seminar. Healthy and happily married, Mary had recently gained 10 pounds and was more anxious than usual.

During our first session, Mary mentioned that she was certain that part of her problem was 'underlying anger I can't seem to get a handle on'. She shared that she believed it was tied to her relationship with her deceased mother and her younger sister (who her parents favoured because she was sickly, needing attention and financial support). I asked Mary to choose an especially disturbing memory involving her mother that also represented the resentment of her sister. We tapped on that, bringing her intensity from '7' to '0'. We also tapped on general stress and cravings, especially feelings that came in the evening after dinner.

During our second and third sessions, we worked on helping her follow through with exercising at least five days a week. She had not been following through with exercise plans even though she had good intentions. Mary sighed, 'I am exhausted in the morning, yet that's when exercise works best for my schedule.' She had no clue why she was so exhausted. I asked what time she went to bed each night. She had been staying up until 1a.m. and then trying to get up to exercise at 7.30 a.m. A lack of sleep was affecting energy level in the morning. We tapped to support an 11 p.m. bedtime, as well as the five-day exercise plan she had been trying to follow. At the end of that session, Mary felt 100 percent certain that she would be enjoying more sleep and exercise in the week ahead.

Here are Mary's results, in her own words, two weeks after our last session: 'I've been working out five out of seven days, not eating after 7 p.m. and charting my calories. I've lost 5 lb and really feel good. I have completely released the anger attached to memories of my sister. When we are together now, I do not have the anger and resentment that just naturally came up prior to my sessions. That discovery was a big one and well worth it. I have stopped wanting to snack all night long. I am generally feeling full after dinner and have none of that restlessness at night that leads to snacking. I am also getting to bed earlier. The questions Betsy asked me in the beginning of each session led to what needed to be tapped on – wonderful realizations about myself.'

RESEARCH ON EFT AND FOOD CRAVINGS

Psychologist Peta Stapleton of Bond University, Australia conducted a study examining the effects of EFT on food cravings. The study examined 96 obese adults, divided into an EFT group and a comparison group. The researchers measured food cravings, capacity to restrain from eating, psychological symptoms, weight and body mass index (BMI); a reliable indicator of body fat, BMI is based on a person's height and weight. Subjects in the EFT group received a two-hour group EFT session for four weeks where they tapped on their favourite foods. Over the course of the study, including a 12-month follow-up, participants in the EFT group experienced significant improvements in weight loss, body mass index, food cravings, restraining capability and psychological symptoms. There was also an unexpected result; two months after the EFT intervention, approximately half of the subjects could not even remember the foods they had previously craved and eaten every day.

Tapping away jet lag

Jet lag occurs after a long flight involving marked differences in time zone. The body's circadian rhythms cannot adjust to changes in local time as quickly as we can travel, and it can usually take a few days for our 'biological clock' to adapt to a new time zone. This particularly affects the body's secretion of adrenaline to wake us up and melatonin to help us sleep. Taming jet lag with EFT is easy. Simply tap the EFT points every two hours and immediately before you land at your destination. First tap for any fatigue, tiredness or travel distress (whether real or anticipated). Then every two hours, tap the Basic Recipe while telling your body, *'It was … o'clock when I left, it is now … o'clock and all parts of me are easily adjusting to this new time zone.'*

Case study: Overcoming jet lag

Psychologist Deborah Miller from Oaxaca, Mexico. shares this experience.

I decided to give EFT a test run on jet lag when I took a trip to Holland at Easter time to visit a friend. I had made several trips across 'the Pond' before and had felt extremely out of sorts and tired for days because of jet lag. I thought this would be a great playground for using EFT in order to enjoy my trip.

Late in the evening on 22nd March I left for Holland from Oaxaca, Mexico, arriving the following afternoon. The time change was a jump of seven hours ahead. I don't normally sleep very well in moving vehicles (car, bus or plane) but I decided that tapping was going to make this a wonderful trip. I tapped every couple of hours, stating that my body rhythms were adjusting to the time change. I tapped that as the plane moved closer to my destination, my biological clock was adjusting to the new time zones as we moved through them and that by the time I arrived I would be completely clocked in. In fact, I managed to sleep more on this trip than normal, a few hour-or-two stints. Every time I woke I tapped to readjust my biological clock and to get some sleep.

I arrived in Holland in the afternoon and spent the rest of the day with my friend. I went to bed at a normal time for Holland, about 11 p.m. I did sleep a little later the first morning. I got up about 10 a.m. but was awake much earlier than that. I was completely clocked in from then on. I was alert and refreshed. My friend asked me several times the first day if I was tired and needed to rest, but I was fine. I only had a 10-minute period where I felt a little tired. After that, I felt fine during the rest of the trip and my friend was amazed since she has travelled extensively.

On the return trip I was awake basically 22 hours because of the time change and travel time. This trip I found I didn't sleep much but still felt fine. I tapped again that my biological clock was adjusting as we travelled. I only felt a little restless towards the very end of the trip. I came home and started in as if I had been there all along.

Tips for successful tapping

Expect success! Expectations are very powerful; in life, we tend to get what we expect. People who expect to be treated with respect generally get respect. Remember, 'Whether you think you can or think you can't, either way you're right.'

Start with simple memories and issues, experience some successes and build from there. Once you have experienced for yourself that tapping works, you will have the confidence to stay positive and persist with more complex issues, even when it seems like it's not working.

Get specific. Just as mechanics use very specific wrenches and tools to repair an engine, so we need to be specific in repairing ourselves. Our issues exist as patterns of very specific thoughts, beliefs, emotions, body sensations and behaviours. The more specific you can be, the more successful you will be.

Break it up, chunk it down. Many EFT newbies make the mistake of trying to tap on global issues, such as 'I feel depressed' or 'my relationship with my mother'. These issues are too broad and too vague to work with effectively. Break big issues into smaller chunks and then tap on the 'chunks', such as 'I felt upset when I lost my job' or 'I felt angry when my mother called five times yesterday'. Do you know how to eat an elephant? One bite at a time!

Keep a tapping journal. Use a tapping worksheet like the one in Appendix 3. Set up a tapping journal and record your successes in your journal. I like to review my journal periodically. It's fun to look back and to see that what I had thought of as being major issues several years ago simply do not bother me any longer.

Exaggerate! If you find yourself stuck or if it's hard to attune to a feeling, try amplifying it with exaggeration. Imagine exaggerating the feelings and sensations, and/or exaggerate the emotional tone and volume of your voice while saying the set-up statements.

Be persistent. Sometimes EFT seems to not work. In these cases the issue may be too vague; it may be a complex issue, with aspects and layers; or you may have a reversal. Break the issue up into aspects and tap on each aspect separately. Be persistent. If at first you don't succeed, tap, tap and tap again.

There are many ways to grow and change and heal. If tapping does not seem to suit you, explore other approaches and find something that works for you.

Energetic self-care

We are energetic beings bathed in fields of energy. Just as we need food, water and exercise for our physical bodies, so we also need to care for our energy bodies as well. Here are some tips for the care and maintenance of your energetic vehicle.

Grounding: Just as we need to ground electrical appliances, so we also need to ground our own bodies periodically. Sleeping outside on the ground periodically reconnects us with the earth's electromagnetic field and literally grounds our body. A very healthy practice is to walk outside barefoot (weather permitting) to ground our energy.

In a recent book, *Earthing: The Most Important Health Discovery Ever?* (2010), authors Clint Ober, Stephen Sinatra and Martin Zucker describe the importance of grounding our electrical bodies with the magnetic field of the earth. Energy medicine researcher James Oschman wrote: 'Earthing seems to do away with or dramatically improve so many health challenges: insomnia, the chronic pain of multiple diseases and injuries, exhaustion, stress, anxiety and premature ageing.'

Hydration: Water is both an electrical conductor and a powerful solvent, and is necessary for all metabolic activities. We need to be properly hydrated to think clearly and to perform optimally. Water comprises a larger percentage of the brain (estimated at 80 percent) than of any other organ. Coffee, tea and caffeinated soft drinks are diuretics and can cause us to lose more water than we take in. I drink tea and coffee but drink filtered water as well. If you're trying to lose weight, drinking a glass of water 30 minutes before meals may help you eat less. Listen to your body; sometimes what we call 'hunger' is actually thirst.

Exercise: Our bodies were made to move. While the heart pumps the cardiopulmonary system, the lymphatic system, which removes the body's wastes, is 'pumped' by muscular action. Walking, running, swimming, any form of cardio workout and (especially) jumping on a trampoline both works our muscles and helps keep all our fluids and systems moving and flowing. Stimulating exercises such as the Four Thumps and qi gong clapping stimulate and energize our inner energetic systems. Sedating exercises such as the Eeman relaxation circuit, Cook's hook-ups and Brain Buttons etc. are useful to calm and sedate our nervous and electrical systems, especially when we feel 'wired' or uptight. See Appendix 5 for energy exercises.

Electromagnetic fields: All appliances have electromagnetic fields. It's best not to use electric blankets because sleeping with it for 6–8 hours affects your own subtle energy field. At the time of writing, there are (as yet unproven) concerns about the effects of cell phones, computers and microwaves. A few minutes checking email is probably not at all harmful, but sitting in front of a screen for hours every day is something else. Until these concerns are resolved, it may be best to keep your cell phone away from your body except when using it and limit your exposure, if possible, to other sources of radiation.

Rest: Be sure to get adequate rest at night, depending on your needs and physiology. If you feel concerned about 'not wasting time sleeping', please note that you will function more effectively and enjoy it more when well rested. Taking a 'power nap' during the day will refresh you and help you perform more effectively as well as live more healthfully.

Tapping into intuition

In the process of doing emotional clearing and inner work, intuition and psychic abilities often develop as well. There are many books and classes teaching methods for enhancing intuition, such as meditating, using pendulums or muscle testing or reading Tarot cards. Meridian tapping is also a very effective way of enhancing intuition and opening our psychic channels. We are naturally psychic and intuitive; what blocks us from exercising these natural abilities are our fears and doubts. When I'm leading seminars, sometimes people are amazed because I seem to be 'reading their minds'. I find that as I continue tapping on myself every day, my intuitive abilities continue to grow and develop and the universe becomes friendly and transparent.

In electronics there is a phenomenon called the signal to noise ratio. The higher the strength of the (radio or television) signal to the background noise, the clearer the reception will be. Many of us cannot hear our subtle signals, the 'still, small voice' within, because we have so much emotional noise going on. As you continue to tap tap tap!, you'll find your inner noise levels decreasing, your sensitivity increasing and you'll find yourself naturally attuned both to yourself and those around you.

Key point

We are naturally psychic and intuitive; what blocks us from exercising these natural abilities are our fears and doubts. As we release these fears and doubts, our natural intuitive abilities begin to develop spontaneously.

Activity: Tapping into intuition

Think of a way you'd like to use your intuition, e.g. being able to read people more easily, listening to your hunches, being able to listen to your gut feelings etc. Then ask yourself:

✻ 'What seems to stop me from using and trusting this......?'
✻ 'What happened, when I was a child, that caused me to doubt or distrust myself?'
✻ 'What specific fears or doubts do I hold around using my......?'
✻ 'Who would dislike or disapprove of me if they knew that I was......?'

These will give you several good tapping targets, aspects to tap on. Then use the EFT Basic Recipe to tap tap tap! and defuse and release each one.

After releasing the blocks to using your intuition, create some positive statements supporting you in your practice:

✻ 'I feel grateful that I am now trusting, using and enjoying all my intuitive abilities.'
✻ 'I feel grateful that my intuition and psychic abilities are growing and developing more and more every day.'
✻ 'I can trust myself to use my gifts safely and respectfully, for the highest good of all.'

Create your own supportive statements and then tap tap tap! until each one feels strong, solid and congruent.

Troubleshooting when EFT seems to not work

Sometimes we can tap (and tap and tap and tap!) and the intensity level does not seem to change. We may feel stuck and the issues do not shift. Here are the most common reasons for this and some suggested solutions.

Problem 1. The issue is too big, too broad or too vague. Sometimes people pick an issue such as 'Nobody loves me' or 'I feel depressed'. These issues are too global to address effectively.

Solution: Break it down. Get very specific. Find specific examples, specific experiences of this issue, specific aspects, and tap on those.

Problem 2. The issue may have different layers, aspects and roots. For example, the person may begin with feeling angry, and the anger shifts to feeling hurt. This is a deeper 'layer' emerging.

Solution: Tap on each layer, one at a time. Tap each one down to '0', until the whole issue feels clear and resolved.

The issue may have different aspects; for example, having a memory of being a passenger in a car accident. Tapping on it gives no relief.

Solution: Break it down into its different aspects. One aspect might be feeling apprehensive *before* the accident; another might be hearing someone say 'We're going to be hit!'; another might be bracing herself just before the impact; another might be hearing the tyres screech, etc. Tap on each separate aspect and often the whole memory will 'collapse'.

You may need to find and tap on the underlying roots. See the discussion on treating roots in Chapter 6.

Problem 3. Psychological reversal: a reversal is a block to healing that is associated with a belief or motivation that is opposed to your conscious intention. You can ask yourself questions such as:

▶ 'If there was a limiting belief blocking my healing right now, what might that be?'

▶ ' If there was some good reason for holding on to this condition, what might that be?'

▶ ' If I was feeling afraid to change, what might I be feeling afraid of?'

Solution: Correct the reversal by naming it and plugging it into the Parts set-up while tapping the Karate Chop point: *'Even though A PART OF ME THINKS that......, the REST OF ME KNOWS that......, and I'M CHOOSING TO......'*

Problem 4. Switching, also called neurologic disorganization, refers to a phenomenon where part of the brain shuts down or 'switches off'. It is possible to test for switching with muscle testing, but this is not easy to do with yourself.

Indicators of switching include: you are making mistakes, which you normally don't do; you've lost your keys today; you're banging into things; you cannot remember names or phone numbers, when normally you can; you feel tired, fatigued, stressed or 'off'.

Solution: Switch yourself back on by doing the Cross-Crawl or the Brain Buttons (see Appendix 5). Then tap again.

Problem 5. Dehydration: our bodies are approximately 75 percent water and our brains are about 80 percent water. Water is vital for all metabolic processes as well as for circulating our blood and cooling our brains. Water is an electrical conductor; you do not want to be in a swimming pool during a lightning storm. Being dehydrated can interfere with EFT and other energy techniques.

Solution: Drink a glass of water, notice any shift and then tap again.

Problem 6. Energy toxins are any substances which 'zap' your energy. It can be anything you are allergic or sensitive to, including stressors such as fluorescent lights, computer monitors or microwaves; synthetic fibres; cologne, perfume or paint fumes; chemical detergents; artificial colours and flavours.

Solution: If possible, determine what you are reacting to. Remove the toxin/allergen from your space; you may need to change your clothes or change environments or wait a few hours after eating and tap again.

While they are relatively rare, energy toxins can occur especially with people who are chemically or electronically sensitive. To treat the toxin, first determine what you're reacting to. Muscle testing can be helpful with this. Notice your state of mind and jot down the intensity from 0–10. Then hold the substance in your field with one hand near your navel, while doing 2–3 rounds of EFT as needed.

The Personal Peace Procedure

I'm including here one of Gary Craig's most outstanding innovations, the Personal Peace Procedure (PPP). It is a very thorough way of identifying and 'handling' every trauma and negative experience in your life. You make a list of every negative experience you've ever had, until you have a list of 30, 50, 100 or more events. Then every day, during your daily tapping time, take one or two events from your list and tap tap tap!

Doing this conscientiously may take several months but it is guaranteed to change your life, sometimes dramatically, for the better.

I will let Gary describe the PPP in his own words.

> The Personal Peace Procedure that I'm about to unfold for you is not just a way to 'feel a little more peaceful'. Properly understood, this technique should be the healing centrepiece for every person on earth. Every physician, therapist, spiritual counsellor and personal performance coach in the world should be using it as a leading tool for helping others (and themselves).
>
> In essence, the Personal Peace Procedure involves making a list of every bothersome SPECIFIC EVENT in one's life and systematically EFTing their impacts out of existence. By diligently doing this we can pull out every negative tree from our emotional forests and thus eliminate major causes of our emotional and physical ailments. This, of course, propels each individual toward personal peace which, in turn, contributes mightily toward world peace.
>
> Here are some uses…
>
> 1 As 'homework' between sessions with a physician or therapist. This is certain to accelerate and deepen the healing process.
>
> 2 As a daily procedure to clear out a lifetime of accumulated emotional debris. This will enhance self-image, reduce self-doubt and provide a profound sense of freedom.
>
> 3 As a means to eliminate a major contributor of a serious dis-ease. Somewhere within one's specific events are those

angers, fears and traumas that are manifesting as dis-ease. By addressing them all, you will likely cover those responsible for the dis-ease.

4 As a useful substitute for finding core issues. If you neutralize all the specific issues you will have automatically included core issues.

5 As a means for consistent relaxation.

6 To become an example to others as to what is possible.

This simple concept should shift the entire healing field. I can state it in a sentence. *Most of our emotional and physical problems are caused or contributed to by unresolved specific events, the vast majority of which can be easily handled by EFT.*

Not bad for a mere engineer, eh? That sentence, if adopted by every healing practitioner and patient, would likely (1) dramatically increase our healing rates while (2) precipitously dropping our costs. Please note that this idea completely ignores chemical causes such as those propounded by the medical model. That's because I have repeatedly seen improvements in clients where drugs and other chemical solutions have failed miserably. This is not to say, however, that drugs, proper nutrition and the like don't have their place. Indeed they do. They can often be vital. In my experience, however, our unresolved specific events are nearer the foundational cause for illness than anything else. Thus they deserve our primary attention.

How obvious! Experienced EFTers are well aware of EFT's ability to cleanly wipe the negative specific events off of our mental walls. This is the area wherein our highest success rates appear. As you eliminate the emotional baggage from your specific events you will have less internal conflict for your system to deal with. Less internal conflict translates into a higher level of personal peace and less emotional and physical suffering. For many, this procedure will likely result in the complete cessation of lifelong issues that other methods have not touched. How's that for peace in a paragraph?

The same applies to physical ailments as well. I'm talking here about everything from headaches, breathing difficulties and digestive disorders to AIDS, MS and cancer. It is becoming more widely accepted that our physical maladies are caused (or contributed to) by unresolved angers, traumas, guilt, grief and the like. I have had many discussions with physicians in recent years and more and more of them echo emotional strife as a major cause of serious diseases. Until now, however, there hasn't been an effective way to eliminate these health bandits. We can mask them with drugs, of course, but true cures have been hard to find. Fortunately, EFT and its many cousins now provide easy and elegant tools that will aid the serious health practitioner in killing the root causes of disease... instead of the patient.

What I share here is NOT a substitute for quality EFT training NOR is it a substitute for quality help from a masterful EFT practitioner. Rather, it is a tool that, properly applied, is capable of wide-ranging relief (quality training or quality assistance will add to its effectiveness). Its simplicity and far-reaching effectiveness give it candidacy as a mandatory method for anyone seeking help for even the most difficult of problems. I know that's a bold statement but I've been at this for over a decade now and have seen so many impressive results over such a wide variety of issues that this statement is easy, if not essential, to make.

The method is simple:

1 Make a list of every bothersome specific event you can remember. If you don't find at least 50 you are either going at this half-heartedly or you have been living on some other planet. Many people will find hundreds.

2 While making your list you may find that some events don't seem to cause you any current discomfort. That's OK. List them anyway. The mere fact that you remember them suggests a need for resolution.

3 Give each specific event a title, as though it was a mini-movie. Examples: Dad hit me in the kitchen; I stole Suzie's

sandwich; I almost slipped and fell into the Grand Canyon; my third grade class ridiculed me when I gave that speech; Mom locked me in a closet for two days; Mrs Adams told me I was stupid.

4 When the list is complete, pick out the biggest redwoods in your negative forest and apply EFT to each of them until you either laugh about it or 'can't think about it any more'. Be sure to notice any aspects that may come up and consider them separate trees in your negative forest. Apply EFT to them accordingly. Be sure to keep after each event until it is resolved.

If you cannot get a 0–10 intensity level on a particular movie then assume you are repressing it and apply 10 full rounds of EFT on it from every angle you can think of. This gives you a high possibility for resolving it.

After the big redwoods have been removed, go to the next biggest trees.

5 Do at least one movie (specific event) per day... preferably three... for three months. It only takes minutes per day. At this rate you will have resolved 90 to 270 specific events in three months. Then notice how your body feels better. Note, too, how your 'threshold for getting upset' is much lower. Note how your relationships are better and how many of your therapy type issues just don't seem to be there any more. Revisit some of those specific events and notice how those previously intense incidences have faded into nothingness. Note any improvements in your blood pressure, pulse and breathing ability.

I ask you to consciously notice these things because, unless you do, the quality healing you will have undergone will seem so subtle that you may not notice it. You may even dismiss it saying, 'Oh, well, it was never much of a problem anyway.' This happens repeatedly with EFT and thus I bring it to your awareness.

It is my hope that the Personal Peace Procedure becomes a worldwide routine. A few minutes per day will make a monumental difference in school performance, relationships, health and our quality of life. But these are meaningless words unless you put this into practice. I will end this article with a quote from my good friend Howard Wight: 'If you are ultimately going to do something important that will make a real difference... do it now.'

Personal Peace to all,

Gary Craig

Things to remember

The main points to remember from this chapter are:

* for best results with EFT or any personal growth technique, it's important to practise it every day
* you can tap while waiting in queues at the bank, grocery or airport using visual tapping or covert tapping
* it's not what we're eating, it's what's eating us. Underlying our cravings and addictions are adverse childhood experiences (ACEs).
* tapping is not just a 'quick fix' or a neat tool to use on others; tapping is a potent tool for personal transformation, for healing ourselves, our families and our world.
* tips to successful tapping include expecting success, getting specific, keeping a tapping journal and being persistent
* energetic self-care includes grounding, drinking water, exercise, recreation and rest
* we are naturally psychic and intuitive; what blocks us from exercising these natural abilities are our fears and doubts. As we release these fears and doubts, our natural intuitive abilities begin to develop spontaneously.

14

On the horizon

Without deviation from the norm, progress is not possible.
Frank Zappa

In this chapter you will learn:

▶ **several tapping innovations**
▶ **EFT in the school system**
▶ **how to do Touch and Breathe (TAB)**
▶ **how to do gratitude tapping**
▶ **how to do surrogate tapping**
▶ **tapping for dead people**
▶ **tapping for animals.**

Meridian tapping is a very robust and fertile field and already it has spawned many innovations. Many of these came through Gary Craig, such as the Movie, Tearless Trauma and Tell The Story techniques, and now others are contributing to the rapidly growing repertoire of tapping techniques. There are many ways to apply meridian tapping; there are different strokes for different folks. Try some of these variations and see what works best for you. In this chapter I will discuss innovations and variations in the tapping world.

Case study: Tapping into creativity

EFT practitioner Sue Hannibal shares how she uses EFT for creative writing.

I use EFT to release unwanted nagging thoughts, anxiety, worry or procrastination that divert the continuous energy flow that creativity requires. Tapping before writing is like clearing a table of dirty dishes. It allows me to more easily bridge the gap between head and heart. Writing from one's head has a flat, book-report quality that readers can sense. Writing from the head and heart is deeper, more expansive and gently enfolds the reader. Tapping promotes peaceful focus and the anticipation of something wonderful about to be manifested, which is literally thought-into-form. The words and concepts slowly take shape on the paper or screen, sweeping me along with it. At that milestone in the creative journey, the writer becomes more tour guide than lone traveller.

The energy of reading

In 2007 Marlene Boltman, a reading specialist, and Mary Hammond, an early childhood development specialist, conducted a study called 'The Energy of Reading Project'. The purpose of the study was to determine whether simple energy interventions could increase children's reading scores. The children selected were the lowest performing readers in an elementary school in Salem, Oregon; their families were below the poverty level. One classroom received the energy interventions, the other did not.

Boltman introduced the exercises to the children by telling them every day, 'We need to wake up our brains!' She then guided them in three exercises: heart tapping, collarbone tapping and cross-crawl marching. The heart centre is a governing energy centre which reaches deeply into the human energy system. Tapping on the heart centre has an immediate calming effect on mind and body, allowing for increased focus and attentiveness. Collarbone tapping refers to tapping on the collarbone points.

Cross-crawl marching guides the right and left hemispheres to coordinate and work together. It involves marching on the spot, with arms swinging and hands alternately touching the outside of the opposite leg on each swing. Many children with learning disabilities are 'switched' or neurologically disorganized; doing the cross-crawl marching corrects this disorganization. (See Chapter 4 for a discussion of switching).

Boltman had the children do all three exercises 'to wake up their brains' at the start of every day. One morning she got a late start with her group and she attempted to dispense with the energy exercises. The students protested, 'But we need to wake up our brains!' She knew then that they valued the process and they knew at some level that it was helping them. Occasionally she would be talking to an individual student or distributing materials and they would begin collarbone tapping without her – no words were ever spoken and she would look up to see the entire group tapping!

For specific issues Boltman used the heart tapping technique as a stand-alone intervention. When a child had problems with reading and said things like, 'I'm not a good reader', 'I can't read' or 'I'll never get this', Boltman would have her students focus on the 'negative' thought while tapping on the heart centre. After releasing the negative thought energy, she guided them to tap on positive thoughts, such as 'I'm a good reader', 'I can do this!' and 'I am getting it'.

The children participated in a half-hour lesson with Mrs Boltman five days a week. (She's a reading specialist, not their regular teacher.) The children's progress over the eight-month school year of 2007–8 was assessed using a standardized assessment called Dynamic Indicators of Basic Early Literary Skills (DIBELS). Both classrooms used a standard curriculum called 'Read Well'. At the end of the school year the comparison group had achieved 8.3 percent growth in reading ability over the eight months. The energy intervention group experienced a 22.9 percent growth in reading ability.

Equally as important as statistics are the personal experiences of the children and their teachers. First, the children:

'I wake up my brain before I do my homework!'

'When I am sad, I tap on my heart centre to feel better and then I can do my work.'

Noticing another child struggling with reading, a child says to him, 'Let's wake up your brain!' And the group of four did the exercises!

'At the beginning of the year I could hardly read at all. I do wake up my brain every day and over Christmas vacation I read a whole Harry Potter book.'

And the teachers:

'I observed that the kids went from sleepy and uninvolved to smiling and glowing and engaged during the wake up your brain exercises!'

'I watched as a 10-year-old big brother showed his younger sister heart centre tapping.'

'A six-year-old told me, "This is just too hard." So we tapped together to let go of that feeling. Within a minute he said, "Oh, I can do it!" and started solving it by himself.'

'One of my eight-year-old students was struggling with reading and burst into tears. We tapped together and his breathing became even, his body relaxed and he started reading accurately.'

'One of my ADHD children is calmer and more focused after she taps.'

Since Boltman and Hammond conducted this study, scores for the entire school have gone from very low to outstanding (compared with other schools in the state). All the grades in the school now start their day with energy exercises to 'wake up their brains', and administrators from other schools are visiting to see what they're doing.

Tapping innovations

Some practitioners suggest doing **continuous tapping.** Right during the initial intake interview, people tell their story and some get emotional. Have your client (or friend or yourself) tap tap tap! continuously while telling their story. With this technique you're not stopping to rate intensity from 0–10, nor stopping to check in after each round. While this technique is global rather than specific and does not necessarily focus on or clear aspects, it can be a fast way to reduce the overall charge of an issue and begin shifting it.

Psychotherapist Dr David Lake and psychologist Steve Wells from Australia use a variation they call **Simple Energy Techniques (SET).** SET eliminates the use of the set-up and reminder phrases, encouraging the client to simply 'be present' with what is occurring now. It also employs the continuous tapping described above. SET has the advantages of being simpler and somewhat easier to learn and use than EFT. For more information, see www.eftdownunder.com.

Another tapping innovation is the **Wholistic Hybrid of EMDR and EFT (WHEE),** developed by psychotherapist Daniel Benor. WHEE is a self-treatment method that is simple to learn and use, yet very rapidly and deeply effective. Within minutes WHEE can often reduce physical and psychological pain, stress and distress, even when these have been present for decades. While there is much more to WHEE than this brief description can cover, the key difference is that WHEE involves tapping alternately on the right and left sides of the body, not necessarily focused on acupoints. (Almost anywhere you touch the body, you will touch acupoints!) See http://wholistichealingresearch.com/whee.

Psychotherapist Meryl Beck has created the **Rapidly Integrated Transformation Technique (RITT).** It uses the same points as EFT, but focuses on clearing the roots in the subconscious (roots to branches), as well as invoking the power of forgiveness and spirituality. See www.energizedforlife.com.

Possibly the most comprehensive approach to Energy Psychology is the **Energy Diagnostic and Treatment Methods (EDxTM™)**

system developed by psychologist Fred Gallo. EDxTM™ involves muscle testing, enhanced intuition and techniques to assist practitioners in custom-tailoring interventions to their clients. Please note that this training is very technical and designed primarily for healing arts professionals. See www.energypsych.com.

Psychologist John Diepold has developed a technique he calls **Touch and Breathe (TAB)**. It is essentially the same as EFT, except that you lightly touch each set of acupoints while repeating your reminder phrase and breathing a relaxed, moderately deep breath. Some people prefer TAB to EFT, as tapping is more active while TAB is slower, gentler and more meditative. See www.answerstochronicfatigue.co.uk/documents/touch-and-breath-eft-with-tapping-points.pdf

Activity: Touch and Breathe

1 Select an emotional memory to release. Give it a name and a reminder phrase.
2 Attune to the memory, locate it in your body and rate it from 0–10.
3 Begin breathing deeply yet comfortably, without forcing or straining.
4 Gently rub the Karate Chop point on the side of the hand while repeating a set-up phrase three times.
5 Gently breathe, touch and hold each set of acupoints, one at a time, while slowly inhaling and exhaling comfortably. Do one (or two) cycles of inhaling and exhaling per acupoint. Say your reminder phrase with each acupoint as you exhale.
6 After one round, check your intensity; how are you feeling now?
7 Do additional rounds of TAB, working with aspects as needed.

Gratitude tapping

Something that is a lot of fun to do is gratitude tapping. People who study the 'Law of Attraction' believe that 'having an attitude of gratitude' is the best way to 'raise your vibration' and attract prosperity into your life. While we know that we 'should' be grateful, it can hard to feel grateful consistently in a very chaotic, fast-paced and, at times, unfair and uncaring world! Gratitude tapping is a way of tuning into the power of Gratitude and anchoring and integrating it into our bodies.

Activity: Gratitude tapping

There are several ways to do gratitude tapping. The 'deeper' method involves first making an inventory and then clearing out the blocks to gratitude: anger, grudges, resentments and disappointments. (For some of us, this will take some time!) The simpler way is to make a Gratitude List and just tap. See methods 1 and 2, below.

Method 1: Sit down and ask yourself, 'What seems to get in the way of my feeling grateful for every aspect of my life?' When you try to think of 'every aspect', some of which are wonderful and some of which are not, you will likely think of several angers, grudges, disappointments and resentments, things that are 'unfair' and 'not right', about which you feel less than grateful. Jot those down on paper, rate each one from 0–10 and tap tap tap!

You can inject gratitude into your set-up phrase by finding something positive – you learned a lesson, you survived, people rallied around you – and inserting it like this:

- 'Even though A PART OF ME THINKS that this was a terrible misfortune, the REST OF ME KNOWS that this is a learning opportunity, and I'M CHOOSING TO turn lemons into lemonade and do the best I can.'
- 'Even though A PART OF ME THINKS that this is really unfair, the REST OF ME KNOWS that I could have checked out the details more closely, and I'M CHOOSING TO be more careful and vigilant in the future.'

This may take several hours – or days if you're being very thorough! You can choose to clear one or two a day. Take your time with it.

After clearing out disappointments and resentments, then move on to Method 2.

Method 2: Make a Gratitude List of at least 10 things you feel grateful for. Your list might include things like:

- I feel grateful for my life.
- I feel grateful for my parents and family.
- I feel grateful for my wife or partner.
- I feel grateful for my career.
- I feel grateful for my vacation last year.
- I feel grateful for EFT.
- I feel grateful to be here.

Then tap tap tap! on each item in your list, while focusing on feelings of gratitude and appreciation.

Psychotherapist David Lake shares his process of **acceptance tapping**. 'Here is a simple method of beginning treatment for many conditions – especially the 'difficult' ones. It paves the way for acceptance of the reality of the problem and reality testing, which is often the missing link for sufferers when progress is blocked. And it can produce surprising results.

'The basic principle is to pay attention to and work with what's there instead of changing it. The solution is in the symptom, so be present to it. In essence you accept that the problem is there before anything else is changed. Then you simply add continuous tapping (described above) into the problem pattern; the person taps continuously along while describing the problem, without trying to change it.

'This process can be taught simply and quickly and clients typically comply, gaining the relaxation of EFT if nothing else. It works equally well in mental rehearsal of a positive behaviour, where presumably unconscious blocking beliefs might be an issue. In many such situations I have found that the addition of tapping changes the routine behaviours of the problem significantly and that kind of change is a sign we want in the beginning. It's a way of getting the client's attention in a new way and of working creatively with the most intense part of the behaviour. You sidestep the thinking mind and just tap.'

EFT master Karl Dawson has created a useful variation of EFT called **Matrix Re-imprinting (MR)**. MR is a sophisticated technique combining EFT with NLP methods. Rather than just tapping on a memory, as in EFT, MR involves going back into the memory, creating safety, bringing in resources, making a new decision and changing the memory, along with tapping. Obviously, there is much more to this than I can describe in a few words; for more information, see www.matrixreimprinting.com.

Yet another powerful tool for personal growth is dreamwork. 'Dreams are the royal road to the unconscious', as Freud wrote, and often show us things about ourselves we don't want to see or look at. Robert and Lynne Hoss have created a powerful method they call the **Dream to Freedom technique**. It involves using gestalt dreamwork to interpret the dream, followed by

EFT to release its associated emotions. See http://dreamscience.
org/articles/Hoss-Dream_to_Freedom_Journal_Article.pdf

Another fascinating development is **intergenerational tapping**.
Have you ever experienced a mood or behaviour that you
could not relate to, that you felt was not really yours? The
theory behind this is that we sometimes pick up unresolved
issues or emotions, very often from our parents but sometimes
from other relatives further back in the family line. The issue is
engaged by first identifying the relative who is the source of the
issue and then tapping for both the relative and yourself. Ways
to identify the source of an issue include using a pendulum or
muscle testing; to use this technique it's best to consult a very
experienced practitioner.

Case study: Tapping on her grandfather's addiction

Licensed professional counsellor Mary Hammond from Salem, Oregon
shares the case of 'June'.

June began drinking when she was 13. It helped her to be accepted among
her peers and it temporarily relieved the pain of her father's death when
she was 10. She also smoked pot and quickly became addicted as she was
unable to predict how much she would drink or use, or how she would
behave when she did. In one of our sessions we accessed the energy of
her maternal grandfather who was a hopeless alcoholic who got drunk
frequently. His drunkenness led to affairs and the affairs caused pain and
humiliation for the family.

We tapped on her grandfather's addiction, his pain and unhappiness, on the
energy of addiction, the energy of infidelity, the energy of the family's pain
and humiliation. We also tapped on the inevitable death wish (the wish to
hurt or kill oneself – which is a reversal) that accompanies addiction.

June had a major 'Aha!' when she realized that by creating more pain for
her family, she was following in her grandfather's footsteps. After working
through many such patterns energetically and establishing a daily
programme of recovery, she has remained sober for over ten years.

Mary adds that 'EFT can be enormously helpful in breaking through denial,
because denial is a form of reversal.'

EFT master Gwyneth Moss from Yorkshire has created a technique she calls the **Web of Life**, which is a group process for intergenerational healing. Based on the family reconstruction work of Virginia Satir that inspired Bert Hellinger's Constellation Work, it involves a group of people tapping as they role-play several generations of one person's family. The people who are role-playing often say and feel the same things the person's relatives would say and feel, and as they tap those feelings change, thus healing tears in the family web of life. The addition of meridian tapping reduces the high levels of emotion that are often present, and clearing energy patterns by 'tapping for dead people' often creates powerful shifts for those still living. Read more at www.emotional-health.co.uk/connected.htm

Surrogate tapping

Surrogate tapping is one of the most fascinating developments in the tapping world. It involves tapping on your own body for the benefit of someone else. Surrogate tapping extends the power of EFT far beyond those people with whom you can be physically present. The other person may be ill, in a coma or an animal, child or teenager who may be unable or unwilling to tap on themselves.

The concept underlying surrogate tapping is that we are all interconnected, especially with family members and people we love. There are numerous stories of mothers waking up at night and suddenly knowing that their husband or child has been injured. The British biologist Rupert Sheldrake wrote a fascinating book, *Dogs That Know When Their Owners are Coming Home*, describing such phenomena involving animals. Doctor Larry Dossey has compiled numerous studies documenting the healing effects of prayer and healing at a distance. Surrogate tapping is similar to prayer, combining focused positive intention with energetic tapping.

Surrogate tapping involves mentally and emotionally putting yourself in the place of another person and then tapping on yourself. It involves the willingness to 'put yourself in the shoes' of the other, to tap and to receive the benefits of EFT for them.

Activity: Surrogate tapping

1 Close your eyes, think of the other and get into rapport with the other.
2 Tune in and imagine what they might be thinking and feeling.
3 Do EFT while staying attuned to the other, with a set-up statement appropriate for the other.
4 Notice any shifts that take place.
5 Mentally let go of and disengage from the other.
6 Give thanks for this opportunity to serve and heal.

I think it is good practice to 'check in' before trying to impose 'healing' on another. People have free will and have a right to choose their experiences, including the right to their own mental states and even the right to be ill if they so choose! A good way to 'get your ego out of the way' is to tap for the highest good of all concerned. Gary Craig does not think we need permission. He makes the point that we pray for other people; do we ask permission before we pray for them?

This is very powerful and exciting work and extends EFT into the realm of the transpersonal, the dimension where we are all interconnected. Some people have had very powerful experiences with surrogate tapping; it's up to you to try this for yourself.

Case study: Surrogate tapping

Psychotherapist Carol Solomon of Libertyville, Illinois, uses surrogate tapping to ease her daughter's dental pain.

While I have used EFT for years, I never understood the concept of surrogate tapping. I often wondered how it could actually work. Then I realized one day that 'it's all energy', so of course if I am tapping for another person and we share the same energy field, they would be impacted as well.

My daughter is 11-years-old, too 'cool' to tap or to allow me to tap on her. However, she was nervous when she had to have some dental work done recently. The dental office is rather long and narrow. The place for the parent to sit is in the opposite corner to where the work takes place. While her work was being done, I was able to do surrogate tapping unobtrusively in my corner. I tapped on myself in the usual manner as if I was her. I spoke the words softly to myself.

* 'Even though it is hard to relax... I know I can stay relaxed and calm.'
* 'Even though I am afraid it will hurt......'
* 'Even though I am not sure what is going to happen......'
* 'Even though I hate the sound of the drill......'
* 'Even though I hate the vibration against my teeth......'
* 'Even though I hate when they put all that stuff in my mouth......'
* 'Even though it feels like this is taking forever......'

My daughter was quiet, relaxed and still for the entire procedure – her best appointment ever. She even remarked later how easy it was!

Tapping for furry and feathered friends

EFT master Gwyneth Moss teaches seminars on EFT for animals. Animals lack the rational thinking mind that in humans is the source of many of our blocks and reversals. They tend to be more open than humans, especially to non-verbal techniques, and they are very sensitive to energy and can sense things that we can't. Animals have meridians as well and you can find meridian charts for cats, dogs and horses on the internet, as well as information on animal EFT.

In her EFT for Animals seminars Gwyneth teaches a simple three-step protocol for working with animals. For articles and stories see www.emotional-health.co.uk/animals.htm

Case study: Soothing the 'raptor pony'

Gwyneth Moss tells how she and riding instructor Heather Smiles soothed the 'raptor pony'.

Imagine the cutest Welsh Mountain pony with a bright chestnut coat and shaggy mane and that is Ruby. You would think she'd be the perfect children's pony and family pet, but in the rescue yard where Ruby had ended up even experienced adult horsewomen were very cautious about going anywhere near her. Ruby was known as the 'raptor pony' because she would strike out with sharp hooves and teeth. Too vicious to be allowed near children and too small to be ridden by adults, Ruby did not have much of a future.

On one of my EFT for Animals days, Heather and I used surrogate tapping for Ruby. We like to tap for animals and others in pairs or groups, though of course you can do surrogate tapping on your own with good results. Tapping together allows one of us to be objective and ask the questions and the other to get into the subjective experience of the animal. We start by tapping and talking about the animal, about the behaviour and whatever we know of the history, breaking the story down into an aspect at a time. We tend not to use 'even though' and just use 'and'. Each one of these statements is a round of tapping.

✱ 'Ruby growls and bears her teeth and deep down she is a good pony.'
✱ 'Ruby kicks and knows how to aim and we still love her.'
✱ 'Ruby hates people and wants to hurt them and she's still goodness inside.'

Heather didn't know much about Ruby's history; a family brought her to the yard because they could not handle her and she had kicked once too often. When we don't know the history, we make it up and somehow images then flow into the person's mind. We move into talking to Ruby.

✱ 'Ruby, you must have been born running wild with your mother in the mountains and you are a beautiful pony.'
✱ 'Ruby, something must have happened, did men take you from your mother?'

At this point Heather feels a physical sensation like a rope around her neck and fighting the rope, so we move into talking as Ruby.

✱ 'There's a rope and it hurts me and I can't run and I'm trapped!'
✱ 'I'm in a box and I can't see the sky, I'm kicking and kicking and I can't get out!'
✱ 'Mother, mother, mother where are you, I'm scared!'

Heather is now feeling Ruby's panic and we tap until that subsides. The next part of the story is at the auction where the foals taken off the mountain are sold. We tap for her fear, confusion and more panic. A family bought Ruby and because she is so small and completely untrained, they pick her up instead of leading her. Having her feet off the ground and being held sends Ruby into complete terror so we tap and tap until that also subsides. The children of the family are enthusiastic to play with their new pony, but Ruby is traumatized and terrified and she bites and kicks at them. Again we tap until the whole story which was so intense fades.

Now Heather as Ruby is more aware of her current surroundings; she knows she is bigger now that there is good grass and horse friends in this place and she is cared for. She knows that she can stand up for herself when she really needs to and that people and other horses are mostly friendly.

The next day Heather walked up to the field and to her amazement Ruby trotted over with a 'smile' on her face instead of bared teeth. Heather was able to lead her by grabbing a handful of her mane and there was no kicking or biting and has not been since. The farrier can pick up her feet, which was previously impossible, and Ruby now has a future.

Things to remember

The main points to remember from this chapter are:

* there are many ways to apply meridian tapping. Try different variations and see what works best for you.
* children are improving their reading skills and grade performance by tapping every day
* we can tune into the 'power of gratitude' by doing gratitude tapping
* tapping on memories, whether real or 'imagined', can be profoundly healing and transformative
* you can tap for other people or for animals, children or teenagers with surrogate tapping
* tapping is not just for ourselves. As we are all inter-connected, tapping affects those around us and contributes to the healing of our world.

Conclusion: The tapping revolution

> There is nothing more powerful than an idea whose time has come.
>
> Victor Hugo

EFT is an idea whose time has come. It is spreading rapidly throughout the world, by books and seminars, on YouTube and other websites, and by word of mouth. There are now over 100 books on EFT and tapping, and more are being published every week. There have been over 1.4 million downloads of Gary Craig's original EFT manual, as well as translations (all by volunteers) into over 20 languages. Before Craig closed his emofree.com website in 2010, it was ranked by Alexia as being in the top 1 percent of most heavily trafficked websites. Craig has recently revived emofree.com and it is already receiving 400,000 minutes viewing time a month. Every year Nick and Jessica Ortner organize an online World Tapping Summit featuring some of the best EFT practitioners in the world; last year over 500,000 people worldwide participated.

People are flocking to lectures, seminars and trainings in EFT, Thought Field Theory and Meridian Tapping Technique. The more serious are attending the practitioner certification programs offered by the Association for the Advancement of Meridian Energy Therapies (AAMET), the Association for Meridian and Energy Therapies (AMT), the Association for Comprehensive Energy Psychology (ACEP) and EFT Universe.

Meridian therapies are spreading rapidly throughout the world because they are so effective, and useful for so many conditions. They have become an internet phenomenon, with many practitioners promoting themselves on websites and with YouTube videos. I see its rapid expansion via the internet as an extension of Gary Craig's tremendous generosity. Rather than attempting to 'bottle' EFT and make a profit on it, he has made his updated EFT tutorial freely available at http://emofree.com.

His example of generosity is being followed as people learn EFT and then share it with their friends, families and clients. EFT is a gift to be shared with all.

Power to the people

We live in a time of rapid change. Among these changes is the digital revolution. Never before in the history of the world has information been so freely available to everyone. Just a few short years ago people had to 'have connections' or pay good money to a doctor, lawyer or consultant for information. Now information on virtually everything is easily available with only a few clicks. A ten-year-old with an iPhone has access to more, and more accurate, information than prime ministers and presidents did only 25 years ago.

For centuries church, business, government and the military have been organized along strict hierarchical lines of authority. This has been true of medicine and psychology as well, where people consulted authority figures about their physical and emotional well-being. Now, power structures are being decentralized and power, in the forms of money, information and decision making, are beginning to be shared by all. While hierarches are not vanishing entirely, the internet and global economies are inspiring new models based in community, collaboration and self-responsibility rather than on hierarchy and control.

EFT is a grassroots movement. Most therapeutic innovations have come from the top down, from a therapist, teacher or researcher who develops training and certification programmes, training other therapists who then dispense it to the masses. EFT came from the 'bottom up'; Gary Craig was not a doctor, therapist or mental health professional.

While many therapists and healing professionals have embraced EFT, the overwhelming majority are average people who have discovered the power of this unique modality for themselves.

Some of you may recall the Human Potential Movement (HPM), based in California, which was at its most influential and popular in the 1960s and 70s. Inspired by the writings of Abraham Maslow, Carl Rogers, Virginia Satir and George

Leonard, the movement's premise was that people can live extraordinary lives of creativity, happiness and fulfilment by tapping their hidden potentials. The HPM has been eclipsed by the more recent self-help movement, which generated an estimated $14 billion in sales of books, training, CDs, DVDs etc in 2012 in the US alone.

EFT is self-help on steroids. It is a self-healing, self-empowerment tool that everyone can use and is dramatically faster and more effective than most. It is the single most effective technology I know for releasing limiting blocks and patterns. Moreover, it is easily learned, whether from books, classes or internet. EFT is 'the people's therapy', and a powerful vehicle for fulfilling the promise of tapping previously untapped human potentials.

Tapping into spirit

Both Roger Callahan and Gary Craig designed their respective techniques, Thought Field Theory and EFT, as secular practices. I surmise that they wanted their techniques to be available to all and did not want them to be seen as religious or cultish. However, I find EFT to be a profoundly spiritual practice. The acupoints are portals into our inner energy system; these are sometimes referred to as subtle or spiritual realms or dimensions. The process of opening our 'inner eyes and ears' occurs spontaneously as we release and remove blocks and issues that impair our perception and drain our time and energy.

While meridian tapping is not spiritually oriented in itself, it can be a powerful adjunct to spiritual practice, no matter what your personal belief system. A central issue that all religions and spiritual systems seek to address is the issue of relationship: our relationship with our families, our communities, the greater world community, the cosmos and with a godhead or higher power. This issue is sometimes referred to as the problem of separation, which appears in the story of Adam and Eve, the Hindu myth of Hanuman and Sita, the Jewish concept of Tikkun and the African myth of the man and the elephant.

One aspect of spirituality lies in the quest for Wholeness. We seek Wholeness because we are conflicted; we have parts, also called subpersonalities, with different wants, needs, beliefs and agendas. These parts are often repressed and 'go unconscious', because they have their roots in trauma, in imprinted experiences.

Healing is connecting. There is an idea in psychotherapy that whatever we are unaware of runs us. Our subconscious programmes, rooted in unmet needs and imprinted experiences, are either sublimated into 'acceptable' behaviours or we defend against them, fighting, resisting or avoiding them. These inner conflicts divide us against ourselves and consume a tremendous amount of energy. The degree to which we can name, accept, transmute and integrate these 'negative' energies is the degree to which we can become more whole. Yin and yang, light and dark, negativity and positivity are all necessary for our greater Wholeness.

Both Gary Craig and I are students of a set of teachings called *A Course in Miracles*. The course was channelled by Dr Helen Schucman, a professor of psychology at Columbia University. The course claims to represent a radical reinterpretation of the teachings of Jesus. Schucman, ethnically Jewish but a self-proclaimed atheist, had difficulty reconciling the course with the rest of her life. She did not discuss it with anyone at Columbia except her supervisor, Dr William Thetford, who assisted her with the material; she would not discuss it with her husband; and she refused to allow her name to be associated with it until after her death.

The course begins with a brief introduction, part of which states:

> The course does not aim at teaching the meaning of love, for that is beyond what can be taught. It does aim, however, at removing the blocks to the awareness of love's presence, which is your natural inheritance. The opposite of love is fear, but what is all-encompassing can have no opposite.

I mention this because EFT and the different forms of meridian tapping are the most powerful techniques I know for removing blocks to the awareness of love's presence. As we remove and release our blockages, rooted in fear, guilt and trauma, we naturally become more patient and compassionate with others and more present to our inner spiritual nature, which is gentle, loving, aware and compassionate. We become whom we are meant to be.

The Golden Buddha

For many years there was an old clay statue of the Buddha in the Wat Traimit district of Bangkok in Thailand. No one knew much about it other than that it was large and very old. The temple did not have a building large enough to house it, so it was kept under a simple tin roof. There are hundreds of temples in Bangkok, so one more statue was nothing special.

In 1955 the decision was made to move the statue to a new location. In the process of attempting to lift the statue from its pedestal, the ropes broke because it was so heavy and the statue fell, damaging the plaster coating. One of the monks noticed a metallic glint shining through the plaster. The temple monks began tapping and chipping away at the plaster and what they found underneath was a beautiful Buddha made of solid gold.

The Golden Buddha is three metres high and weighs 5.5 tons; it is the largest Buddha of its kind in the world. It is believed that it was made during the Sukhothai period, in the 13th to 14th centuries. Burmese armies invaded Thailand in 1767, so it would appear that the monks covered it with stucco to protect it, and thus its secret was hidden for almost 200 years.

This is both a true story and a metaphor. Within each one of us is a secret, a priceless treasure, but it has been covered over to the point where we have forgotten it. This treasure lies hidden, just waiting to be rediscovered. As we tap and chip away at the stucco, our walls of fear, guilt, shame and reactive patterns begin to release and fall away, revealing the treasure of our inner spiritual Nature, our inner Genie.

Joining the revolution

Several years ago, I taught an EFT training seminar in Las Cruces, New Mexico. It was 5th May, commonly called *Cinco de Mayo*, when Mexico's victory in the Battle of Puebla is commemorated, and people were preparing to celebrate. When we think of revolutions, normally we think of guns, bombs, fighting and people doing heroic deeds. But there is another, quiet revolution going on in the world. It is a revolution of Consciousness, a revolution of Spirit.

For the first time in history, large numbers of people have the time, money and awareness to devote to themselves. Millions of people are meditating, doing yoga, practising t'ai chi, qi gong and martial arts, hypnosis and autogenic training etc. This movement has had many names: the Human Potential Movement, the Recovery Movement, the self-help movement. But whatever it is called, it represents a seismic shift in the collective consciousness of our time.

One of my mentors is Greg Nicosia, a psychologist in Pittsburgh, Pennsylvania, and past president of ACEP. Two years before ACEP was founded he had a vision of an army of healers moving out to heal the suffering of this world. Many others have had similar visions and inspirations. The tappers of this world are helping fulfil these dreams and visions.

Meridian tapping is a part of this greater revolution. Many who have been dissatisfied with the healthcare systems are taking their health and healing into their own hands. While we will always need doctors, psychologists and healthcare professionals for more serious ailments, there is much we can do for ourselves regarding both prevention and treatment.

By reading this book and learning to tap, you are joining the worldwide tapping revolution. Your initial desire may have been to release a fear or phobia, to solve a problem or to be more effective in your business. You may want to 'raise your vibration' in order to attract a partner or more abundance. But EFT is not just for ourselves. There is a Hopi (Native American) saying, 'We dance not just for ourselves, but for the good of the whole pueblo.' Similarly, we tap not just for ourselves, but for the good of all humanity.

You have been given a very powerful Gift. I gently urge you to take this gift and use it, for the benefit of yourself, your friends and family and our entire human community.

Appendix 1: How tapping works

The discussion of mechanisms of treatment is interesting, especially since we don't really know how any psychotherapy works. Theoretically, each method has its formulation, but underlying physical mechanisms are harder to discern. And when an explanation of mechanism of functioning is discovered, it just gives rise to questions about the next lower level of analysis. Therefore it is remarkable that physiological mechanisms are already being discovered for energy psychology, even though it is younger and stranger than more established methods.

An anonymous reviewer, commenting on David Feinstein's paper 'Acupoint stimulation: Evidence for efficacy' (2012)

Various theories have been proposed to explain how meridian tapping works. One is that EFT is a form of hypnosis. This is not true, as the client is fully aware while doing EFT and no attempt is made to induce, or even suggest, a trance state. Another theory is that EFT works by 'distracting' people from their pain. This also is patently not true, as meridian tapping involves focusing on the issue by using a reminder phrase. Another criticism is that any success from EFT is due to elements it has in common with other therapies. While EFT does share some common elements, notably psychological exposure and cognitive restructuring, with other therapies, these 'common elements' do not begin to explain the sheer rapidity and effectiveness of tapping modalities. Cognitive behavioral therapy (CBT) cannot effectively treat PTSD in one session, or even six sessions.

The last objection is that EFT is effective because of the placebo effect. It is likely that there is a placebo factor in all therapeutic interventions. Randomized controlled trials, which compare an active intervention with a control (non-active) intervention, are designed to address this issue. In several randomized controlled trials, subjects receiving EFT experienced dramatic reductions in their symptoms, while those in comparison groups or groups waiting for treatment experienced no reduction (Feinstein, 2012).

The energetic hypothesis

The energetic hypothesis, originally proposed by Roger Callahan, is that negative emotions are caused by a disruption (what Callahan referred to as a 'perturbation') in the body's energy system. Tapping and stimulating acupuncture meridians is theorized to remove the blockage or disruption, thereby restoring the free flow of meridian and emotional energy (Callahan & Perry, 1991; Callahan & Callahan, 1996). This can be verified with muscle testing; for example, an indicator muscle may test 'weak' while the client recalls a certain issue, but after tapping on the Collarbone point the muscle will test 'strong', indicating that the tapping has released stress associated with that meridian.

From the viewpoint of mainstream science, there are issues with this explanation. Meridians are invisible, and there is no standardized, agreed method for detecting or measuring chi, the flow of energy in the meridians. While there is some evidence for the existence of meridian pathways (Gerber, 2000; Pomeranz, 1989), this evidence is not widely accepted outside the field of energy medicine.

Another theory is the counter-conditioning hypothesis. Counter conditioning refers to the practice of using classical stimulus-response conditioning to replace bad or unpleasant emotional responses to a stimulus with more pleasant, adaptive responses. It was first demonstrated by Mary Cover Jones, based on the conditioning theories of the Russian physiologist Ivan Pavlov (Jones, 1974).

What we sometimes forget is that we are all Pavlovian dogs. Once experiences are conditioned (associated with other stimuli), then whenever we see, hear or smell anything similar to these (repetitive, conditioned) memories, we will re-experience the same feelings and sensations automatically, mechanically and unconsciously (Wolpe, 1969). Tapping on acupoints is believed to desensitize conditioned emotional responses and reassociate a relaxation response with the formerly stressful stimuli (Lane, 2009).

Meridian tapping combines acupoint stimulation with psychological exposure. Exposure is a component of several PTSD treatments, including cognitive behavioural therapy, Eye Movement Desensitization and Reprocessing (EMDR) and exposure therapy. In these therapies the subject is deliberately exposed to a fearful or traumatic stimulus, which activates neural circuits related to fear, pain and anxiety. Acupoint tapping is theorized to reduce hyperarousal in the limbic system, thus reciprocally inhibiting and counter-conditioning the threat response, while simultaneously rewiring neural pathways whereby reduced arousal is reassociated with the triggers that were mentally activated (Feinstein, 2010). This rewiring of neural pathways is a form of neuroplasticity (Doidge, 2007), and is similar to the reprocessing aspect of EMDR (Shapiro, 2001). (Neuroplasticity refers to the brain's ability to rewire neural pathways in response to changes in behaviour, environment and other neural processes.)

The reconsolidation hypothesis

It has been known for many years that emotional memories are extremely difficult to change, if not indelible. Memories formed in the presence of intense emotion during childhood tend to be locked into neural circuits by durable synapses that continue throughout the person's life. Ecker (2011) observed that 'the tenacity of such symptoms reflects the durability of the underlying emotional schemas, which persist through decades'.

Recent discoveries in neuroscience are building evidence for *reconsolidation*, a form of neuroplasticity which allows emotional memories to be extinguished, not just overridden and suppressed by learning a preferred response. Consolidation – a process by which newly learned information is stored in memory – was previously believed to occur only at the time of its initial formation. Research studies at New York University led by Joseph LeDoux have demonstrated that 'consolidated memories, when reactivated through retrieval, become labile (susceptible to disruption) again and undergo reconsolidation' (Debiec, Doyere, Nader, & LeDoux, 2006). Thus, if a sufficiently strong therapeutic action challenges and contradicts the memory before it reconsolidates, the memory can change – permanently.

Ecker et al (2012) describe three steps necessary for consciously engaging the labilization-reconsolidation process:

1 vividly accessing emotional memories that are involved in the targeted symptom

2 concurrently activating an experience that contradicts implicit models or conclusions drawn from the original experiences, i.e. a 'juxtaposition experience'

3 verifying that the change has occurred.

In a 2012 paper, 'What does energy have to do with energy psychology?', David Feinstein points out how Energy Psychology protocols implicitly utilize these steps. Thought Field Therapy juxtaposes activation of a disturbing memory or issue with tapping acupressure points, which is believed to reciprocally inhibit the arousal associated with the issue. EFT utilizes juxtaposition in two places: in tapping on points (just described), and in the set-up phrase, where the client holds (juxtaposes) the issue ('Even though I have this......') with internal resources of love and acceptance ('I deeply and completely love and accept myself').

Many people associate 'negative' experiences with anxiety, guilt and shame, believing that they caused or were somehow 'responsible' for them. Even simply recalling these experiences may retrigger old feelings of fear and guilt. Recalling such an experience while repeating, 'I deeply and completely love and accept myself', followed by the tapping-induced relaxation response, may create an 'experiential disconfirmation' (i.e. a mismatch between former expectations and current experience) resulting in extinction of the old response and reconsolidation of the new one.

Appendix 2:
Research on EFT

EFT is part of a larger field called Energy Psychology. While Energy Psychology as a field is relatively new, the use of energetic metaphors to illuminate psychological processes is not. Sigmund Freud explained his theories using energetic concepts such as libido, repression, cathexis and catharsis in terms of the physics (Maxwell's thermodynamics) of his time (Galatzer-Levy, 1976; Sulloway, 1992). Carl Jung related new discoveries in physics to explore his notions of synchronicity and acausality in terms of quantum mechanics (Jung, 1969; Enz 2009). Energetic concepts were central to the work of Wilhelm Reich and have been retained in contemporary somatic psychotherapies (Shapiro, 2002; Pierrakos, 1990; Kurtz, 2006). Notions of 'energy' play a central role in cross-cultural healing traditions worldwide, such as the Christian practice of laying on of hands, shamanic healing practices (Krippner & Rock, 2011), Native American healing (Braswell & Wong 1994), and traditional Chinese medicine (Hammer, 2005). Ninety-seven cultures have been identified whose healing traditions refer to a human energy field (White & Krippner, 1977).

Energy Psychology is grounded in classical behavioural theories of exposure, conditioning, and reciprocal inhibition (Wolpe, 1969; Ruden, 2005; Lane, 2009). The stimulation of acupuncture points has been shown over the course of a ten-year research programme at Harvard Medical School to rapidly reduce limbic system arousal (Fang et al., 2009). Energy Psychology methods are behavioural desensitization techniques which combine imaginal exposure with the stimulation of acupressure points (Gallo, 2004; Feinstein, 2010; Church & Brooks, 2010). In a comprehensive assessment of the evidence on psychological and pharmaceutical treatment outcomes, the Institute of Medicine (IOM) of the National Academy of Sciences found that the single type of intervention (psychological or pharmaceutical) whose efficacy was judged to have been established according to the rigorous standards used in the IOM's review was psychological exposure (Committee on Treatment of Posttraumatic Stress Disorder, 2008). Energy Psychology methods combine psychological exposure and cognitive restructuring with the stimulation of acupoints, which is based on the well-documented phenomenon of acupuncture and acupressure analgesia (e.g. Kober et al., 2002; Birch et al., 2004; Sun et al., 2008; Fang et al., 2009; Claunch et al., 2012).

Evidence of strong clinical outcomes following Energy Psychology interventions has been accumulating. In a review of 51 published outcome reports or systematic investigations, including studies conducted by independent researchers, each reported evidence for efficacy (Feinstein, 2012). Moreover, several of the studies used only a small number of sessions in treating symptoms of PTSD and produced strong outcomes whose results held up three, six, 12 and/or 24 months later (Church, 2010; Church et al., 2012; Connolly & Sakai, 2011; Karatzias et al., 2011; Sakai, Connolly & Oas, 2010); the outcomes appear to be robust and durable.

Energy Psychology methods are eclectic, drawing upon Gendlin's notion of the felt sense (Gendlin, 1996), the TOTE model (Miller, Galanter & Pribram, 1960), and the use of the Subjective Units of Distress (SUD) scale (Wolpe & Lazarus, 1966). Mechanisms of action for these techniques have been proposed (Ruden, 2005; Lane, 2009). One theoretical model hypothesizes that:

1 imaginal exposure activates an amygdala threat response

2 stimulating selected acupoints reduces limbic arousal (Kober et al., 2002; Sun et al., 2008; Fang et al., 2009; Claunch et al., 2012), thereby

3 reciprocally inhibiting and counter-conditioning the threat response, and

4 rewiring neural pathways where reduced arousal becomes reassociated with the triggers that were mentally activated (Feinstein, 2010; Lane, 2009).

Some sceptics about Energy Psychology methods have suggested that early positive findings may be attributed to poor research methodology, experimenter bias or expectancy effects. Following this line of reasoning, one would expect that as these issues are overcome, the positive findings would diminish. However, although research methodologies have become more rigorous (e.g. Church, Yount & Brooks, 2012; Connolly & Sakai, 2011) and these techniques are being studied by teams of independent researchers (Karatzias et al., 2011), Energy Psychology methods continue to demonstrate high levels of clinical and statistical significance on both psychological and physiological measures. Energy Psychology protocols have been shown to:

- reduce levels of the stress hormone cortisol (Church, Yount & Brooks, 2012)

- activate stress-reducing genes (Feinstein & Church, 2010)

- normalize aberrant brainwave patterns (Diepold & Goldstein, 2009; Lambrou, Pratt & Chevalier, 2003; Swingle, Pulos & Swingle, 2004)

- increase production of serotonin, opioids and other neurotransmitters associated with pleasure (Church & Feinstein, 2012).

For further information, see the research pages at www. energypsych.org.

Appendix 3: My tapping worksheet

Memory or Issue	Rate (0–10)	Set-up and Tap Karate Chop points	Tap points and Reminder	Test (0–10)	Adjust and Aspects
		'Even though I'm feeling this......'			

Appendix 4: Probing questions

Asking questions sensitively is a way of gathering information, and getting to know the other person. It's just as important to listen to *what* they say as to *how* they say it.

It is also a way of building rapport. EFT will work much better if you have rapport and feel connected with your partner than if you just start tapping immediately after she or he has walked through the door.

Asking questions is also a way of going deeper, and of uncovering tapping targets, aspects and roots. Questions, like the question mark itself, are hooks; you toss them out into the great sea of the subconscious and they will hook memories, feelings and associations.

Do not attempt to ask the other person (or yourself) every single question here. Some of these are repetitive, and often just asking 3–4 questions will be sufficient. You will know that you've hooked something significant when your partner has an emotional reaction to the question, when they try to avoid the question (she/he doesn't want to go there) or if she/he has an 'Aha!' moment while answering the question.

▶ What do you notice in your body when you attune to this issue?

▶ Where in your body do you feel this?

▶ Where did this come from?

▶ What do you think might be the cause, source or origin of this......?

▶ What do you tell yourself when......?

▶ What are you telling yourself about......?

▶ What does this issue/symptom remind you of?

▶ About how old do you feel when.......?

- When did you experience this…… before?

- If there was an emotional contributor to this issue, what might it be?

- If this issue/symptom were trying to communicate something to you, what would that be?

- If this issue/symptom were trying to get you to do something, what would that be?

- What image, symbol or metaphor comes to mind when……?

- What fears do you have, about either keeping or releasing this issue?

- If there was a person or event in your life you'd rather have skipped, what would that be?

- What seems to be stopping/preventing you from……?

- What are the advantages of holding onto this issue? (What are you GETTING OUT OF holding onto this issue?)

- What are the disadvantage(s) of giving up this issue? (What is holding on to this issue COSTING you?)

- What happened the last time you tried to…… (e.g. lose weight)?

- What was going on in your life in the 3–6 months BEFORE this symptom/condition first showed up?

- What will you have to give up in order to get……?

- What else comes to mind, when you think of this issue?

When using this technique, notice how your body responds, with any emotional shifts, shivers or 'Aha's. The body holds the truth of what happened whether you can recall a specific memory consciously or not. Even if you cannot recall a specific memory, you can always tap on the symptom itself and on your body sensations (i.e. body memories) as well. Remember that *feeling is healing*; listen to your inner 'truth bell', which will tell you when you've found your truth.

Appendix 5:
Energy exercises

These exercises are designed to stimulate and balance your inner energies. Some of them, like the Cross-Crawl, coordinate and balance the two brain hemispheres. The Cross-Crawl and Four Thumps are energizing exercises, while the Brain Buttons, Eeman Relaxation Circuit and Hara Alignment are calming and balancing exercises. The Cross-Crawl and the Brain Buttons are also corrections for switching (neurologic disorganization). As part of good energetic self-care, it will be helpful to practise one or more of these exercises every day.

CROSS-CRAWL
Stand and march on the spot, raising your knees high.

While marching, tap the outside of the left knee with your right hand, and the outside of your right knee with your left hand. Do this for 30–60 seconds.

FOUR THUMPS
In this exercise we'll be thumping ourselves in four different places. Begin by finding the collarbone points, just below the collarbone and 1–2 inches to the side of the midline.

1 Thump these two points with both hands for 10–15 seconds.

2 Thump your thymus! The thymus lies between the heart and the sternum (breastbone), and helps to regulate the immune system. Make a gentle fist and thump the middle of the sternum vigorously while making loud 'Ha, ha, ha, ha, ha' sounds for 10–15 seconds.

3 Thump the Under Arm points with both hands, either by crossing both arms over the chest or by bringing each hand back to thump the points, for 10–15 seconds.

4 Slap the sides of your ribs with open flat hands for 10–15 seconds.

EEMAN RELAXATION CIRCUIT

This works best if you lie flat on your back on a bed or couch.

1 Cross your ankles.

2 Place your right hand under your tailbone, and your left hand under the occiput (under the 'bulge' at the back of your head, just above the neck).

3 Breathe comfortably in this position for 2–10 minutes.

THE BRAIN BUTTONS

This is another exercise for balancing your energies and getting you 'unswitched'.

1 Gently press on your navel with three fingers of your left hand while rubbing both Collarbone points with your right hand, for about 10 seconds.

2 Gently press your navel with the fingers of your left hand while rubbing the Under Nose and Chin points with your right hand, for about 10 seconds.

3 Gently press your navel with the fingers of your left hand while rubbing your tailbone with your right hand, for about 10 seconds.

4 Switch hands and repeat steps 1–3.

COOK'S HOOK-UPS

There are several versions of this exercise for balancing and centring.

1 Sit in a chair with your back straight and cross your right ankle over the left.

2 Extend your arms in front of you, point the thumbs down, cross the right wrist over the left and interlace the fingers.

3 Bring your crossed wrists in towards your chest and then up under the chin.

4 Breathe deeply, with your tongue touching the roof of your mouth while you inhale and your tongue relaxed as you exhale, for 2–3 minutes.

HARA ALIGNMENT

1 Sit in a chair with your back straight and your feet flat on the ground.

2 Imagine sinking your energy down through your feet deep into the earth, as though you are grounding your energy in the earth. Then imagine extending your energy up through the crown of your head and making a connection with the sky above.

3 Breathe gently while feeling the energies from above and below connecting and merging in the *hara*, the lower abdomen below the belly.

Appendix 6:
The Original EFT Recipe

Gary Craig developed the 'original' EFT Basic Recipe in the early 1990s. It is longer than the revised Basic Recipe given in Chapter 5 as it includes tapping on finger points, plus the nine-gamut sequence (see below). Craig uses the analogy of a sandwich; the recipe is like two pieces of bread (the sequence) with the nine-gamut as the 'meat' in the middle. While most practitioners now use the revised (and greatly simplified) Basic Recipe, I still find the full Original Recipe, especially the nine-gamut sequence, very useful.

The Original Recipe also includes the option of tapping the Karate Chop point *or* rubbing the Sore Spot while repeating the setup affirmation. While most practitioners use the Karate Chop point, some prefer the Sore Spot. You can find this spot by placing the fingers of either hand on the U-shaped notch on the collarbone; drop your hand down about 3 inches, then move your hand laterally (to either side) another 3–4 inches. Poke around in this area until you find a sore spot.

I will first list the points, on the head, torso and hands; and then the nine-gamut procedure, followed by the Original Basic Recipe. A diagram showing the head and torso tapping points may be found in Chapter 5.

Tapping points

You are already familiar with the first eight tapping points in the Basic Recipe. There is also an optional point, the Side of the Ribs point, which is described below.

Top of Head	Right on the crown of your head.
Eyebrow	At the inside edge (toward the midline) of either eyebrow.
Side of Eye	On the flat bone bordering the outside corner of either eye.
Under Eye	On the upper edge of the lower eye socket, right below the pupil of the eye.

Under Nose	On the midline, halfway between the bottom of the nose and the top of the upper lip.
Chin	On the midline in the middle of the crease, between your lower lip and the chin.
Collarbone	At the junction where the collarbone, breastbone (sternum) and first rib meet. Find the 'U' in the middle of the collarbone. Slide down one inch and then slide laterally across 1–2 inches, to a tender spot that's just outside the breastbone. The correct point is *below* the collarbone and in a small 'hollow' where the sternum drops off.
Under Arm	On the side of the body about four inches below the armpit. This point is exactly parallel with the nipple on men and approximately in the middle of the bra band on women. It will be tender when you find it.
Side of Ribs	The location of this point is about 2 inches below the nipple. As this is a sensitive area for women, it's easier (and less embarrassing in public!) to slap the side(s) of the lower ribs with one or both flat, open hands, with your middle fingers touching the approximate midline of the body.

THE FINGER POINTS

The four points on the thumb and index, middle and little/baby finger are all in the same location but on different fingers. A diagram showing the hand tapping points, as well as the Karate Chop and the Gamut Spot may be found in Chapter 4.

Thumb	On the lower edge of the fingernail, where the nail touches the skin, on the side closest to the midline of the body.
Index finger	On the lower edge of the fingernail, on the side closest to the midline.
Middle finger	On the lower edge of the fingernail, on the side closest to the midline.
Little/Baby finger	On the lower edge of the fingernail, on the side closest to the midline.
Gamut Spot	In the valley between the knuckles (metacarpophalangeal joints) of the 4th & 5th fingers, on the back of the hand.

The nine-gamut procedure

As the name implies, there are nine steps to the nine-gamut procedure. Look straight ahead and keep your head level while tapping continuously on the Gamut Spot; you should be moving your eyes, not your head!

While tapping the Gamut Spot:

1 Close your eyes.

2 Open your eyes.

3 Look hard down to the right while keeping your head level and facing straight ahead.

4 Look hard down to the left while keeping your head level and facing straight ahead.

5 Slowly roll your eyes in a large circle.

6 Slowly roll your eyes in the opposite direction.

7 Hum two bars of any song or melody.

8 Count a few numbers, e.g. 1–5.

9 Hum the two bars of music again.

The nine-gamut procedure is certainly the oddest part of EFT! However, it can be very useful. The right-hand side of the brain governs the left side of the body, and the left-hand side governs the right side of the body. Looking down to the right activates the left side of the brain, and looking down to the left activates the right-hand side. Humming music is a right-brain function, and counting (mathematics) is a left-brain function. This exercise coordinates and balances both brain hemispheres, while attuned to a memory or issue.

The EFT Original Recipe

1 Select a specific memory or experience.

2 Tune and rate its emotional intensity from 0–10.

3 Set-up: Tap the karate chop point on the side of the hands, or rub the Sore Spot while repeating aloud three times: *'Even though I have this......, I deeply and completely accept myself.'*

4 Tap the full sequence of points, with a reminder phrase.

5 Tap the Gamut Spot while doing the nine-gamut procedure.

6 Tap the full sequence of points again, with the reminder phrase.

7 Test: Tune and rate again.

8 Adjust: If not yet finished, return to step 3 and repeat the sequence as needed. For subsequent rounds, use this set-up: *'Even though I'm STILL feeling SOME of this......, I deeply and completely accept myself.'*

9 Continue tapping on additional aspects as needed, until the intensity is down to '0.'

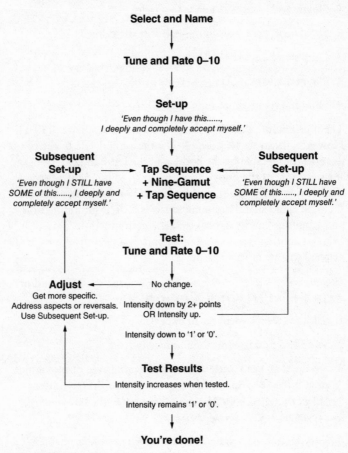

Figure 16: The EFT Original Recipe

Appendix 7: Associations and practitioners

The following organizations sponsor training, conferences and certification in EFT and related energy therapies:

Association for Advancement of Meridian Energy Therapies
www.aamet.org

Association for Meridian and Energy Therapies
www.theamt.com

Association for Comprehensive Energy Psychology
www.energypsych.org

EFT Universe
www.EFTUniverse.com

I am profoundly grateful to the following psychotherapists and EFT practitioners, who generously shared cases, stories and/or discussions with me during the writing of this book:

Martina Becher, Siegen, Germany
www.eft-verladetraining.com

Meryl Beck, Cleveland, OH, USA
www.stopeatingyourheartout.com

Daniel Benor, Guelph, Canada
www.wholistichealingresearch.com

Judy Byrne, London, UK
www.judybyrne.co.uk

Gary Craig, Sea Ranch, CA, USA
www.emofree.com

Jaqui Crooks, Leicester, UK
www.beacontraining.co.uk

John Diepold, Moorestown, NJ, USA
www.heartassistedtherapy.net

David Feinstein, Ashland, OR, USA
www.innersource.net

Alina Frank, Seattle, WA, USA
www.tapyourpower.net

Mary Hammond, Salem, OR, USA
www.maryhammond.net

Susan Hannibal, Vista, CA, USA
www.guidedhealing.com

Crystal Hawk, Toronto, Canada
www.therapeutictouch.com/crystal.html

Rhonda Heyns, Albuquerque, NM, USA
roma1358@hotmail.com

Robert and Lynne Hoss, Cave Creek, AZ
www.dreamscience.org

Philip Friedman, Philadelphia, PA, USA
www.philipfriedman.com

Lindsay Kenny, San Francisco, CA, USA
www.lifecoachingwithlindsay.com

Tim Kremer, Jupiter, FL, USA
www.myspiritofgolf.com

David Lake, Sydney, Australia
www.eftdownunder.com

Karen Ledger, Vancouver, Canada
www.at-one.ca

Tam and Mair Llewellyn-Edwards, Yorkshire, UK
www.tickhillclinic.com

Paul and Val Lynch, East Sussex, UK
www.theheartcentre.co.uk

Gwyneth Moss, Yorkshire, UK
www.emotional-health.co.uk

Lorna Minewiser, Charlotte, NC, USA
www.emotionalfreedomcoach.com

Deborah Miller, Oaxaca, Mexico
www.oaxacaproject.com

Betsy Muller, Cleveland, OH, USA
www.theindigoconnection.com

Lynne Namka, Tucson, AZ, USA
www.angriesout.com

Gregory Nicosia, Pittsburgh, PA, USA
www.thoughtenergy.com

Sandi Radomski, Atlantic City, NJ, USA
www.allergyantidotes.com

Mike Rotheram, Bamford, UK
www.metaphorics.co.uk

Carol Solomon, Libertyville, IL, USA
www.carolsolomon.com

Mary Stafford, Tucson, AZ, USA
www.mindbodytherapy.com

Stacey Vornbrock, Scottsdale, AZ, USA
www.breakthroughperformance.net

Greg Warburton, Corvallis, OR, USA
www.gregwarburton.com

Yves Wauthier-Freymann, Brussels, Belgium
www.therapeutia.com

Steve Wells, Perth, Australia
www.eftdownunder.com

Phyllis Winslow, Tucson, AZ, USA
www.energybalancingaz.com

Susi Wolf, Albuquerque, NM, USA
www.wolfsongcreative.com

Appendix 8:
Further reading

Adams, A. & Davidson, K. (2011). EFT Level 1 Comprehensive Training Resource. Fulton, CA: Energy Psychology Press.

Arenson, G. (2001). Five Simple Steps to Emotional Healing: The last self-help book you will ever need. New York: Fireside.

Ball, R. (2006). Freedom at your Fingertips. Fredericksburg, VA: Inroads Publishing.

Becker, R. & Selden, Gary. (1985). The Body Electric: Electromagnetism and the foundation of life. New York: Morrow.

Benor, D. (2008). Seven Minutes to Natural Pain Release. Bellmawr, NJ: Wholistic Healing Publications.

Benson, H. (1976). The Relaxation Response. Farmington Hills, MI: Gale Cengage.

Bohm, D. (2012). Wholeness and the Implicate Order. Abingdon: Taylor & Francis.

Bruner, P. & Bullough, J. EFT and Beyond : Cutting edge techniques for personal transformation. Saffron Walden : Energy Publications Ltd.

Burr, H.S. (1972). The Fields of Life: Our links with the universe. New York: Ballantine.

Callahan, R. & Perry, P. (1993). Why Do I Eat When I'm Not Hungry? New York: Harper.

Callahan, R. & Trubo, R. (2002). Tapping the Healer Within. New York: McGraw Hill.

Carrington, P. (2007). Multiply the Power of EFT. Kendall Park, NJ: Pace.

Church, D. (2007). The Genie in Your Genes: Epigenetic medicine and the new biology of intention. Santa Rosa, CA: Elite Books.

Coca, A. (1994). The Pulse Test: The secret of building your basic health. Fort Lee, NJ: Barricade.

Craig, G. (2008). The EFT Manual. Fulton, CA: Energy Psychology Press.

Craig, G. (2008). EFT for PTSD. Fulton, CA: Energy Psychology Press.

Csikszentmihalyi, M. (1990). Flow: The psychology of optimal experience. New York: Harper and Row.

Diamond, J. (2012). Men Alive: Stop killer stress with simple energy healing tools. Willits, CA: Fifth Wave Press.

Diamond, J. (1979). Your Body Doesn't Lie. New York: Warner.

Doidge, N. (2007). The Brain That Changes Itself: Stories of personal triumph from the frontiers of brain science. New York: Viking.

Ecker, B. , Ticic, R. & Hulley, L. (2012). Unlocking the Emotional Brain : Eliminating symptoms at their roots using memory reconsolidation. London: Routledge.

Eden, D. & Feinstein, D. (1998). Energy Medicine. San Francisco: Jeremy Tarcher.

Feinstein, D., Eden, D. & Craig, G. (2007). The Promise of Energy Psychology. San Francisco: Jeremy Tarcher.

Flint, Garry. (2001). Emotional Freedom: Techniques for dealing with emotional and physical distress. Vernon, BC, Canada: NeoSolTerric Enterprises.

Fone, H. (2008). Emotional Freedom Technique for Dummies. Chichester: John Wiley & Sons.

Friedman, P. (2009). The Forgiveness Solution : The whole-body Rx for finding true happiness, abundant love, and inner peace. San Francisco: Conari Press.

Gallo, F. (1999). Energy Psychology: Explorations at the interface of energy, cognition, behavior and health. Boca Raton, FL: CRC Press.

Gallo, F. (2002). Energy Psychology in Psychotherapy: A comprehensive sourcebook. New York: W. W. Norton.

Hartmann, S. (2000). Adventures in EFT. DH Publications.

Hartmann, S. (2003). The Advanced Patterns of EFT. Eastbourne: Dragon Rising.

Hartung, J. & Galvin, M. (2003). Energy Psychology and EMDR: Combining forces to optimize treatment. New York: W. W. Norton.

Kabat-Zinn, J. (2005). Coming to Our Senses: Healing ourselves and the world through mindfulness. New York: Hyperion.

Levine, P. (1997). Waking the Tiger : Healing trauma – the innate capacity to transform overwhelming experiences. Berkeley, CA: North Atlantic Books.

Levine, P. (2010). In An Unspoken Voice: How the body releases trauma and restores goodness. Berkeley, CA: North Atlantic Books.

Lipton, B. (2008). The Biology of Belief. Santa Monica, CA: Hay House.

Lynch, V. (2001). Emotional Healing in Minutes: Simple acupressure techniques for your emotions. London: Thorsons.

Mollon, P. (2008). Psychoanalytic Energy Psychotherapy. London: Karnac.

Muller, B. (2011). Energy Makeover: A conscious way to stay young, have fun and get more done! Henderson, NV: Motivational Press.

Norretranders, T. (1999). The User Illusion: Cutting consciousness down to size. New York: Penguin.

Ober, C., Sinatra, S. & Zucker, M. (2010). Earthing: The most important health discovery ever? Laguna Beach, CA: Basic Health Publications.

Oschman, J. (1998). What is Healing Energy? The scientific basis of energy medicine. Dover, NH: Nature's Own Research Association.

Schwarz, R. (2002). Tools for Transforming Trauma. New York: Psychology Press.

Seligman, M. (1998). Learned Optimism: How to change your mind and your life. New York: Pocketbooks.

Shapiro, F. (2001). Eye Movement Desensitization and Reprocessing (EMDR): Basic principles, protocols, and procedures. New York: Guilford Press.

Shealy, N. & Church, D. (2008). Soul Medicine: Awakening your inner blueprint for abundant health and energy. Santa Rosa, CA: Elite Books.

Sheldrake, R. (2011). The Presence of the Past: Morphic resonance and the habits of nature. London: Icon.

Swanson, C. (2010). Life Force, the Scientific Basis: Breakthrough physics of energy medicine, healing, chi and quantum consciousness. Tucson, AZ: Poseidia Press.

Talbot, M. (1992). The Holographic Universe. New York: HarperCollins.

Appendix 9: Sources

CHAPTER 1

Selye, H. (1956). The Stress of Life. New York: McGraw-Hill.

Pert, C. (1999). Molecules of Emotion: The science between mind-body medicine. New York: Scribner.

Solomon, G. F., Amkraut, A. A. & Kasper, P. (1974). Immunity, emotions and stress: With special reference to the mechanisms of stress effects on the immune system. Annals of Clinical Research, 6(6), 313–322.

Goleman, D. (1995). Emotional Intelligence. New York: Bantam Books.

Leonoff, G. (1995). The successful treatment of phobias and anxiety by telephone and radio: A replication of Callahan's 1987 study. TFT Newsletter, 1, 2.

CHAPTER 2

Montagu, A. (1971). Touching: The human significance of the skin, New York: Columbia University Press.

Keltner, D. (2009). Born to Be Good: The science of a meaningful life. New York: W. W. Norton.

Harlow, H.F. (1962). Development of Affection in Primates. In E.L. Bliss (Ed.) Roots of Behavior. New York: Harper.

Blum, D. (2002). Love at Goon Park: Harry Harlow and the science of affection. New York: Perseus.

Tor Nørretranders, T. (1998). The User Illusion: Cutting consciousness down to size. New York: Viking.

Benson, H. (2000). The Relaxation Response. New York: Avon.

CHAPTER 3

White, J. & Krippner, S. (1977). Future Science: Life energies and the physics of paranormal phenomena. New York: Anchor.

Milloni, P. (1994). The Quantum Vacuum: An introduction to quantum electrodynamics. San Diego: Academic Press.

Burr, H. S. (1972). The Fields of Life. New York: Ballantine.

Perry, P. (1997). The Healing Art of Qi Gong: Ancient wisdom from a modern master. New York: Warner.

Keyes, L.E. (1982). Toning: The creative and healing power of the human voice. Camarillo, CA: DeVorss.

Chan, C.L. & Leung, P.P. (2012). Clapping Qi Gong. In R. A. Neimeyer (Ed.)., Techniques of Grief Therapy: Creative practices for counselling the bereaved. Abingdon: Routledge.

CHAPTER 4

Csikszentmihalyi, M. (2009). Flow: The psychology of optimal experience. New York: Harper Collins.

Bracha, H. S., Bracha, A. S., Williams, A. E., Ralston, T. C. & Matsukawa, J. M. (2005). The human fear-circuitry and fear-induced fainting in healthy individuals: The paleolithic-threat hypothesis. Clinical Autonomic Research, 15, 238–241.

Frost, R. (2002). Applied Kinesiology: A training manual and reference book of basic principles and practices. Berkeley, CA: North Atlantic Books.

Thie, J. (1973). Touch for Health. Camarillo, CA: DeVorss.

Callahan, R. & Trubo, R. (2000). Tapping the Healer Within. New York: McGraw Hill.

Dennison, P. & G. (1989). Brain Gym: Teacher's edition. Hearts at Play, Inc.

Hannaford, C. (1995). Smart Moves: Why learning is not all in your head. Great River Books.

Swack, J., originator of the concept of blocked access and developer of Healing From the Body Level Up: www.hblu.org

Levine, P. (1997). Waking the Tiger: Healing trauma – the innate capacity to transform overwhelming experiences. Berkely, CA: North Atlantic Books.

Lieberman, M.D. et al. (2007). Affect labelling disrupts amygdala activity in response to affective stimuli. Psychological Science, 18(5), 421–428.

Rogers, C. (1961). On Becoming a Person: A therapist's view of psychotherapy. London: Constable.

CHAPTER 5

Craig, G. (2008). The EFT Manual. Santa Rosa: Energy Psychology Press.

EFT Tutorial: www.emofree.com

CHAPTER 7

Shapiro, F. (2001). Eye Movement Desensitization and Reprocessing: Basic principles, protocols and procedures. New York: Guilford Press.

Ecker, B., Ticic, R. & Hulley, L. Unlocking the Emotional Brain: Eliminating symptoms at their roots using memory reconsolidation. Abingdon: Routledge.

CHAPTER 9

Sarno, John. (1991). Healing Back Pain: The mind body connection. New York: Warner.

Ader, R. & Cohen, N. (1975). Behaviorally conditioned immunosuppression. Psychosomatic Medicine 37(4).

Coca, A. F. (1958). The Pulse Test: The secret of building your basic health. New York: Carol Publishing Group.

ACE Study: The enduring effects of abuse and related adverse experiences in childhood. Anda R. F., Felitti V. J. et al. (2006). A convergence of evidence from neurobiology and epidemiology. Eur Arch Psychiatry Clin Neurosci 256(3):174–86.

Dong M., Anda R. F., Felitti V. J. et al. (2005). Childhood residential mobility and multiple health risks during adolescence and adulthood: the hidden role of adverse childhood experiences. Arch Pediatr Adolesc Med. 159(12):1104–10.

Church, D. (2011). The utilization of energy psychology in primary care. Energy Psychology Journal, 3(1).

Littrell, J. (2008). The mind-body connection: Not just a theory anymore. Social Work in Health Care, 46(4), 17–37.

CHAPTER 10

Scaer, R. (2006). The precarious present. Psychotherapy Networker, 67: 49–53.

Tanielian, T. & Jaycox, L. (2008). Invisible Wounds of War: Psychological and cognitive injuries, their consequences, and services to assist recovery. Rand Corporation.

Church, D. (2009). The treatment of combat trauma in veterans using EFT: A pilot protocol. Traumatology, 15(1), 45–55.

Church, D., Hawk, C., Brooks, A., Toukolehto, O., Wren, M., Dinter, I., Stein, P. (2012). Psychological trauma symptom improvement in veterans using EFT (Emotional Freedom Techniques): A randomized controlled trial. Journal of Nervous and Mental Disease.

Sakai, C., Connolly, S. & Oas, P. (2010). Treatment of PTSD in Rwandan child genocide survivors using Thought Field Therapy. International Journal of Emergency Mental Health,12(1), 41–50.

CHAPTER 11

Seligman, M. (1991). Learned Optimism: How to change your mind and your life. New York: Alfred A. Knopf.

Sophie Kinsella interview: www.time.com/time/magazine/article/0,9171,2019622,00.html

Setting SMART Goals: www.oma.ku.edu/soar/smartgoals.pdf

CHAPTER 12

Gallwey, W. T. (1974). The Inner Game of Tennis. London: Pan.

Jorge Reyes interview: www.youtube.com/watch?v=8bBEtzLQ1qM

Tim Kremer: http://prezi.com/qigkzk6fiar1/spirit-of-golf-10-key-principles/

Church, D. (2009). The effect of EFT (Emotional Freedom Techniques) on athletic performance: A randomized controlled blind trial. The Open Sports Sciences Journal, 2, 94–99.

Llewellyn-Edwards, T. & Llewellyn-Edwards, M. (2012, Spring). The effect of EFT (Emotional Freedom Techniques) on soccer performance. Fidelity: Journal for the National Council of Psychotherapy, 47, 14–19.

Rotheram, M., Maynard, I., Thomas, O., Bawden, M. & Francis, L. (2012). Preliminary evidence for the treatment of Type 1 'yips': The efficacy of the Emotional Freedom Techniques. The Sports Psychologist, 26, 551–570.

CHAPTER 13

Wright, J. (2006). The Soft Addiction Solution. New York: Penguin.

Stapleton, P., Sheldon, T. & Porter, B. (2012). Clinical benefits of Emotional Freedom Techniques on food cravings at 12-months follow-up: A randomized controlled trial.

Energy Psychology Journal, 4(1), 13–24.

Ober, C., Sinatra, S. & Zucker, M. (2010). Earthing: The most important health discovery ever? Laguna Beach, CA: Basic Health Productions.

The Personal Peace Procedure originally appeared on Gary Craig's website: www.emofree.com

CHAPTER 14

Energy of Reading Project: www.energyoflearning.com

Lake, D. & Wells, S. (2010). Enjoy Emotional Freedom: Simple techniques for living life to the full. Wollombi, NSW: Exisle Publishing.

Benor, D. (2008). Seven Minutes to Natural Pain Release. New York: Midpoint Trade Books.

Gallo, F. (2002). Energy Psychology in Psychotherapy. New York: Norton.

CONCLUSION

Houston, J. (1997). The Possible Human: A course in extending your physical, mental, and creative abilities. Los Angeles: Jeremy Tarcher.

Vanderkam, L. (2012). The Paperback Quest for Joy: America's unique love affair with self-help books. New York: Manhattan Institute for Policy Research.

Kuhn, T. (1996). The Structure of Scientific Revolutions. Chicago: University of Chicago Press.

Talbot, M. (1992). The Holographic Universe. New York: HarperCollins.

A Course in Miracles. (1976). Mill Valley, CA: Foundation for Inner Peace.

APPENDIX 1

Callahan, R. & Perry, P. (1991). Why Do I Eat When I'm Not Hungry? New York: Avon.

Callahan, R. J., & Callahan, J. (1996). Thought Field Therapy and Trauma: Treatment and theory. Indian Wells, CA: Author.

Debiec J., Doyere V., Nader K., Ledoux J. E. (2006). Directly reactivated, but not indirectly reactivated, memories undergo reconsolidation in the amygdala. Proc Natl Acad Sci, 103(9), 3428–33.

Doidge, N. (2007). The Brain That Changes Itself. New York: Penguin.

Ecker, B. (2011). Unlocking the Emotional Brain: Finding the neural key to transformation. Psychotherapy Networker, 32(5), 42–47, 60.

Ecker, B., Ticic, R. & Hulley, L. (2012). Unlocking the Emotional Brain: Eliminating symptoms at their roots using memory reconsolidation. New York: Routledge.

Feinstein, D. (2010). Rapid treatment of PTSD: Why psychological exposure with acupoint tapping may be effective. Psychotherapy: Theory, Research, Practice, Training, 47(3), 385–402.

Feinstein, D. (2012). Acupoint stimulation in treating psychological disorders: Evidence of efficacy. Review of General Psychology. Advance online publication. doi: 10.1037/a0028602

Feinstein, D. (2012). What does energy have to do with energy psychology? Energy Psychology Journal, 4(2).

Gerber, R. (1996). Vibrational Medicine: New choices for healing ourselves. Santa Fe: Bear.

Jones, M. C. (1974). Albert, P., and John B. Watson. American Psychologist, 29, 581–584

Lane, J. (2009). The neurochemistry of counterconditioning: Acupressure desensitization in psychotherapy. Energy Psychology: Theory, Research, & Treatment, 1(1), 31–44.

Pomeranz, B., Strux, G. & Han, C. (1989). The Scientific Basis of Acupuncture. New York: Springer Verlag.

Shapiro, F. (2001). Eye Movement Desensitization and Reprocessing: Basic principles, protocols and procedures. New York: Guilford Press.

Wolpe, J. (1969). The Practice of Behavior Therapy. New York: Pergamon Press.

APPENDIX 2

Birch S., Hesselink, J. K., Jonkman, F.A., Hekker, T. A. & Bos, A. (2004). Clinical research on acupuncture. What have reviews of the efficacy and safety of acupuncture told us so far? Journal of Alternative and Complementary Medicine, 10(3), 468–80.

Braswell, M. E. & Wong, H. D. (1994). Perceptions of rehabilitation counselors regarding Native American healing practices. The Journal of Rehabilitation, 60(2), 33–37.

Church, D. (2010). The treatment of combat trauma in veterans using EFT (Emotional Freedom Techniques): A pilot protocol. Traumatology, 15(1), 45–55.

Church, D. & Brooks, A. J. (2010). The effect of a brief EFT (Emotional Freedom Techniques) self-intervention on anxiety, depression, pain and cravings in healthcare workers. Integrative Medicine: A Clinician's Journal, 9(5), 40–44.

Church, D. & Brooks, A. (2010b). A Review of the EFT (Emotional Freedom Techniques) Method, Research, and

Application. Integrative Medicine: A Clinician's Journal, 9(4), 22–26.

Church, D., De Asis, M. & Brooks, A. (2012). Brief group intervention using EFT (Emotional Freedom Techniques) for depression in college students: A randomized controlled trial. Accepted for publication in the Journal of Depression Research and Treatment.

Church, D. & Feinstein, D. (2012). The psychobiology and clinical principles of energy psychology treatments for PTSD: A review. In T. Van Leeuwen and M. Brouwer (Eds.), Psychology of Trauma, (in press). Hauppage, NY: Nova Publishers.

Church, D., Hawk, C., Brooks, A., Toukolehto, O., Wren, M., Dinter, I., Stein, P. (2012). Psychological trauma symptom improvement in veterans using EFT (Emotional Freedom Techniques): A randomized controlled trial. Accepted for publication by the Journal of Nervous and Mental Disease.

Church, D., Yount, G. & Brooks, A. (2012). The effect of Emotional Freedom Technique (EFT) on stress biochemistry: A randomized controlled trial. Journal of Nervous and Mental Disease, 200(10), 891–896.

Claunch J., Chan S., Nixon E., Qiu W., Sporko T., Dunn, J., Kwong, K. & Hui, K. (2012). Commonality and specificity of acupuncture action at three acupoints as evidenced by FMRI. American Journal of Chinese Medicine, 40(4), 695–712.

Committee on Treatment of Posttraumatic Stress Disorder. (2008). Treatment of posttraumatic stress disorder: An assessment of the evidence. Washington, DC: Institute of Medicine of the National Academy of Sciences.

Connolly, S. M. & Sakai, C. E. (2011). Brief trauma symptom intervention with Rwandan genocide survivors using Thought Field Therapy. International Journal of Emergency Mental Health, 13(3), 161–172.

Diepold, J. H., Jr., & Goldstein, D. (2009). Thought field therapy and QEEG changes in the treatment of trauma: A case study. Traumatology, 15, 85–93.

Enz, C. P. (2009). Of Matter and Spirit: Selected essays. Hackensack, NJ: World Scientific Publishing.

Fang, J., Jin, Z., Wang, Y., Li, K., Kong , J., Nixon , E. E., Hui, K. K.-S. (2009). The salient characteristics of the central effects of acupuncture needling: Limbic-paralimbic-neocortical network modulation. Human Brain Mapping, 30, 1196–1206.

Feinstein, D. (2010). Rapid treatment of PTSD: Why psychological exposure with acupoint tapping may be effective. Psychotherapy: Theory, Research, Practice, Training. 47(3), 385–402.

Feinstein, D. (2012). Acupoint stimulation in treating psychological disorders: Evidence of efficacy. Review of General Psychology. Advance online publication. doi: 10.1037/a0028602

Friedman, N. (2004). Eugene Gendlin's approach to psychotherapy. Annals of the American Psychotherapy Association, 7.

Galatzer-Levy, R. (1976). Psychic energy: A historical perspective. Annual of Psychoanalysis, 4, 41–61.

Gallo, F. (2004). Energy psychology: Explorations at the interface of energy, cognition, behavior, and health. New York: CRC Press.

Gendlin, E. (1996). Focusing-oriented Psychotherapy. New York: Guilford Press.

Hammer, Leon. (2005). Dragon Rises, Red Bird Flies: Psychology and Chinese medicine. New York: Eastland Press.

Jung, C. G. (1969). Synchronicity: An acausal connecting principle. Princeton, NJ: Princeton University Press.

Karatzias, T., Power, K., Brown, K., McGoldrick, T., Begum, M., Young, J. & Adams, S. (2011). A controlled comparison of the effectiveness and efficiency of two psychological therapies for posttraumatic stress disorder: Eye Movement Desensitization and Reprocessing vs. Emotional Freedom Techniques. Journal of Nervous & Mental Disease, 199, 372–378.

Kober A., Scheck, T., Greher, M., Lieba, F., Fleischhackl, R., Fleischhackl, S. & Hoerauf, K. (2002). Pre-hospital analgesia with acupressure in victims of minor trauma: A prospective, randomized, double-blinded trial. Anesthesia & Analgesia, 95 (3), 723–727.

Krippner, S. & Rock, A. J. (2011). Demystifying Shamans and Their World: A multidisciplinary study. Exeter, UK: Imprint Academic.

Kurtz, R. (1997). Body-centered Psychotherapy: The Hakomi method. Mendocino, CA: LifeRhythm.

Lambrou, P., Pratt, G. & Chevalier, G. (2005). Physiological and psychological effects of a mind/body therapy on claustrophobia. Journal of Subtle Energies and Energy Medicine, 14(3), 239–51.

Lane, J. (2009). The neurochemistry of counterconditioning: Acupressure desensitization in psychotherapy. Energy Psychology: Theory, Research, & Treatment, 1(1), 31–44.

Llewellyn-Edwards, T. & Llewellyn-Edwards, M. (2012, Spring). The effect of EFT (Emotional Freedom Techniques) on soccer performance. Fidelity: Journal for the National Council of Psychotherapy, 47, 14–19.

Miller, G., Galanter, E. & Pribram, K. (1960). Plans and the Structure of Behavior. New York: Holt, Rhinehart & Winston.

Pierrakos, J. C. (1990). Core Energetics: Developing the capacity to love and heal. Mendocino, CA: Liferhythms.

Rotheram, M., Maynard, I., Thomas, O., Bawden, M. & Francis, L. (2012). Preliminary evidence for the treatment of Type 1 'Yips': The efficacy of the Emotional Freedom Techniques. The Sports Psychologist, 26, 551–570.

Ruden, R. A. (2005). A neurological basis for the observed peripheral sensory modulation of emotional responses. Traumatology, 11, 145–158. doi: 10.1177/153476560501100301

Sakai, C. S., Connolly, S. M. & Oas, P. (2010). Treatment of PTSD in Rwandan genocide survivors using Thought Field Therapy. International Journal of Emergency Mental Health, 12(1), 41–50.

Shapiro, D. (2002). Theoretical reflections on Wilhelm Reich's character analysis. American Journal of Psychotherapy, 56, 338–346.

Sulloway, F. (1992). Freud, Biologist of the Mind. Cambridge, MA: Harvard University Press.

Sun, Y., Gan, T. J., Dubose, J. W. & Habib A. S. (2008). Acupuncture and related techniques for postoperative pain: A systematic review of randomized controlled trials. British Journal of Anaesthesia,101(2), 151–60.

White, J. & Krippner, S. (1977). Future Science: Life energies and the physics of paranormal phenomena. New York: Anchor.

Wolpe, J. (1969). The Practice of Behavior Therapy. New York: Pergamon Press.

Wolpe, J. & Lazarus, A. (1966). Behavior Therapy Techniques: A guide to the treatment of neuroses. Oxford: Pergamon.

Zhang Y., Feng B., Xie J. P., Xu F. Z. & Chen J. (2011). Clinical study on treatment of the earthquake-caused post-traumatic stress disorder by cognitive-behavior therapy and acupoint stimulation. Journal of Traditional Chinese Medicine, 31, 60–63. doi: 10.1016/S0254-6272(11)60014-9.

Index